THE BOY HAS GONE

How 16 weeks of training
changed him forever

JOHN J. GREEN

One Printers Way
Altona, MB R0G 0B0
Canada

www.friesenpress.com

Copyright © 2024 by John J. Green
First Edition — 2024

All rights reserved.

No part of this publication may be reproduced in any form, or by any means, electronic or mechanical, including photocopying, recording, or any information browsing, storage, or retrieval system, without permission in writing from FriesenPress.

All contents of this book are the intellectual property of John J. Green. Written permission must be granted from John J. Green for the use of any part of this book.

This book is factional—facts inspired by real life experiences are shared within the fictional writings. All names and characters have been changed or created for the purposes of this book.

ISBN
978-1-03-830827-6 (Hardcover)
978-1-03-830826-9 (Paperback)
978-1-03-830828-3 (eBook)

1. BIOGRAPHY & AUTOBIOGRAPHY, MILITARY

Distributed to the trade by The Ingram Book Company

Doug & Mal
Many Thanks and look after yourselves
John Gree.

This book is dedicated to:

My parents John and Catherine Green
for all their unfailing belief in me.

My wife Joan,
who must have felt that she herself
had joined up at times.

All my family and friends
for bearing with me,
while I kept saying, "Not long now."

A special mention to my friend Hazel Butterworth,
without whose help this dinosaur would not
have been able to get this book into print.

WHY I WROTE THE BOOK

Like many people who grew up at the end of the Second World War, I soon discovered that a sense of humour could be a great asset. After my army service, I was encouraged by my parents to write a book as I had so many stories to tell. Seven years after I was demobbed, around 1980, I wrote about twenty pages. When I retired in 2016, I found that old original writing pad among a pile of other books, which had now yellowed with age, and I decided to finish writing my book. Not being tech savvy, I wrote the entire book in freehand then had to learn how to type to prepare it for a publisher. This was definitely a sense-of-humour test.

I wanted to write about my sixteen weeks of basic training as I believe this was the turning point for me, and a great foundation for the remainder of my life. I wanted to show how people from all walks of life and backgrounds could be gathered together and re-moulded into a well-disciplined unit but still keep their individuality.

The skills I learned during training still serve me well today. This is written with the humour and hardship showing the realistic way that this was achieved.

FROM BOY TO SOLDIER
HOW IT BEGAN
1960s

"Son, if balls were brains, a splinter on a toilet seat would totally destroy anything you ever learned."

How did I end up here? In a foreign world, no family, no feelings, just a spotless soldier in an unforgiving land.

"You're an intelligent boy with the world at your feet. Discipline—a few years in the navy will make a man out of you. I was in, your mother was in, her father and brother were in and the cat and the budgie were in. We all served before the mast."

My Dad's answer to everything. Brilliant, two fingers to all except the budgie. *I'll show them I'll join the Guards, the world respects real men.*

"Heels together, toes apart forty-five degrees, shoulders back, stomach in and clench the cheeks of your arse together, that way it doesn't hurt so much when I put my boot in it. Does Mummy want pictures of a Guardsman's well kicked rectum? If she recognises it, we'll get you in the WRAC (Women's Royal Army Corps) or do a check for piles."

I must find out about piles, never heard of them but no one else seems to be struggling about what's being said, I must be naïve. I wish I was strong enough—I'd tell them where to stick it but they don't shut up long enough, and if I told them where to stick it then the subject of piles would only crop up again. Eighteen years old, a man, the police said, you can vote, drink beer, chase women and have erections. A king in your own castle, but nobody mentioned this lot, they must have been born when they were fifteen years old to understand all of this. I'm totally convinced that sanity is a word that hasn't penetrated this little piece of God's kingdom.

My village was home and everyone knew and was concerned about their neighbours. If you got out of hand they would box your ears, but at the end of the day father was The Man. Inborn to the Royal Navy at sixteen, everything he said had a salty tang; his bearing was upright and the world had been his oyster. All the massive oceans had been his plaything. Exotic names like India, Hong Kong, Malta and Gib (Gibraltar). He was forever rolling out countless tales of his naval exploits. This was going to make a man of me.

Well, I'll be my own man and just to get up his nose the British Army it will be. It would have been the navy but they were shut when I went.

"Stand still you perverted waste of breathing space. You make the queen's uniform look like a used pleasure skin (later identified as a durex or a rubber), except they don't make them big enough for you pricks."

Is this why I am red faced on the tarmac parade ground of a million boot prints, breathing like a bulldog in a heat wave?

Eighteen years old and the eldest of five children, I'd been around. I once even got to Manchester (fifteen miles away), stayed all day and had to catch two buses and a train each way. I knew all about travelling, so why was I standing outside a large, long London railway station, suitcase in hand, weak kneed, with a stomach like a bucket of month-old tripe? *Where are all these people going?* The noise was absolutely deafening, buildings claustrophobically scrambling upwards to get at the fresh air. It must be up there somewhere, and with all the cars in the world in one area, I must have arrived on a Sunday market day.

Was it only six hours ago that I was saying goodbye to my family, feeling a real man of the world?

"Don't be upset, this is what I want, in four months I will be a trooper in The Life Guards and we will all feel as proud as I will." (Was I to remember *this* remark over the coming weeks.) A last casual wave to everyone at home, a cocky saunter onto the train—it was beginning.

As I sat on the train, I wandered into a fantasy world. Sat astride an Arabian charger, breastplate glittering, riding behind the queen with sword in hand, defender of the realm, super fit and bronzed. The whole world now *my* oyster. All the people back home who gave me a month at most before finishing, would be averting their eyes to avoid the sun bouncing off my breastplate. "Sir Lancelot, you're a learner."

Then the grim reality of a London railway station—Lancelot never had this to contend with. "Just around the corner for your connection," I was told but they failed to mention the wall-to-wall mob who seemed to view me as something to clean the dust off their sleeves. It had only taken me ten minutes to get there, but my bucket of month-old tripe was aging fast. I collapsed onto the last train and now I was only forty-five minutes from Windsor and this would be my final destination said the joining instructions.

When I first laid eyes on Windsor, (such a beautiful town I had been told and this was to prove to be the truth) my first sight of it left much to be desired.

As I left the railway station, I heard a loud shout: "You for Combermere Barracks?"

I looked around and saw a tall sprawl of a man, beret casually hanging off his head, an open-necked shirt under a baggy khaki pullover, wide stable belt holding up his large stomach, khaki trousers, and boots that had rejected polish in their infancy.

"Yes, my name is—"

"Couldn't give a bollocks, toss your gear in the back of the Land Rover and get in, I've a session to get to and you are holding me up."

I fell into the passenger seat as he shot the Land Rover off up the road. Traffic lights weren't driven through, they were attacked. Keep-left bollards were only there to see how close a vehicle could be got to them, and all bends appeared to be set to ninety degrees. It only took a few minutes but I did a fair impression of a pea on a drum in the seat. We arrived at the Guard Room and for the first time that day I wasn't just apprehensive, I was bloody terrified.

A tall man, totally opposite of the budding stock-car driver who had just roared off, strode out of the Guard Room door. A red and dark blue cap with gold braid on the slashed peak over his eyes and onto the tip of his nose, made him stand as straight as a steel rod. He wore an immaculate khaki jacket and trousers atop a pair of boots that absolutely gleamed on that cold, crisp January evening. Hair cropped skull tight, a riding whip held one end in his right hand the other end under his right armpit. This was all complemented by a white, Blanco-ed belt around his waist. (Blanco was a compound used to clean, colour, and waterproof equipment.) The brass buckle and badge on it shone as did the brass crown over the three stripes on the upper half of each arm.

"I am Corporal of Horse Tighe and from the beginning of your course tomorrow I will be your senior instructor," he said in a soothing, reassuring voice. "Until then I will send someone with you to issue you with bedding and show you to your quarters. Good luck."

This will be alright, he is a gentleman, was my first impression as he turned and marched back into the Guard room.

Fifteen minutes later, I arrived on the first floor of a fairly new-looking barrack block, bedding under one arm, suitcase in the other hand, facing a room full of hopefuls who looked as lost as I did. There were eight beds, four on each wall, of which five were already taken.

A voice said, "Help yourself to any of the spare beds; your locker is on the left of your bed as you face the wall."

I put my bedding and suitcase onto a metal-framed bed at the top of the room and sat on the end of it. A stocky, powerfully built youth with a shock of dark, curly, unruly hair came across. He held out his right hand, "Timmy More, ye's fair lookin' ashen hinny, first time away fer yame?" (Rough translation—You are looking pale, is it your first time away from home?) and I realised I'd never met a Geordie before.

"I'm John Green, you'll have to speak slower than that," I said as we shook hands. "I only understood your name."

Someone misheard my name as Jim and because of this I was never called John again during my service, only Jimmy, except by my family.

A monster of a fellow who was hanging clothes in the locker opposite Timmy More's turned and said, "It's nae worry man I canna understand neither, its yaws (years) of pain caused by Newcastle Broon Ale." They both laughed; it was infectious and soon we were all laughing.

Within five minutes, we were all chatting, names known and for a while surroundings forgotten. Timmy and the big fellow, whose name was Alex, lived close to each other in Newcastle. Of the others, one was Scottish, one from Devon, one from Yorkshire, and me from Lancashire, it was necessary to open the windows to let all the accents out. Time flew, more hopefuls arrived, same procedure, more chat, more accents.

Suddenly, in the time-honoured tradition of all good gatherings, "The pubs are open!" and the room emptied quicker than a pint at closing time. An hour later the accents had gotten stronger and the conversation made the bar sound like a beehive. There didn't seem to be anyone in the place who wasn't primed and ready for tomorrow.

By closing time at 10:30 pm, a gaggle of meandering youths, the world at their feet, staggered back to the barrack room totally convinced between hiccups and wind that life was a ball. Fairly quickly all had sunk into a heavy sleep, being the hallmark of a good flow of brewery juice.

WEEK 1

MONDAY, DAY 1

"Wakey-wakey, this is your last lie-in for four months. Get washed, shaved, and over to the cookhouse and muster by the main doors for 0730hrs. Move it."

By the time I rolled over the voice was already in the next room. "What time is it?"

"Six-fifteen."

"Morning or evening, it's still bloody dark outside."

But by 0730 hrs, thirty tired looking individuals were milling around the main foyer, all talking at the same time.

"Shut up you lot and listen." The voice came from a slim, athletic, blond-haired man who appeared from a door at the end of a corridor.

The hubbub stopped as if a light switch had been thrown.

"Get in a straight line facing the door and shut up unless you are told to speak."

This was done and one by one we were shown into a storeroom.

"Name?"

"Green."

"Neck size, height, shoe size?"

"Fifteen and a half, five foot eleven, nines."

A horse-hair shirt, beret, a pair of denim coveralls, socks, and boots were slapped on the counter. "Upstairs—put these on, place all civilian clothing on a hanger and in the bag provided, and bring them back here by 0800hrs. Next."

We were all having the same problems with the shirts; they itched like hell and the tails nearly reached the back of our knees. Within ten minutes, we were all wandering around downstairs in baggy coveralls, rigid boots, a beret that looked as if it was to double as a flying saucer, and the inevitable impression of a waist-up version of St. Vitus Dance. Then we went upstairs to await the next orders. Within five minutes, the most prized possession was a corner to scratch your back on, the whole landing alive with bodies vainly trying to get some relief.

"Get down here. Faster." The blond-haired man was now wearing a uniform with two stripes and a crown on each upper arm. "Fall in outside, get into two ranks."

Outside was the edge of a large tarmac square with two-storey barrack blocks on three sides and the cookhouse straight across. After much jostling, two lines were formed looking like a dog's back legs.

"The first thing is an opening address from the course officer, Captain A.J. Forbes-Hart." (A bit impressive—I later found out that it appeared to be an accident of breeding that mass initialling and double-barrel names separated them and us.)

We were marched across to another block. The blonde NCO (non-commissioned officer) went through a door and then almost immediately reappeared and ushered us into a large room. A desk had been placed opposite the door with chairs in four rows facing it.

"Sit down, shut up and do not move."

Don't move? Thirty men were doing the horse-hair boogie on the backs of their chairs. Just as it was getting unbearable the inevitable voice. "Room atten-shun," and four rows of carefully placed chairs crashed in all directions.

"Stand still, look to the front."

There was a crunching of highly polished shoes and boots and Captain Forbes-Hart was at the desk flanked by Corporal of Horse Tighe on his right and the blond corporal plus two others on his left. He sat down and Corporal of Horse Tighe told us to sit down. (I later noticed that commissioned officers usually ignored the more mundane aspects of life—there was always an NCO on hand to do it.) Corporal of Horse Tighe and the three corporals took up what was to be a fairly common stance. Legs apart, whip held under right armpits, and eyes darting across the hopefuls from under the slashed peaks like weasels in a wood pile.

"Good morning, gentlemen, I am Captain Forbes-Hart and I will be your course officer for its full duration." The accent was pure Eton College and he exuded education and good breeding. He had a nine o'clock shadow and was fairly slim but absolutely immaculate in his uniform, with a highly polished Sam Browne Belt around his waist and over his right shoulder. His riding crop was different from the NCO's (shorter) but always there. His most striking feature was his mouth—tight lips pulled across beautiful teeth. It appeared as if a smile was beginning when it wasn't.

"You will not see much of me—Corporal of Horse Tighe will deal with all matters unless you specifically request to see me on a private matter about home, or your instructors are too hard on you, ha-ha-ha."

We laughed politely and Corporal of Horse Tighe gave a mirthless grin. The three wise men never batted an eyelid. That should have been the first warning signal, but I was entranced by the bearing of Forbes-Hart. For the first time, I noticed the black Labrador at his feet, totally unbothered, idly keeping the flies off his master's highly polished brown shoes with an occasional flick of his tail.

Still smiling, Forbes-Hart sat down, removed his cap, and placed it on the desk with his short leather riding crop, to show dark hair parted close to the centre and combed back and flat. "I would briefly like to explain what is going to happen to you over the next four months as now you have all enlisted in the Household Cavalry as a trooper in The Life Guards or The Royal Horse Guards for mainly six or nine years. This will be your training centre for all of your training. In normal times, it is a very busy barracks with the two regiments alternately spending six years here then six in Germany. The Royal Horse Guards are currently eighteen months into their Germany tour and The Life Guards are in Cyprus with the United Nations on peace keeping duties for the foreseeable future.

"Those of you who finish training..." a pregnant pause for effect... "and all of you will not, will be posted to your respective regiments. Those who elect to go to the Household Cavalry in London for ceremonial duties will commence riding school when the course finishes. You have now joined the senior regiment of the British Army and will be trained accordingly. Everything you do will be in the tradition of a great regiment. We will turn the survivors into fit, highly trained soldiers capable of surviving collectively or individually under great stress, with a sense of belonging and intense pride in yourself and your regiment. You, in turn, will give us the right to feel proud of you, and be obedient and disciplined. If your standards are high enough, for long enough, you'll have an ongoing future in a regiment made famous by the high achievements of your predecessors. If you fail in any of these areas, we will have no hesitation in kicking your arses out through the gates. We hope this will not be necessary as no one likes to invest time and money on failures." He paused and the silence was almost deafening.

Thirty bodies took in air simultaneously and a quick twitch on Forbes-Hart's face indicated he knew he had struck home.

"Corporal of Horse?"

"Sah."

"Take over."

"Sah."

Forbes-Hart replaced his cap and in reply to Corporal of Horse Tighe's crisp salute, tipped it with his riding crop, "Tiber Out" and with that, captain and Labrador took their leave.

The ensuing buzz was quickly nipped in the bud by Corporal of Horse Tighe. "Did I say you can talk? Then don't, from this moment in time, you won't breathe unless you are told, you will not answer back unless you are instructed to, and you will always stand to attention when addressed. You refer to me as Corporal of Horse or sir, and my corporals as Corporal. Do you understand?"

A pregnant pause. I was just thinking this guy was a schizophrenic when he shouted, "*Understand!*?"

Mumble, mumble. "Yes, Corporal of Horse, sir."

"From now we will begin. I don't have time to play bloody games, because I have only a short time to turn you into soldiers. Judging from first impressions, God has failed the human race. I will correct these failings because as far as you are concerned, I am God. My way is the way things will be done and done quickly, without hesitation and to the best of your ability. If you question this, we will crawl up your arses and choke you. You will not know a moment when we are not chasing you around and you will measure up. Do you understand?"

Thirty voices as one jolted from a state of deep shock. "Yes sir!"

Talk about hit them hard and fast.

"Louder."

"*Yes sir*!"

He must like this sir thing, I thought, but at this moment if he wanted to be called Esmerelda, there was nobody going to object.

"You will not fraternise with regular soldiers left in the barracks; they are either sick, lame, lazy, or due for discharge, and they will eat you alive. You will shortly be split into four groups under myself, Corporal Miles, Corporal Wheeler, and Corporal Fletcher and then we will prepare you for tomorrow. Any questions? None, Good." (There was never a pause here.)

Groups were formed and in double-quick time, vanished to all corners of the barracks.

I was among the lucky ones who drew Corporal of Horse Tighe. "You can't march, so everything will be done while jogging."

I think he was getting his voice sharpened up as every few seconds it was "Quick mark time," until he caught up and then we'd go again.

Finally, we arrived at a block marked "Orderly Room" and we were lined up by the door. One at a time we were marched in and processed. We were given our army identification number, eight figures long, and told that whatever else we forgot in life, this we would always remember, and to this day it has proved to be true. Everything was laid bare. Details of each life were checked: previous employment, schools, hobbies, birthmarks, scars, inoculations, with everything subject to supposedly hilarious remarks.

"From Manchester—somebody has to be, don't worry we will speak very slowly."

"An electrician's mate—bright spark, probably used to pulling his wire, never mind we'll bring him down to earth."

"Inoculation's up to date. From Manchester? It's always raining we'll just put a damp-proof course in."

I was not used to all this what with the loose boots, baggy clothes, stupid beret, and now the funniest person in the world having a go. But I was soon to learn a very important lesson of recruit life: there is a time to speak and a time not to speak.

"Ever had any kind of clap?"

"Only once when I was twelve."

"Twelve?"

"Yes, I was Puss-In-Boots in the school play, brought the house down."

"Don't take the piss out of me, boy. Think you're a funny bugger, do you?"

"Green, atten-shun." Tighe was on my shoulder. "I'll deal with this, Corporal Major. About turn, double quick time through the door and onto the edge of the square. I told you to shut up unless told to speak, round the square eff-ight, eff-ight, eff-ight (It was too quick to fully say left, right) and report back here to me."

On my return he looked at me and I said, "He asked me if I had..."

"Eff-ight, eff-ight, eff-ight, get around the square again."

I'd done two laps and was moving at the speed of a bulldog in heat when he called me in. "Understand?"

"Yes, sir."

He liked the "sir" and I'd had enough effin-ights to last me a lifetime. By the time I was back at the Orderly Room desk, I didn't have the wind to be funny. I was still trying to pull pockets of air from my feet.

Eventually we were all processed and were lined up again outside. It was only a short distance we thought to our next port of call... the NAAFI (Navy, Army and Air Force Institutes; an organisation providing canteens, shops, etc. for British military personnel at home or overseas). But next to it was another legendary sign: "Regimental Hairdresser."

"Squad halt." Corporal of Horse Tighe looked inside. "Ready for the next lot Corporal Pyle?"

Pyle nodded, and Corporal of Horse Tighe said to the room, "Outside you lot and get in line."

Eight very sorry looking individuals trooped out of the room and all of us outside began to laugh. I only recognised Timmy More by his tattoos. Gone was his shock of dark, curly hair to reveal a half-inch of hair over the top of his head and from half an inch above the ears...nothing. He pulled a funny face and referred to Corporal Pyle's lack of parentage as we were marched in, while Tighe took Timmy's group to the Orderly Room. There was mayhem for a few seconds as everybody tried to get in the chair farthest away from Corporal Pyle's.

"Right," he said, pointing to a youth from Yorkshire, "you first."

"Ok, just a trim, sideburns level with the bottom of my ears and I'll have a square neck."

"Ah, the usual."

Five minutes later, with one half-inch over the head and nothing from half an inch above the ears sat a Yorkshire youth struck dumb, unseeing, and unbelieving as shock set in.

"Next!"

A youth from Birmingham, with naturally wavy, dark hair, took his place on Pyle's castration chair. "Can you shorten the front by an inch and step the back, so it just reaches my collar and same over the ears?"

"What about your sideburns?"

"Just clean them up, please."

"Ah, the usual."

Five minutes later—one half-inch over the head and nothing from half an inch above the ears, Brummie youth joined the unspeaking, unseeing and disbelieving in the shock seat.

"Next!"

I sat down and five minutes later, one half-inch over the head, and nothing from half-inch above the ears. A Manchester youth joined the unspeaking, unseeing, and disbelieving in the shock seats.

Thirty minutes later, we had been marched back to the block, dismissed, and told to report back to the muster area at 1330hrs, lunch being at 1230–1300 hrs. We ran upstairs to the nearest mirrors, took an overall look at the lack of hair, and revisited the world of shock, but as the other squads returned the bantering and good-humoured remarks began.

"You only need a lion stamping on it." (A lion was stamped on eggs to show they were fresh at this time.)

We went for dinner at 1230 hrs and got the same treatment from the "Old Sweats" who were just leaving. (Old Sweats: long-serving soldiers who knew the system). We found they weren't allowed in the same section of the cookhouse where we were, part of the decontamination process.

The cooks had a field day though. "I could make a dozen omelettes if I could get my hands on that one."

"Chefs, you need dark glasses to protect your eyes from the glare."

We ate well and then returned to our barrack block, where shirts were thrown off and thousands of hairs washed off bodies. I lay back on my bed thinking about how much could be got into a day, was it only this morning all this had begun? What would I be doing at home? What was everyone else at home doing? Could I handle all this? But it was quickly 1330 hrs and back to the muster area.

"Fall in outside."

We fell in after a fashion and my group was quickly marched back inside and lined up outside the storeroom where we had been that morning.

"Shut up and stand still."

Tighe was warming up his vocal cords. "When you have all your equipment, take it and throw it on your beds, then get back down here."

I was called in and this was the first time I came across the curious phenomenon of the army issuing everything backwards:

Boots —Ammunition—Pairs two

Socks— Khaki-Wool—Pairs four

Shirts— Red—PT—Pairs two

Shorts—Blue –PT—Pairs two

The voice droned on as gear came from all angles and was rammed into the issued suitcase and kit bag hung around our necks with bedding piled into open arms and then put upstairs on the bed. On my return downstairs, I was also issued with my "Cap-Forage-Size seven," a smart red and dark blue cap, and a black peak with a single gold braid running along the rim. Name and number were written inside the sweat band, and then two of us were marched to the tailor's shop.

He took the caps, which he was going to slash in the traditional Guards style, and then measured us up for our two uniforms.

These were the traditional khaki uniforms worn by soldiers for parading and drilling and they would take approximately four weeks. I was marched back to the storeroom and issued with a diagram of a locker layout, bed layout, and numerous other pieces of everyday useful and "essential" information. How to clean brass buttons, badges, and belt buckles; how to whiten a No-2 dress belt; and the best polish for boots. How had I ever lived without this vast array of knowledge?

"Upstairs, stand by your beds."

When everyone had been kitted out and back upstairs, we were told we would occupy the entire first floor. The staircase came up centrally from the foyer in a dog-leg shape and turned onto the centre of a landing approximately twelve-feet wide and fifty-yards long in total, with a wider area at the top of the landing leading to windows on the far wall over-looking the square. The other side overlooked a grass area and then another block. The rooms at each corner were bedrooms and on each side of the staircase were a large washroom, showers, and toilets. The cleaning rooms were across the corridor from the washrooms and were two long, fairly empty rooms with large sinks and long draining boards, plus a couple of tables. Washroom floors were tile and the remainder of the floors were vinyl squares. The tiles were a mix of light-blue and white and walls were rough textured—greenish-blue lower and white upper.

We were divided into two rooms of eight and two of seven with all rooms having spare lockers for cleaning equipment.

"Stand by your beds, unpack bed packs as per diagram, gear in lockers as per diagram, and be ready for an inspection at 1600 hours." With that, he vanished, probably gone for a drink as per diagram.

We just had time to roughly sort it all out when Corporal of Horse Tighe returned and the rest of the mean machine entered the other three rooms. In our room, eight bodies leapt to attention with all the split-second timing of a dyslexic drum roll as Tighe shouted, "Stand at ease-shun!"

"Stand at ease-shun."

"Stand at ease-shun."

Oh hell, he's slipped into overdrive again.

"I know bad when I see it and you are a disgrace to the word. It will take some weeks to get you to just bloody awful, but you won't care, you'll be so knackered that the weak, lame, and lazy who are gone will make you think they were right. Now, dismantle all spare beds and place them on the truck outside the main doors. Two spare lockers into the main cleaning rooms for larger equipment, one in each room for smaller stuff, any left take out to the truck."

Later we realised that in spite of our under-breath mutterings, this was a good move as it was a lot less stuff to clean.

"Three men from this room follow me." This had simultaneously happened at the other end. Ten minutes later, they had all returned with our new best friends for the next four months.

Buckets- Steel Galvanized—Twelve

Brush — Stiff—Sweeping—Twelve

Brush — Soft—Sweeping—Twelve

Rolls — Toilet—Not Soft—One hundred

Mops — Handles—Long— Twelve

By the time it was all laid out, it resembled a hardware-store delivery day.

Polish—Floor—Lots of...all divided between the two main cleaning rooms to be kept in the now bulging lockers, except for the floor buffer, which was the equivalent of a road gang's tarmac flattener. This had to stand in its gleaming elegance as the granddaddy of all cleaning tortures.

"Fall in at the muster area. Faster."

Wow, in one half-day we had learned where the muster area was, and that "faster" meant a lot more than very quickly.

Hanging on the wall by the main-door muster area was a large notice board.

"Your weekly routine will appear here every Friday along with daily routine orders and anything else we want you to know," Tighe said, pointing to a printed sheet with his riding whip. "This is the remainder of this week. Mealtimes are the same every day, including weekends, as you don't have weekends. Activities are shown and we will inform you how you are to be dressed. Highly polished means *highly* polished. When I tell you to fall out, get to your rooms, prepare for tomorrow, and all equipment had better befit the senior regiment of the British Army. Fall out."

Everyone stayed to look at the notice board:

Reveille —0600hrs.

Breakfast —0700–0730hrs.

Lunch —1230–1300hrs.

Evening Meal—1630–1700 Hrs.

Lights Out —2300hrs

The weekly routine was a dazzling piece of literary precision up to Friday.

0740–0800—Room Inspection

0800–0900—PT Shirt—Shorts—Socks—Plimsolls.

0915–1045—Drill-Beret—Shirt—Coveralls—Boots.

NAAFI BREAK:

1100–1230—Drill or PT

1315–1445—PT or Drill

1445–1630—Drill or PT

1700–1930—Cleaning

1930–2030—NAAFI Break

2030–2300—Cleaning

All activities subject to alteration.

The last line could be roughly interpreted as, if the instructor was having a rough day, we as the germs who were causing it, were subject to his particular brand of medicine.

We all trooped off upstairs into our different rooms and looked at the pile of equipment on our beds, but it was close to feeding time so off we went.

"Get into twos and double march across the edge of the square to the cookhouse and the same when returning." Corporal Wheeler was working on his vocal cords as well.

The meal was very good and plentiful and as usual the banter from the cooks was the same, but who cared, by now we were getting used to it. Double march back and upstairs to rest.

On the bed was more essential information for a recruit to live by: How to shrink a beret to fit, base preparation for whitening Regimental belts with Blanco, preparing boots for highly polishing. New locker-door diagrams showed sizes of folded sheets and blankets, what shelf gear went on, and distances apart for everything. Even suitcases had a distance set to make it central on the top of the locker. Then there was how to clean web belts and brasses. *Oh yes, this is living the dream.*

We spent the evening laying out lockers, cleaning rooms, preparing boots, and...we thought, making a great job of it.

TUESDAY, DAY 2
"HANDS OFF COCKS, ON WITH SOCKS!"

Who the? What the f...? Then the dozy realization that it was the dulcet tones of Corporal Wheeler, just before reveille was blown.

"It's 0600hrs. Shit, shave, shower, soap, and shampoo, clean the room, tidy the lockers, and be at breakfast 0659 hours. One minute late and it's Tango Sierra."

In shock, the room came slowly from sleep to sitting and standing, saying, "What did he say?" But thirty minutes later, we were internally and externally cleansed. We were sweeping and mopping rooms and toilets, all laughing because Timmy, who had previous experience with the territorial army, answered the burning question of the day: "Tango Sierra?"

"Tough shit."

Ok, that's par for the course so far.

We were all back in the room by 0740 hours and Corporal of Horse Tighe entered the room. "Open your lockers." And our gleaming layouts were systematically pulled, pushed, and shoved, all accompanied with various terms of disgust. "The only thing I can say is that to a man, you are going to improve—you will not live in a shit pit, understand?"

"Yes sir."

With that, he left and we all looked at each other without speaking but with a deep look of *holy shit*. We heard the other rooms getting the same treatment and we realised all thirty of us had a common bond; we were all a disgrace.

But before we could take it in, a voice shouted, "Three minutes, downstairs, PT kit."

It took about a minute to find where our gear had finished up, but in three minutes we were all in the muster bay, bang on 0800hrs and were lined up on the edge of the square as per rooms in two ranks.

"In future, line-up in this order when told. Double quick time, follow me." And Corporal Wheeler was off, with Miles and Fletcher on either side and Tighe behind us.

He didn't need to run—he had a bellowing voice and a knowledge of short-cuts. He was like a bad smell, turning up just when we thought he had gone. It didn't take long to get back to jogging and fast walks; we weren't the fittest guys in the world and it was showing. We went around the back of the blocks. Not too far at first, but enough to let the ones who had not gone with the regiment abroad know that a new bunch of fodder was being processed.

We finally returned to the starting point and heard the reassuring words from Corporal of Horse Tighe: "Unfit, filthy, and fucked. Give me strength. Upstairs and into drill kit, back here at 0915hrs."

And we all huffed and puffed up the staircase.

But, at 0915hrs, we were back on the edge of the square, looking resplendent in our flying saucer berets, hairy shirts, over-sized coveralls and "highly polished" boots.

"Always take these positions, until told otherwise."

Cavalry line-up in twos as opposed to other regiments, who line-up in three ranks. Then, from the upstairs window, Tighe changed some more positions and came down onto the parade ground. "Now all we have to do is make soldiers of you. That may be impossible, but when I'm finished with you, you'll either be at home with the regiment, or just at home."

There goes that weasel in the wood-pile look again.

The next two hours were definitely tiring and we never moved from the spot. How to stand easy, stand at ease, attention, left and right turn on the spot. At attention, turn foot to ninety degrees, then swing other leg parallel to the ground, ninety degrees at knee then slam that foot down—great in ammo boots that had studded soles, so were noisy. Somehow left and rights were mixed up and it seemed really funny, until the one who got it wrong did ten more press-ups in front of everybody. We all at some stage screwed up and took centre stage for our sins. All the time, the three wise men were pushing feet to forty-five degrees, holding thighs parallel, kicking boots not at ninety degrees during turns, pulling arms back, pushing stomachs in, shoulders back, their voices sometimes at fever pitch and using new words.

No one knew names although we had name tags, it was just as easy to be Trooper Pillock at this point. Except for a smoke break, this continued until 1220hrs.

"What a pack of human screw-ups we have been given this time. Some people here are in for a big shock and it will not be us. Back here at 1305 hrs."

At lunch we had plenty of laughs about the sheer number of cock-ups, but one or two were feeling a bit tired, and one was complaining about being screamed at directly into his face. We knew everyone was getting a good shouting at, but some were taking it personally.

"Get outside."

It was 1301hrs. and we clattered, slipping and sliding downstairs and mainly forgot our positions—well it was forty minutes ago—so it all began again. The good thing, though, was consistency—we were crap this morning and crap again this afternoon.

"Stand at ease, attenn-shun, chest out, stomach in-shoulders back." They were teaching us how to stand. Apart from two short breaks, this went on until 1620 hrs, being pulled, pushed, and loudly cajoled into various human contortions. But we maintained our inconsistency; we were still a useless band of human screw-ups.

At least we had more good food and then a quick relax before cleaning all our new equipment that Corporal of Horse Tighe had kindly arranged in a heap for us, though on the bright side, we now saw everything we had.

"What's this?"

"A brass button and badge cleaning stick. Slide it behind them prior to highly polishing."

"What's this little white cotton pack with needles and thread in it?"

"A housewife."

"You're kidding."

"Nope, for darning socks, etc."

"Ha-ha, screw you."

"No, I'd rather have a housewife."

Soon we all marched down to the NAAFI, drank pop, ate pies, swapped stories of the day, and got back at 2030hrs.

Corporal Fletcher came in and got us all into one of the large cleaning rooms. "You will all be allowed to phone home once a week for fifteen minutes. If it is an emergency, your families have a central number for us, and we will contact you. Each room will be allocated a night. Stick to it—if you overrun, you miss next week's call. Questions?"

"Yes, Corporal. Once a week?"

"Why? Is that too often?"

"Well, I thought that we..."

"You don't fucking think, I do."

Thirty sets of eyes with a group feeling of *wow!*

"Right, get on with cleaning." And with that, he was gone.

After five minutes, a voice said very quietly, "Has he gone?"

"Yes, I saw him leave."

"Bloody pillock." Not so quiet now, and once again we all agreed. Now that's consistency.

More cleaning. Highly polishing two sets of boots took most of the time, but I thought: *These are good, they will impress.* With that, a shower, then into bed and although restless to begin with, it turned into a good night's sleep.

WEDNESDAY, DAY 3
"HANDS OFF COCKS, ON WITH SOCKS!"

No! Impossible—I've just got in bed, but reveille was being played under the windows and then the musician moved on.

We slowly set off to the washrooms. We had seized up a bit, feeling sore in other areas after yesterday's little efforts.

It took until after breakfast to get reasonably mobile again, just in time to be stood by our beds, ready for our morning kit inspection by Corporal of Horse Tighe...and he was on form.

Fifteen minutes later and we virtually had a kit-exchange programme in operation. My highly polished boots apparently weren't and one ended by Timmy's bed, but that was okay, his button stick and PT vest landed by Alex. In turn, Alex's plimsolls and housewife sailed over Keith's bed, whose apparently highly polished boots also weren't, and they ended up under another bed. At least nobody could get upset about being left out, so we felt as if we were beginning to bond.

"Outside 0800hrs, we will discuss this after evening meal."

This made us a little apprehensive but we had no time to think.

Bang on 0800hrs we were lined up in our correct formation on the edge of the square. No Corporal of Horse Tighe, just three wise men.

More pushing, prodding, and shoving with a huge splash of shouting. Left turn-Right turn-Shun, for about an hour, then..."Upstairs, back here in ten minutes in PT kit."

At 0920hrs we were back on the edge of the square looking resplendent in red, short-sleeved shirts, baggy blue shorts, socks, and plimsolls. The plimsolls had very low soles and it was like constantly running on concrete.

We ran around the edge of the square (never across it) and were lined up outside. We were handed over to Corporal Kelly and Lance Corporals Jones and Thomas, all dressed in perfect-fitting red shirts; long, blue, light-weight trousers; smart red cloth belts; and good-looking footwear. We looked like the poor relatives as we were taken inside, put in three teams of ten, and then introduced to the physical training instructors.

Corporal Kelly looked really fit prancing around on his toes, no excess fat, and apparently, he just couldn't stand still. "For the rest of the day we will be assessing your fitness at different skills and deciding what level you are at now. Don't want to kill you on your first day in here."

Must be in the food, all this pleasantry.

The gym was very much like our school one. A large, open space, wall bars on two opposite walls, lots of mats, medicine balls, vaulting horses, and small springboards stored in a room at the front. High ropes tied to the ceiling when not in use, and a particular form of torture that took place on beams lowered from the ceiling called pull-ups.

It was nearly always cool in the gym at the beginning of a session just to keep us on our toes, I think. They slowly began putting us in three teams, initially using the eyeball method: is fit—looks fit—needs help. We were then shown all the various pieces of equipment one at a time and how maximum pain could be extracted from it, plus what would be expected from us over the coming weeks. We pulled out the ropes, made a circuit of vaulting horses, ramps, and mats, by which time it was close to lunch, so we jogged back to the block to change for lunch, and be back in PT kit on the edge of the square at 1300 hrs.

During lunch, we talked about Corporal of Horse Tighe's rummage sale, and how the gym had been a fairly easy start. But talk about the calm before the storm. By 1305 hrs we were back in the gym facing the new version of the Three Musketeers.

First a bit of leg stretching, touch toes, flail arms around like a demented windmill, then line-up in our teams. This was almost always the start of each session.

My team under Lance Corporal Jones was on the wall bars first. We did various exercises, then while still ticking boxes, Lance Corporal Jones told us to rest.

We sat and watched the others, as big Alex dismantled the horse's top section, while trying to vault it. (As Lance Corporal Thomas put it, "with all the finesse of a ruptured hippopotamus") and the nickname Big Hippo was to stick with Alex.

Then off to the ropes with Corporal Kelly. We had to climb them twice, the second time waiting at the top until told to come down, but some guys struggled with this. We did a couple of laps of the gym, then went to Lance Corporal Thomas at the vaulting horse.

"Run down the next mat, vault over the horse, touch the far wall and run back."

Two did it, two hit it low and got crushed nuts, the other four of us landed on it and shuffled off. All the while, Lance Corporal Thomas bemoaned the fact that we were crap material to work with, and he must have been bad in a previous life.

Then he did a brilliant demo of running to the pommel horse, springing high in the air, barely touching the two handles at the centre, and landing with all the flair of a man in total control.

The first recruit to try it didn't get very high. He caught his toes on the horse and did a perfect dive headfirst into the floor…nose burst and blood everywhere. Three of us ran to him aided by the sympathetic words of Lance Corporal Thomas.

"You pillock, you've got blood on my clean floor."

We helped stop the bleeding, and Corporal Kelly came and took the dazed recruit to the office, to check him over.

"Okay, the rest of you get my floor gleaming again."

This put a damper on things for a while, but it did prioritise life as a recruit. Clean kit, clean floors, do as you are told, Tango Sierra if hurt.

On the plus side, it gave us all five minutes to get our breath back and the pommel horse was never used again.

The recruit who burst his nose was a Royal Horse Guard recruit from London called Pete Hughes, who had a way with words, and from nose dive to stopping the bleeding, he got in at least twenty "Facking hells and Fack me's." To the end of the course, he was known as "Facking Pete."

During a break, they told us that every two weeks there would be assessments, emphasising, "With pass or fail."

This day brought us closer together. Going in and out of each other's rooms, there was plenty of chat about the day's events. A couple of guys were looking serious and we all tried to tell them it wasn't personal. One of them was a bigger, slightly overweight individual in Room Two, who was already becoming mentally and physically bogged down—not a good sign.

Corporal of Horse Tighe did promise us a visit after evening meal this evening, so a wary eye was kept on the outside doors, while we prepared our wayward gear again for cleaning, waiting all the time for a visit from God.

He arrived with Corporals Wheeler and Fletcher, and this time we were given the whole double-barrel expectancies.

"This is the only time I will explain what we require from you. You have four to five hours minimum every night to work on your equipment, plus weekends for getting washrooms, toilets, showers, and floors in the rooms fit for royalty. I want every piece of equipment you own to be gleaming. I don't know what 'highly polished' means to you, but I have not seen even the remotest attempt to achieve this. My corporals will show you what we expect, then it will improve every single day of your training. If it doesn't, I will throw it out of the window, or you off the course. The choice is yours."

I remember thinking at the time: *He really is an immaculate lunatic.*

But it was collective big gulp time.

"Corporals take over." And with that, his boots made a loud clacking sound in the totally quiet room as he marched out.

Then began a fairly long preamble, explaining how the next sixteen weeks would make men of us, push us to our limits, and weed out the weak, but that the end result would be even above our own belief. They went through every piece of equipment methodically and precisely, missing nothing. What it is, what it's for, what will we do with it. (This one always brought a laugh.) How to wash, fold, iron, starch, where to place locker layout plans, what shelf, how far apart, fold shirts to a certain size, order of hanging clothes...but army logic was a pleasure to behold.

"How will we know if they are the correct size and spacing?"

"Because we will not have pulled them apart."

I glanced at Timmy and we grimaced and rolled our eyes back at each other...then:

"Green, More, do you find this funny?"

"No Corporal. Very enlightening, Corporal."

"Well enlighten the floor with ten press-ups."

Timmy said, "Ten press-ups?"

"Okay, fifteen."

Then on and on. Brass cleaning, badge cleaning, webbing belts cleaning, and how to whiten regimental belts. Highly polish belt brasses and no cracking marks on white belts. No signs of Brasso or whitening, other than where it should be.

Berets, keep putting them in hot then cold water to shrink, keep them on until dry, if not perfect, second verse same as the first. But the crowning glory, as always, would be our boots.

"You have two pairs: one for everyday use and these will always have a deep shine. The second pair will be so highly polished that countless layers of spit and polish will make them like deep, deep gleaming mirrors. To prepare them, either dip them in horse urine or put lighted candles under the leather to remove all traces of grease, and then you can begin building up the polish in layers."

(That night, the NAAFI sold out of candles and the horses were free to pee at their leisure.)

"Questions?"

Well, we were ten minutes into NAAFI break by now, so no questions.

"Right, NAAFI, then get started at 2030hrs." And like two ghosts in the night, they were gone.

By 2035hrs, the big sinks were full of water and the ceremonial dipping of the berets began, while some began burning off their boots. It took hours and the rooms smelt like a Chinese brothel, apparently!!

The beret fitting took time. When the beret was shaping on your head, you could start on other things, though at times as they shrunk it was like having your head in a vice. We all spent about three hours on these tasks, and then began to shave and shower. We soon cottoned on to this night shave and shower idea, as there was not much time in a morning, and it was easier to clean the washrooms. By 2300 hrs, lights were out and everyone was flat out asleep.

THURSDAY, DAY 4 – FRIDAY, DAY 5
WASH, RINSE AND REPEAT

For two days, on the drill square, we were pushed and prodded into shape. We were taught how to stand, breath, and how to shut up and listen. Every move was subject to scrutiny, and none of it was ever right, but there was lots of encouragement.

"If that's a stride, you're going for a medical."

"I could stride farther than that in high heels—do you normally wear high heels?"

We did laps of the square each time we got it wrong, and there were many laps.

There were inspections upon inspections. They could see a flea's left-ball size of Brasso at ten feet and react as if someone had shot the pope. Anything larger than two fleas' left-ball sizes of Brasso warranted apoplexy.

They didn't bother with names at first. If an individual made a mistake, they were called out to the front of the squad to explain why they were Trooper Pillock. If anyone even risked a smile, the squad went for a run round the square.

The first time we marched and halted on the square, three men went arse over tit, and the rest of us hung on to each other to stay upright.

This led to one pair of ammunition boots (ammo boots), which were studded, being changed for a pair of boots—ankle—DMS (direct moulded sole) and the rubber soles gave us a better grip.

"In future you will only wear ammo boots when told, as they can only be worn by people who have a clue what they are doing. Both pairs will always be immaculate."

We paid another visit to the gym. I was in Team Two with Lance Corporal Thomas, and each team had different levels of goals. The first visits were to get under-used bodies gradually up to speed.

As is almost traditional, out of earshot, the PTIs were given nicknames.

Corporal Kelly was "Gimme" from "Give me one more."

Lance Corporal Thomas was "Ticker Thomas" as he was always ticking (complaining).

Lance Corporal Jones was "Jeeves Jones" as he was always waiting on something or someone.

At this time, a few of us were getting a few sore red areas on our feet. Corporal Kelly said, "If they turn to blisters, don't pop them and get them looked at later; your feet will toughen up soon."

After evening meal, I was talking to Baines from Room Two. He was nicknamed Banjo because he was highly strung. He told me he was fed up with all the constant shouting and he seemed a bit down.

I later mentioned it to Timmy (as he was old and wise at twenty-three) and we decided to keep an eye on Banjo.

To be honest, many of us were having quiet times in the evenings, thinking of what was happening at home but keeping busy with things to do here.

After NAAFI, it was back to the never-ending cleaning and then off to bed.

SATURDAY, DAY 6 – SUNDAY, DAY 7
A CLEAN SWEEP

The weekends were initially for huge clean-ups, but soon evolved into a mix of the daily routines.

We had a quick kit inspection, involving tossing the towels and lobbing the PT kit, and then we were lined up in the corridor.

This produced another large array of cleaning aids: sprays, powders, polish, scrubbing brushes, all coming with instructional use.

Just when we thought the worst was over, out came the "buffer," the granddaddy of all tortures affectionately known as...the Bumper. (It couldn't pass anything without bumping into it).

There was a heavy base with an attachment underneath on which to attach seventeen-inch-diameter pads. It had a thin, four-foot stem, and a "T" handle across the top, with holding levers controlling on/off. If you let go of the levers, it would stop...eventually. A fifty-foot lead, and two small wheels on the back to help it along, and let battle commence.

Corporal Miles proceeded to demonstrate and made it look easy. Then he took his eye off the ball and let go of the lever, causing him to fall one way while the Bumper went the other.

We were enjoying this as Corporal Miles said, "Just to show you what could happen if you lose control."

Corporal of Horse Tighe found this amusing. "Much appreciated, Corporal Miles."

After lunch, Corporal Miles showed us what they expected, including: dust off bed frames, clean windows, wash walls, and toothbrush in small areas, including toilets. He left us to get on with it and told us he would be back tomorrow morning.

Next day, plan A was all lockers and beds into the middle of the room, clean and polish this area, then replace them. Afterwards, Bumper corridors and hand polish the staircase. Mop out and clean washrooms and clean rooms—it was endless.

Corporal Miles left mid-morning saying, "Don't forget your personal gear."

We put everything in the middle of the room. Thinking I was a confident operator, I put a pad on it and plugged in the Bumper.

I pushed into a large dollop of polish and promptly splattered the lower back wall, two backs and sides of lockers, and three pissed-off recruits, including myself. I let go of the levers and in its death throes the Bumper swung into the side of Bob's locker.

I looked around and said, "Fucking hell, do you think there was too much polish on the floor?"

"There's fucking not now," Keith said as we burst out laughing.

This probably saved me from a lynching.

After lunch, more cleaning and while in the washroom one of the guys from Room Two mentioned that Banjo never seemed to sleep and had to be pushed to help out.

We went and got Banjo, and chatted to him while he helped us in the washroom.

He was very helpful and even managed to clear a very dodgy looking build-up in a toilet. We paid for a pie for him in the NAAFI that evening—high praise indeed.

Corporal Miles came in later to tell us that commencing tomorrow, Room One would be on phone calls, Room Two on Tuesday, and so on.

These phone calls became important to all of us, and we only ever discussed positive things.

It had been another long and tiring day and I'm sure I went to bed with my arms still doing circular motions.

WEEK 2

MONDAY, DAY 8
"HANDS OFF COCKS!"

Shut up you noisy prick (I shouted very loudly, but only in my own head). Everyone had a last room clean, dried out the washroom and cleaning room, then went off to breakfast feeling very pleased with themselves.

At "Stand by your beds" we were already there, chests puffed out, totally at ease with a good expectant air about everything.

"Room atten-shun, What the fuck is this?" And the feelgood factor rapidly left. He was by Alex's bed and had put on a white glove with one finger held out after it had gently caressed the inner hinge of the open locker door.

"It looks like a speck of dust, Corporal of Horse."

"A speck! a speck! No such bloody thing! This is dirt, filth!"

(I still don't know how a speck of dust causes plimsolls to fly or bed packs to unravel).

By the time he left us, the room was looking very familiar for 0750hrshrs on any given morning. It was hard to believe that only ten minutes ago the rooms had been a blitz-free area.

Edge of square at 0800 hrs, then double back upstairs, get sheets, pillow slips, and towels. Change for clean ones, place neatly in middle of earlier carnage, then onto the square.

We ran through our drill moves with an excess of encouragement. (Monday seems to do that to people). In our defence, we hadn't drilled for three days. One recruit failed to get his timing at the command "Halt" and marched straight into the stationary soldier in front of him.

He was doubled to the front of the squad where the immortal words of an irate instructor rang out. "Son, if balls were brains, a splinter on a toilet seat would totally destroy anything you ever learned."

Moving on, saluting.

Even this had its own learning curve: right arm longest way up, shortest way down. Demo: arm swung out to right and bring flat of hand, palm out, to a position where index finger/middle finger are approximately one inch over right eye. We went over and over this timing: up two-three, down two-three. Hands and arms pulled and pushed, adjusted and re-adjusted. A short break then straight back on the square, but now up a notch, saluting to the front after "Halt" was given. Piece of cake...well rock cake really. Halt, check one-two, up two-three, down two-three. More demos, more encouragement. We looked good alone, but saluting collectively were a nightmare. It looked like one drawn-out movement with an arm wave all the way from front to back as we were still concentrating on not clobbering the guy in front of us.

A Trooper Pillock was brought to the front. "Show them, Trooper."

When he'd finished, Corporal Wheeler observed that Trooper Pillock looked more like "a fucking window cleaner."

I don't know whether Trooper Pillock grimaced or smiled at this, but there followed the inevitable.

"Round the square, back here, salute the squad."

He did and Corporal Wheeler said, "Who told you to stop?"

Off he went, rolling his eyes at the squad in passing, which caused many to smile.

"If you like Trooper Pillock that much, follow him."

We all did two laps. Shit, it's that army logic again. Are we beginning to understand it? Not really, but getting there.

Eventually it was lunchtime, upstairs, quick wash, and cookhouse.

We lined up at the hotplate, and the three cooks behind it all smirked and saluted. The square was highly visible from the cookhouse.

Big Hippo said, "You look fucking stupid."

Immediately they all looked really angry, but before they could react, Big Hippo said, "Thank fuck, you are all good cooks."

"Give that man an extra roast, Chef," said the cook corporal and tension was gone. I like to think it was because Big Hippo was quick thinking, and nothing to do with being six-foot-two and over 200lbs.

New routine orders had been posted in the foyer on the way back. Only the date was changed, but of course all was subject to change.

At 1301hrs we were on the square in PT kit doing the usual couple of laps around the square. Then we lined up and were taken into the gym… more demented wind milling and then into teams.

It was apparent now that numbers one and two in Team One had been born fit. Even Corporal Kelly seemed impressed.

I think some of us were also feeling better. Lots of exercise, running, good food, no beer, more energy, and the morning soreness easing out quicker. Sometimes it was a good feeling but mainly it was a constant effort to keep going as everything was met by "gimme more."

The afternoon soon passed and it was time for evening meal and then back to our extended cleaning routine. In my room's case, we were all excited about using the phone. Alex was first and got straight through, and then I followed him.

I heard Mum's voice at the other end and felt a strange feeling in the pit of my stomach, but I had to stay positive. "Hi Mum, it's great to hear you. How is everything at home?"

"Oh John, it's quieter without you around. We all miss you, how is it all going?"

(As I mentioned previously, in the army I was called Jimmy right from the start and it stuck. I was only reacting to Jimmy at this point, except to my family.)

"Well, it's not boring. Plenty of exercise, shouting, drill, good food, and lots of cleaning."

"What? You? I'll have to save some cleaning for you when you get home."

I had a quick word with the family. Dad asked when I was coming home, a bit sarcastically, and I said for three days at the end of March/

April. "Good lad," and then the last five minutes with Mum explaining the phone routine and not to worry if it changed a bit.

"Okay love, my time's nearly up, I'll call you next Monday."

Mum, a little emotional, said it reminded her of when she joined the navy, and all too soon the fifteen minutes was over.

I went back to the room, and just sat on my bed feeling absolutely mentally and emotionally drained. My head was just full of mixed thoughts and my stomach was churning.

"Jimmy, are you okay?"

It was Timmy, and I said, "Hopefully in a few minutes."

"It's called home sickness."

"What is?"

"You and how you feel. Keep busy, focussed, and eventually it will get easier. It happened to me when I left home three years ago. Come on, let's get bulling."

We spent a while chatting then he went to the phone.

Soon it was NAAFI break. The majority of us who had phoned were quiet. I couldn't eat and even Banjo noticed.

"Are you alright, Jimmy?"

"Just a passing phase, Banjo."

We carried on personal cleaning, and for the last hour or so did another blitz of the rooms, ready for tomorrow's assault.

Then to bed and I had a lousy night. My mind was playing games, mostly wide awake, then dozing, strange dreaming and it all revolved around being at home. I felt so upset that I sat up once with tears rolling down my cheeks, but eventually fell asleep just before they woke us.

TUESDAY, DAY 9
"HANDS OFF COCKS!"

I slowly got up and wandered off for a wash and shave and got everything ready for inspection, feeling brighter now with all the chatter. I was really hungry and ate a huge breakfast and talked with Banjo. He wasn't sleeping well and couldn't wait for tonight to phone home. Then it was back to our rooms for inspection.

"Form up in your washrooms."

"Why does that toilet door squeak when it opens?"

Silence.

"Green, answer me. Why?"

"Is it because this comes under routine maintenance, not cleaning Corporal of Horse?"

"Fucking maintenance! Corporal Wheeler, have you ever heard such a crock of shit?"

"Never ever, Corporal of Horse." But there was a faint smile forming on Tighe's face.

"It can't get any worse, but it does. By tomorrow morning, every window and door hinge will be rubbed down, cleaned, and oiled. If I hear another squeak from any hinge, I will take it personally, understand?"

"Yes, Corporal of Horse."

The weather was getting worse this morning, much wetter and chillier. "PT kit, plimsolls, camouflage jackets, foyer 0800 hrs."

By 0800hrs it was really persisting down, so..."Upstairs, DMS boots, plimsolls in pockets, plus towel."

We reformed in the foyer looking at each other as if *What the F****.

"Don't want to upset you by missing your jog. Hopkins, (one of our two top fitness recruits) in twos, jog them around the square." And off we went. To give the instructor his due, he did stand near the foyer door, under cover.

As we were finishing the lap: "Carry on again and go to the gym."

The doors were opened and we took off our jackets and boots, towelled dry, and put on plimsolls. The hairs on my legs felt as if a static charge had been applied to them.

Corporal Kelly put us in our teams and said, "Shut up. If I hear anyone moaning, we'll go outside all morning."

This was followed by another classic, "War don't wait for weather."

I'm sure they must go to classes for these.

"Okay, warm up." Burpees (for a warm up, come on) press-ups, touch toes and, of course, demented windmills. We spent the next hour in teams, sprinting to one end of the gym, picking up a medicine ball, sprinting back, and then giving it to the next man. Twenty press-ups for the losing team. We got in a few press-ups this morning. We had a guy who could lift the London Bridge with one hand (Bull Durham), the problem was he had the running speed of a herniated duck, but who was going to tell him?

We had a NAAFI break, and then back in for part two, setting up a kind of obstacle course with different expectations for Teams One, Two and Three. Banjo was in Team Two and reasonably fit, but if he could get away with the minimum he would, and he got a hefty bollocking as we were putting everything away.

"Baines, you lazy wanker, I am watching you," said Kelly. "Get your finger out, you bloody dead leg."

Banjo didn't even acknowledge him, just picked something up and carried it to the store.

The main topic at lunch was Banjo's bollocking. Everyone laughed at this, except Banjo. I spoke to him on the way back and he had definitely had a humour transplant.

"Fuck 'em, but at least I can phone home tonight."

"Yes, great," I said, "Something to look forward to."

Soon it was 1305hrs and the weather was much better. We formed up on the square doing re-runs of everything from stand easy to saluting. It looked like the beginning of a hard afternoon as we heard "Atten-shun, Two ranks right dress." Twenty-nine eyes went right, and the right arm was raised to the next recruit's left shoulder, except one who did eyes left and left arm, and then realized his mistake but not quickly enough.

"That useless piece of skin, get out here."

I don't know why but to this day this kind of cock-up is nearly always impossible not to laugh at.

"Raise your left arm, keep it in the air and turn it in a left circle until I tell you to stop." After a few twirls, it was biting cheek time, our shoulders moving with suppressed laughter.

"Repeat after me, I am the stupid pillock who does not know his left from his right."

"Right Trooper Pillock, double quick time, and the rest of you follow him."

A few left and rights later we ended back where we began, with all thoughts of laughing subdued. We asked the trooper about it later, and he said it was just nerves. We tended to agree as we were all dropping clangers somewhere in the day. We pounded away, had a quick NAAFI break for a smoke, then lined up again.

"We will move on to about-turns on the march. Demo, going forward about turn, halt, check one-two and swivel right heel left toe through 180 degrees. Lift leg at knee and bring down alongside right foot two-three, then step off on left foot."

The next fifteen minutes were utter chaos. We had numerous demonstrations, followed by numerous cock-ups.

"I knew you would not be able to grasp anything above the level of a five-year old, we'll do it stationary until you get it."

We did the halt, then a stationary 180-degree swivel, wobbling all over the place, with loads of shuffling and more encouragement. We spent the rest of the afternoon halting, turning, wobbling, and making left knee adjustments and foot positions before stepping off. With no small relief it was eventually evening mealtime.

Banjo was like a dog in heat and at 1755hrs he was at the door ready to head for the phone. At about 1830hrs he was back but the guy after him, called Parkin, was annoyed as they had nearly come to blows to get Banjo off the phone.

This started again later, and a few punches were thrown before they were separated. The air was tense and Banjo wouldn't come to the NAAFI.

When we got back, he was sitting on his bed staring at the floor, seemingly in his own world.

We carried on with personal cleaning. Our equipment was beginning to look much smarter now. The ammo boots with not being worn and still being bulled, were gleaming. Even our camouflage suits were pressed, and they were hung up like mirror images of each other.

A last clean-up of the washrooms where we checked all hinges and door movements. They were good and un-squeaky clean, so then it was off to bed and after a restless couple of hours I managed to fall asleep.

WEDNESDAY, DAY 10
"HANDS OFF COCKS!"

I'm sure there is no night—it seems to be head down, then up. The stiffness on getting up is improving and the feet are not needing much attention, so it's getting better.

I saw Banjo at the sinks, and he looked rough and apparently hadn't slept.

"Banjo, you look like shit; you need to settle down and just get on with it."

"Who really gives a shit, Jimmy?" And he went back to his room.

After breakfast we returned to the block.

"Stand by your beds."

We should have known it would not be a squeaky door test; the army doesn't work that way. Corporal of Horse Tighe had just begun his morning air-borne assault on our equipment when he was called by Corporal Wheeler to go next door.

A few minutes later he came back and said, "On the yard for drill in five minutes."

Now this was unusual even for them. As we were going down the stairs, one of the guys in Room Two said, "It's Banjo."

Corporals Fletcher and Miles shouted, "Shut up and line-up on the square."

We all fell in but saw no sign of Corporal of Horse Tighe, Corporal Wheeler, or Banjo. We were put through our paces right from square one. It was hard to concentrate, as three rooms hadn't much of an idea, and the room that did couldn't talk.

We were practicing about-turns when we saw Corporal of Horse Tighe, and another man we didn't know walking towards the MI room (medical inspection) and going inside. It was not far, just at the end of the blocks on our side of the square.

Around 1015hrs we were marched to the NAAFI and told to stay there until we were told differently. The squad was buzzing and the guys in Banjo's room all told roughly the same story.

From stand by your beds, Corporal Wheeler entered the room and saw Banjo at the other end, half dressed and bed pack all over the place. Wheeler marched down and said, "Baines, you lazy, idle, little shit clean that mess up, I will see you after this is over."

Banjo said, "If you are that fucking worried, clean it up yourself," and threw something on the floor.

They all agreed, though, that Banjo didn't look good.

Corporal Wheeler called in Corporal of Horse Tighe.

"Baines, are you refusing an order to pick up your equipment?"

Banjo just stared at him and never moved.

"Did you hear me?"

Banjo apparently muttered something about all this being a load of fucking bollocks."

Corporal of Horse Tighe had then told everyone to get into drill kit and sent Corporal Wheeler to instruct Corporals Fletcher and Miles to run the drill session.

He told Banjo to stay put until we were all out of the block.

About 1050hrs we were marched back to the square. Corporals Fletcher and Miles carried on with drill and we were immersed in it until around midday.

At approximately 1200hrs, we were instructed to go to the floor on our block. Upon arrival we were met by Corporal of Horse Tighe and Corporal Wheeler, who said, "Line-up in pairs along the corridor."

We couldn't do it quickly enough—the suspense was killing us.

"After seeing the medical examiner, Recruit Baines exercised his right to leave the army. He has handed in his equipment and is gone."

Talk about hearing a pin drop. A long, stunned silence ensued, broken by Corporal of Horse Tighe saying, "If anyone else is not man enough to carry on, see me now and don't infect the ones who can."

Phew, let's take a while to get to the nitty-gritty, or not.

"Room two get his locker and bed and put them in the corridor next to the storeroom downstairs then clean his space up. Lunch is at 1230hrs and 1305hrs edge of square for PT. Questions?"

"Dismiss."

We walked back into our rooms, and it was as if someone had lifted a sound curtain. Suddenly Ginger said, "One down, twenty-nine more to go."

"Twenty-eight. I'm going nowhere," said Dave Marx.

"Nor me," said the rest of us in the room, and in a selfish kind of way, we were feeling relief that it wasn't us. Strangely, it strengthened our resolve to see it all the way through. This was the only topic of conversation at lunch, with a thousand theories as to what the cause was, and a bit of a realisation that Banjo would not be the last.

But soon it was business as usual and we were going into the house of body reconstruction for our demented windmill session, and our daily dose of the quest for perfection.

Later I learned the meaning of pain. I had just got to the wall when Alex threw me over his shoulders and did his kind of herniated duck run to the far wall. It took forever. By the time he put me down, I felt like I'd been kicked in the nuts...and we still had to get back.

I got him on my shoulders (he was nearly touching the floor with his hands and feet) and off we went. Soon my knees began to feel as if they were bending, and halfway through I realised I was going off diagonally. My legs felt as if the muscles had turned to lead. As I staggered along, everyone was telling me to keep going.

My pride said *Yes*, but my body was having none of it and about eight or nine staggers more and the floor came up to meet me. We both ended up on the floor, exhausted, and Alex by now also had the sore nut treatment.

As I stood up, my legs had gone to jelly and I was all over the place. After that, Alex was a carry-free zone. Although not on the same team, he had grabbed me as I was nearest. Ten minutes later, Bull Durham was put in Team Three with Alex, to have a regular clash of the titans, and a more human-sized human was put into ours.

My legs were still a bit shaky and later, after sitting still for twenty minutes eating, it was hard to get them going again. I think Alex was also getting some stick as he kept looking across, pretending to rub his nether region and shaking his fist. I gave him my best shock and horror look.

That afternoon, it was a strange atmosphere during cleaning, with Banjo being the main topic of conversation and everyone having different ideas of why.

For me, later in the NAAFI, while talking to Timmy, Alex, and Dave Marx, it was the defining moment of my training. I said I couldn't even think of leaving, I didn't have the courage to quit and let myself and my family down. From then on, quitting was never an option, and it was never again discussed positively.

After NAAFI to lights out, throughout the increasing cleaning routines, everything was as normal, if we knew what normal was anymore. One thing for certain, it was amazing how much effort and drama could be fitted into any given day. The effect on the squad was now transferred from how we'd felt at lunch time, to a strangely positive theme that had spread amongst all of us. We were boosting our own confidence amongst the inevitable bravado that took place.

I slept really well that night. I had totally convinced myself that whatever was going to happen from now on, I would be part of it.

THURSDAY, DAY 11 – SUNDAY, DAY 14
A BLISTERING PACE

Through this period, drill was the order of at least half of every day. It was becoming more automatic, and we were feeling more in tune. Pity it was only us, though. The instructors practised new words of encouragement, plus tried and tested ploys such as pretending someone had smiled when they hadn't, just so we could go for a jog around the square. They were loud, and in your face, with little or no respite. We were pleased when it was over, but also always pleased to have survived.

During a drill period, Bull Durham decided to do a bit of bum wiggling and was spotted by Corporal Wheeler, who made him come to the front and take over, "…being as you are a smart arse."

Bull was flustered and set us off but then went quiet.

Corporal Wheeler shouted, "Say something, or they will vanish up Windsor High Street."

Bull shouted "Halt!" but on the wrong foot and chaos ensued.

Corporal Wheeler said, "I think you want to address the squad."

Bull went to town on how big a pillock he was, and Corporal Wheeler thanked him for confirming that.

That night in the NAAFI we ribbed Bull unmercifully.

The NAAFI lady, whose name was Alice, and who looked on us as more of a vocation than a job, said to Bull, "You don't have to put up with that."

"Yes, I do, Alice," Bull said. "I had a big cock-up today."

It was the only time we saw her lost for words, but these events were helping us to get to know each other better.

Later that evening I was talking to a guy in Room Three, who was the dog's bollocks of boot bulling, but not so good with his belts. My world got decidedly better when after a quick discussion, and for the rest of the course, Don did my boots, and I did his belts.

Room inspections were still a gamble as to what would happen. Quite often it was totally unexpected. The morning after Banjo finished, we heard, "Both rooms, washroom, now."

Corporal of Horse Tighe was pointing into a toilet bowl. "Who used this last? ...Nobody? So, we have a phantom crapper. All of you look in here."

Lying there in all its glory, was a single, pristine piece of toilet tissue.

"Disgusting, obviously we will have to keep an eye on your dirty habits." And off they went.

"Who the hell did that? If I find out, I'll beat the shit out of him." This was the guy who had come to blows with Banjo.

"Look properly before you start gobbing off, you are too quick with your mouth," Danny Williams said. "Not even a crease in the paper."

Then it dawned on us *who* had put it there.

As the recruit now known as the Mouth walked away, Danny said, "I liked Banjo."

Around this time, on a room inspection, Corporal of Horse Tighe, from ten feet away, saw Ginger's bedpack was a quarter of an inch too small and tossed one of his blankets out of the window.

That evening Ginger had a brainwave. He bought a tape measure from the NAAFI and made a cardboard template. It was hidden in a suitcase, and the instructors only became aware of it during the last week, when Ginger informed them about it.

The gym was a hive of industry, and our fitness was definitely improving. On the Friday we did a big workout, ready for the first assessment next Monday. It was a hard-worked workout and by the end of it we were knackered, but at least the first wave of blisters were settling down.

They were also establishing a regular run around the barracks, the only criterion being that one of us led and we had to go farther than the last run. Jim Jones in Room Three soon cottoned on and went one lamp-post farther. This only added a few seconds each time, and from then, whoever led, followed his lead.

It was a very busy period, but by now we knew that this was the way it was going to be.

WEEK 3

MONDAY, DAY 15 – FRIDAY, DAY 19
A FLEA'S LEFT BALL

This week carried on in the same vein, but the drill and gym were getting more strenuous.

Morning room inspections were still in full swing, with nothing escaping the eagle eyes of the instructors: from the lowly shaving brush thrown through the window, "I've seen more hair on a squirrel's arse," to towels floating across the room like a ghostly apparition.

This was carried onto the drill square, where we had more inspections on the level of a flea's left ball speck of dust from ten feet. No matter how good you thought you were, if it was your turn then you got it.

Corporal of Horse Tighe said to Don Davies, "Show your dirty beret to Green. Green, would you wear this dirty beret?"

"No Corporal of Horse," I said.

"See Davies, it's too dirty for Green to wear."

I couldn't risk my new boot buddy getting all twitchy, and without thinking I said, "No Corporal of Horse, it's because it's too small for me."

Kaboom, apoplexy, but at least after two laps of the square I had warmed up.

Drills were getting more prolonged now, as we were learning more and more new movements, and along with the gym were our primary day-fillers. We were doing far more in ranks of four, which is how we would line-up for the passing out parade. Hour after hour we would spend practising, small things could take dozens of attempts to get right, but we could feel some overall improvement.

Gym assessments were carried out and it really pushed the limits at times. For periods of it I was feeling some hurt, and what didn't hurt didn't matter.

Eventually it was finished, and we dragged our sweaty bodies over for a shower.

The next day our results were in. I remained in Team Two. The Mouth came into Team Two and Williams went to Team One. We also had to pick a personal achievement. I decided to try a forward somersault in the air. It was totally impossible at first, and it normally ended with an ignominious back splat.

The momentum was now going to pick up again, ready for the next assessments.

Later, the Mouth said he was only put there to get some of the pricks in Team Two moving.

Someone said, "It takes one to know one."

He jumped up, but Bull shut him up saying, "If I was in Team Two, I would take that personally." The Mouth was not endearing himself to us, and he didn't seem to care.

One morning it was raining hard, and we thought, *Good, no run,* but that only led to, "War don't wait for weather," and off we went.

Bull was leading off for this one and Corporal Wheeler shouted, "No arse wiggling, Durham."

"It's no longer in my arsenal, Corporal."

"It's not your arsenal I'm going to put my boot in, but it's close."

The highlight of this week was our first Pay Parade. We were paid fortnightly. I received £18.00 of which £6.00 went home. (When we started work, we "tipped up" some of our wages, to show our parents we appreciated all they had done for us). I saved £8.00, and received £4.00 to carry on my pie, pop, and polish lifestyle.

These parades were held in the foyer on the ground floor and consisted of a pay officer and pay corporal, Captain Forbes-Hart and his dog

Tiber, and a Life Guards warrant officer, who were all seated behind two six-foot tables.

The first to march out was Trooper Allen, who had a lot of loose change. Halt-salute-name-rank-and-number, pick-up-money, salute, right turn, and march off. Somehow as he turned, his change ended all over the floor. The procedure was amended to: pick up money-put in pocket-salute.

The best was yet to come. Towards the end, Trooper Bell marched across, and in doing an extra smart halt he hit the table with his knee, and upended it.

The officers jumped back, knocking their chairs over, and Tiber shot across the foyer.

They put it all back together and Ding Dong looked like a man having a nervous breakdown. He'd gone as white as a sheet and developed a stammer.

The warrant officer said, "Go back and try again, son, but this time without the full-frontal assault on the table."

Corporal of Horse Tighe gave the other officers a look of resigned indifference, but by now they were all smiling.

During the morning, a full-length mirror had been placed in each cleaning room, for us to practice in front of. We all had to march up to the mirror and salute, which led to a few lighter moments.

That night, Alex, naked except for his forage cap, socks, and plimsolls marched to the mirror and saluted. Immediately Timmy ran up to him, smeared Alex's best friend with boot polish, and legged it out of the room. Timmy was quite safe, though, as Alex spent the next half-hour in the shower, delicately trying to coax polish off his now very tender best friend.

There were other things that happened right out of the blue. One evening a captain came in with Corporal of Horse Tighe, and asked if we had any musicians for the Officer's mess. He got five straight away. He asked if anyone could play a piano, and Jim Jones told him he could, but hadn't played for a while.

"That's good." And they were taken off to the mess.

We all went to the NAAFI, feeling a little bit envious, but were surprised to see our musical ensemble enter ten minutes later.

Jim told us they went into a large room with a dance floor, and a grand piano at one end. They lifted the grand piano very carefully and carried it to the opposite corner. At this moment they realised that they had been conned.

We were in hysterics when he finished, and we learned first-hand how the old adage, "Never volunteer" had originated.

All the hard work was pulling some of us together and friendships were forming. Timmy, Ginger, Alex, Dave (Karl) Marx and myself got on well with each other, and our room all worked well together. If something dodgy or personal was happening, we would involve one or all of us, and discuss it.

There were no long chats tonight on this tiring Friday, as we all wanted a good sleep ready for the promised, "Bloody big block clean-out tomorrow." I was restless, but eventually my mind straightened out, and I slept well. The morning routine would fill any hollow brain space.

SATURDAY, DAY 20 – SUNDAY, DAY 21
"HANDS OFF COCKS!"

Oh *shit, it's him again.* Bring back the prime minister before I leap out of here and annihilate this prick. He must realise how close he is coming to harm because his rallying call is far away so quickly now.

After breakfast, we got back into the block thinking we had an entire day to just clean. Or was it?

We were just getting out the cleaning equipment when Tighe showed up. He marched into the centre of the room, briefly glanced around, informed us we were bone idle and taking advantage of his good nature, so dress for drill 0815hrs on the square.

At 0815hrs we were lined up outside, receiving words of encouragement centred around our requiring a reminder as to why we were there. The only bright spot appeared to be that we were all dysfunctional together, thereby maintaining consistency.

In no time at all, we were displaying our consistency across the parade ground, and we carried on saluting, quick marching, and about-turning to our hearts' content.

By 1215hrs we'd had one short break and absolutely hammered away at left and right wheels. This was a turn more gradual then the ninety degree turns, where the inside man took small steps and the outside man took much longer ones.

Most of us were realising that there's no sense worrying about these sudden changes in the program. We were being pushed and prodded and reprogrammed into fitting into the "army mould."

None of it was personal, not always easy to appreciate when tired, and bombarded with constant "encouragement" at close range, but no one knows their limits until pushed to them.

It must have been alright as after lunch we were allowed the great pleasure of beginning the big clean-up, so all hands to the pump. We began to form a clean-up by consensus, routines worked out and who did what, where and who with. We realised that they were going to get their way, so no point kicking against the system. Initially, odd arguments broke out, mainly due to personality clashes, mostly good natured but occasionally physical, but they were soon broken up.

We went to the NAAFI that evening and Alice had a new assistant called Jenny, a very attractive older woman of about twenty-five, who was the talk of the NAAFI.

After the initial rush Keith Durban said, "Ok I'm going to chat her up."

We all sat and watched his approach work, which was about on par with a monkey scratching his nuts.

He shuffled over to Jenny, and loud enough for us all to hear said, "Have you got a suggestive biscuit?"

"A *what?*" said Jenny.

"You know something sweet and soft to chew on."

But all too soon he realised Alice had overheard him.

"Jenny, serve this man. I will deal with *him*."

Keith's bravado just seemed to evaporate.

"I'll suggestive you—get to the back of the queue until I decide if you will be served."

"But there is no queue," Keith stammered out.

"Then you could be there for a long while. Play with something while you wait."

At this point a totally deflated Keith made his way back to the table amid thunderous applause. This was carried on for the remainder of the night until we turned in.

Next morning, we were beginning to relax into more cleaning. The block was nice and warm and most of us were in T-Shirts, shorts, and plimsolls. In Room Two a couple of guys were on their beds chatting, no big deal, until out of the blue Corporal Fletcher appeared.

"What are you two doing?"

As quick as a flash Tom Peters, between coughing and spluttering, managed to get out, "Working on locker layout, Corporal."

"Do I look fucking stupid? Room Two dress for a run outside in two minutes. You want to run round the barracks? Then I'm happy to oblige."

Rooms Three and Four were laughing at this as they were leaving and also got a run for their troubles, joined by Room One to ensure no one felt left out.

Cpl Fletcher made a comment as he was getting ready to leave about weapon training beginning on Monday, then promptly left. This was around the block with the speed of a carrier pigeon with its arse on fire, and was the main topic of conversation for the rest of the weekend.

Great start to a Sunday, totally unpredictable and stops us getting bored. It did lead to an argument getting out of hand between Tom Peters and the Mouth, who was holding Tom responsible for their run out earlier. It was only stopped by Bull, who on hearing the noise went in and stopped it. The Mouth always seemed to want to blame somebody when these things happened, so much so that guys either gave him a wide berth or only dealt with him when necessary.

"How come Rooms Three and Four also went for a run and Tom wasn't with them?" said Bull.

"He'd better keep his fucking mouth shut in future," said the Mouth, being an expert on this.

"Listen to your own advice; you might benefit from it yourself in the future," replied Bull, but for now another flashpoint was averted, and the Mouth had run out of friends.

We were getting more confident with the Bumper these days, to the point of being blasé. Sunday afternoon saw Tony Mahoney displaying his total mastery in front of about ten of us. We applauded, and Tony removed one hand to take a bow, and the Bumper's handle hit his leg. It took almost two weeks for the bruise to disappear. From this day forward, Tony never went near the Bumper again, his belief being it was possessed.

Most of us went down to the NAAFI and Alice saw Keith and pointed towards her eyes and then at him. Jenny laughed out loud and Keith went bright red.

"You won't be laughing when I crack it," Keith muttered to the rest of us.

"I know, we will all be pensioned off by then."

On return to the block we carried on cleaning, leaving a small path to walk on until morning, turned in and were soon fast asleep.

"Fire! Fire! Fire!"

What a racket—alarms going off, people shouting and running in all directions and then...

"Downstairs now all of you."

Twenty-nine recruits in all kinds of disarray. Mostly half-awake and half dressed, staggering around wholly confused, bumping and barging down the staircase, to be met by Corporal Miles and a Corporal of Horse we didn't know.

"Line-up in the corridor."

We did, breathing heavily. It was slowly dawning on us that this was a drill.

"One minute and twenty seconds, not good enough. Back to your rooms we will discuss this later."

We wandered back cursing and swearing.

"What time is it?"

"0230hrs."

"Fucking hell that's crazy."

"The shite hawks," and "What a load of wankers," were among the nicer remarks.

We were soon back in our pits, although it took a while to settle down and return to the land of nod.

WEEK 4

MONDAY, DAY 22 – FRIDAY, DAY 26
BREECH BLOCKS AND BLINDFOLDS

The day began with an air of excitement about the weapon training, but first the routine.

"Stand by your beds." Tighe was in the room almost in front of his voice. "Run downstairs to the far end of the corridor and back."

This was repeated in all four rooms.

He lined us up and said, "The slowest time today was thirty-five seconds, on Sunday it took one minute and twenty seconds. Walters, why?"

"We were all asleep, Corporal of Horse."

"You are always asleep you dozy pillocks. Thirty seconds is now the benchmark. It will not take longer than that next time." *Ouch, there is a next time.*

The gym remained a constant, everything geared up for the next set of assessments. Plenty of "gimme more, gimme another."

Afterwards, for a relaxing bonding session, we would form two teams and throw bean bags at each other. If hit, lie on floor and get run over. If hit in nose, do not bleed on the floor, hold it and run to the sink.

By the time we had lunch it felt as if we had been steam-rolled, but nothing a good meal couldn't fix. One positive in all this was being able to eat three good meals a day, plus NAAFI pies, and still lose weight.

Drill carried on relentlessly with an unfailing barrage of encouragement. "Sims, that was lazy, do a halt-check-one-two around the squad."

Jake only managed to do four impressions of a frog on a hot plate, and we fully earned our two laps round the square. We were getting more accustomed to these outbreaks now, knowing that come hell or high water they would happen, so mainly, nobody blamed anyone else for these consequences.

Nicely spread out across the next five days was our weapon training. We were taken across to a large room in the lecture block where Corporal of Horse Tighe opened the proceedings in his own inimitable way. "I didn't sleep well last night thinking of you lot with a gun in your hands, but against my better judgement I decided to go ahead." He handed us over to Corporal Fletcher and left.

"You will not use this weapon until you know every piece by name, its capabilities, and safety aspects. This is the L1A1 Self Loading Rifle (SLR) 9.62mm-weight 9.5lbs-range 875yds(800m) overall length forty-five inches."

He showed us the inner parts, breech block carrier, gas plug cylinder (piston and spring) etc. until the rifle was completely in pieces.

For five days, for at least three hours every day, we learned the parts off by heart, until we could do it blindfolded. Who could believe that a toilet part could be confused with a rifle part?

By the third day we were assembling it and stripping it down very quickly, then trying it blindfolded.

By the fifth day we had to crawl across the floor of a darkened room and strip it down, then the next person would crawl along and put the parts back together.

Safety was paramount. First, always cock the rifle, hook your finger in the breech, then look down the barrel, then show it to the instructor (cock, hook, and look).

"Never point it at anyone unless you are going to use it."

"Never let it out of your sight."

"If you break any of these rules, I will make you wish you had never been born."

"Yes, Corporal." Although wishing we had never been born was not a new concept recently.

We had a spare hour and Jay took us for a jog around the barracks, increasing it by one lamp post. On our return, Tighe said he had seen Billy laughing and sent us off again.

We got back in the block and Billy was telling anyone who would listen that he didn't smile, "...and the bastard set me up."

Suddenly a voice in the corridor said, "Are you calling me a liar Jackson?"

Billy drained of all colour and froze.

"Well, are you?"

And Billy turned to see...Alex in the doorway.

Billy went off on a relieved rant, and Alex nearly had a laughing hernia on his way up the corridor.

It was events like this that kept our spirits up along with unplanned cock-ups, as in the Friday run.

Don had been told to lead off, and we followed our normal route, until he suddenly veered off onto an unused area of road.

"Where the fuck are you going, Davies?"

"Unsure, Corporal."

"You are in charge, why don't you know?"

"No more lamp posts, Corporal."

"Squad halt, what the fuck is going on in that tiny mind?"

"I was going to jog one more lamp post, then turn around."

"So, are you just going to carry on into oblivion?"

"Into where, Corporal?"

By this time everyone was laughing out loud. Don was bright red, and totally unable to see the funny side of it.

It got even funnier when telling the PTIs about it later Don said he thought oblivion was an area in the barracks.

I had made my phone call and Mum was very happy about the allowance, which made me feel happy as well.

I noticed that evening that my home sickness, that awful feeling in the pit of my stomach, was becoming much less of a worry now.

I also realised I had never seen Jay go to the phone. He told me he had no family, that he had been in an orphanage before enlisting, and had joined the army to get some stability in his life. He was a self-motivated person who rarely complained, and he was popular amongst the squad. It made me realise how lucky I was to have my family behind me.

In the NAAFI one evening, I was asked about my family. I was the eldest of four siblings (two sisters and a brother) all born within six years after the end of the Second World War, and then another sister who was only seven months old. Dad used to say he had celebrated the end of the war very enthusiastically and relaxed again when he was sure he couldn't be re-enlisted.

It was hard to believe how much smarter our gear was looking, especially as we had deals with each other. I was pleased to have worked it out early with Don and he was still the crème de la crème of the boot bulling world. The nights were good for getting together, and over a period of time we began to talk more personally between ourselves, as we were in each other's pockets for twenty-four hours a day. This was like home, but with a much more diverse family.

Timmy told me he had chatted to Jake, who'd told a couple of them that Corporal of Horse Tighe was going to give him a few days to go home to sort some personal problems out, they just had to decide when.

SATURDAY, DAY 27
"HANDS OFF COCKS!"

G*ive it a break you gob shite, or stay there and take your beating like a man.* Well tomorrow then, I'm a bit stiff this morning.

We were back from breakfast and ready for inspection. Surely there would be one today, but before we had time to ponder on it, the crunch of boots heralded the all-too familiar battle cry of the advancing instructors.

"Stand by your beds."

We were ready for anything, but usually not the anything they had thought up that morning. All the rooms were subjected to the same routine, an instructor at the top of the room looking slowly over us.

"Open your suitcases on your beds."

We looked quizzically at Ginger, as he'd been the last to use the template, suspecting that they had got wind of our short cut.

Corporal of Horse Tighe marched up and down glancing into each one and said, "Put them back. Downstairs, combat gear, boots, webbing, and berets ready for a road run at 0820hrs." Then like a well-rehearsed exit stage right, they were gone.

We all looked at Ginger who burst out laughing, more out of relief than anything, at his narrow escape. "You know I was last to use it, and they were on the stairs by the time I had finished." He turned his bed pack sideways, pulled the top blanket out, and with all the timing of a seasoned magician slid the template from the middle of it.

Fack said, "What would you have done if he had pulled your facking bed pack apart?"

The whole room fell apart laughing as Ginger said, "I would have saved him the trouble, and thrown myself out of the window."

It was a chilly morning but no rain or high wind, so all in all a fair morning to jog, accompanied by Corporals Wheeler and Fletcher.

"Do you know where oblivion is Green?"

"No Corporal."

"Thank fuck for that, lead off."

And away we went for a full run around the barracks and ended up in the garage area.

It was raining by now as we practiced sprinting in the rain and soaking in a downpour with a ten-minute break to show that no matter how bad the weather was, we could still keep a cigarette lit long enough to enjoy a good cough.

By around 1200hrs a bunch of soaked and bedraggled recruits arrived back at the block. We showered and changed and ran over for lunch.

After lunch it was into the beginning of the big clean-up. We were getting more into our routines by now. Move everything to the centre of the rooms. Wash down the walls and skirting boards, rub down the back and sides of our lockers, then the bed frames, and put them back. The Bumper was red hot during these sessions. As soon as it was finished in one room it went straight into the next. It was always a hectic time and non-stop, but lots of banter and joking around kept everyone involved.

Around this time Bob said he saw Jake on the stairs talking to Corporal Fletcher, and a short while later Corporal of Horse Tighe appeared. All three had a conversation and then the two NCOs left without coming upstairs.

At evening meal, Jake sat talking to Timmy in a quiet voice all through their meal. Most of the squad knew by now that Jake was wanting to go home, so we were not too bothered about it, just curious as to how it would work out.

We got back over into the block and carried on cleaning. Timmy told us that Jake had told him Corporal of Horse Tighe was going to speak to him, as soon as possible, to give him permission.

Around 1830hrs Corporal Fletcher briefly called in to tell us that there would be a full inspection tomorrow, then he left and Jake walked down to the foyer with him. We heard Jake thanking him very loudly and he came back much more cheerful.

Later we all went to the NAAFI except Jake and Jay Bird.

We got stuck into some heavy cleaning on our return. Jay went and told Jake's room that Jake was in civvies around 2000hrs, and he'd had a quick chat with him. Jake had gone home saying he would be back soon. Jay wished him all the best.

We carried on with our cleaning and then turned in at midnight as there was still another day to finish off what was left. We chatted for a while about Ginger's close escape, but as a priceless painting stolen from the Officers Mess toilets was still the best theory about the suitcases, we quickly slipped into a deep sleep.

SUNDAY, DAY 28
"HANDS OFF COCKS!"

You monotonous prick, get a life, unless you fancy a hospital food diet. Oh, it's Sunday, so it will have to keep.

We returned from breakfast, put the finishing touches to our spaces, and stood ready for the inevitable.

"Stand by your beds."

Corporal of Horse Tighe had barely begun his demolition work when Corporal Fletcher came into our room. Very briefly, Corporal of Horse Tighe flashed a look of annoyance at him, until Corporal Fletcher whispered in his ear.

They both immediately turned and hurried out of the room in a mix of hot boot soles and mystery.

One minute later, the NCOs were in a huddle in the middle of the corridor, having an animated discussion.

A voice yelled out, "Rooms One, Two, and Three dress for drill. On the square in five minutes."

Damn, every time a sniff of a mystery was in the air, we all end up on the drill square.

After ten minutes, most of Room Four were joining us, except Jay Bird, who had stayed behind with Corporal of Horse Tighe and Corporal Fletcher.

At 1045hrs we were marched back into the block. It soon became apparent what the problem was—Jake had gone over the wall AWOL. (Absent With-Out Leave).

An angry Corporal of Horse came into each room and asked if anyone had spoken to Sims in the last twenty-four hours about his leaving.

Timmy said he had, so ten minutes later Timmy, Jay, and one very pissed off storeman, who had been woken up early today, went to make statements.

The rest of us lucky ones got to pound the drill ground until lunch time.

We were all straining for some information.

The cooks, who had seen the storeman earlier, had been informed that, "One of those stupid bastards has fucked off over the wall and made me look a right prick."

Timmy and Jay came over and said they were still making statements.

Jay took what seemed an age to sit down and told us about the early part, when Corporal Fletcher had marched in to do his inspection and quickly saw that Jake was not standing by his bed.

"Where is Sims?"

Alan Ladd said, "He's gone home, Corporal," and Corporal Fletcher ran up the corridor as if his arse was on fire. It was dawning on Room Four that something was amiss.

We had been told to return to the block after lunch and carry on with the cleaning. Twenty minutes later, Timmy and Jay joined us and got stuck into the cleaning, but they couldn't say anything as Corporal Wheeler and Corporal Miles were wandering around.

This being the army, it didn't take long to move on and at about 1415hrs Corporal Fletcher appeared and shouted for Room One to go to their room.

We were thinking, *Shit, now what?* but the waters were already closing, as Corporal Fletcher said, "One volunteer to move to Room Four. Hughes, pack your gear and move to Sims' bed."

This caught us all by surprise, especially Pete, who couldn't even get a "fack" out before Fletcher had turned and gone. All Jake's bedding and gear was returned to the stores.

We helped Pete take all his gear down to Room Four, take over Jake's bed and locker, and put Pete's bed and locker downstairs.

The remainder of the afternoon was taken up by Corporals Wheeler and Miles showing us that there is a price to pay for someone else's misdemeanours, as they proceeded to get us to flatten out all areas of the parade ground.

Everyone went over for evening meal after being told that Corporal of Horse Tighe would be in at 1830hrs to talk to us all. We were all over Timmy and Jay, but they both said to wait until Corporal of Horse Tighe had spoken to everyone.

As we heard a door slam around 1830hrs it was pretty obvious that Corporal of Horse Tighe was not the happiest of humans. He stormed into the cleaning room where we were all gathered, his opening remark being, "Don't anyone else piss me off, or I will teach you the meaning of pain."

He then proceeded on a ten-minute rant, at no point coming up for air, while we all stood frozen and very quiet.

Eventually he began his descent in the area of, "If any more of you want to run off to Mummy, stand by the perimeter wall, and I will gladly kick your chicken-shit arses over it. Any more of you got any fancy arsed ideas?"

Do we look insane?

Not a rustle or a murmur came from a room of recruits who had the look of deer caught in the headlights.

"Inspection tomorrow at 0800hrs; it had better be above excellent." Then he spun round and faded off into the night. We all automatically seemed to decide to make major efforts tonight—no sense tightening an already over-wound watch spring.

Everybody in the NAAFI was on about it; most hadn't a clue this was on the books. Those who had heard a little thought it was all above board.

About halfway through NAAFI break we could hear Keith talking loudly, and then Alice saying to Jenny, "It makes sense in a way—running away from some of this lot." Then laughing, she looked at Keith. "Please, tell me you are thinking of joining him."

We really got stuck into the work when we got back. Not one of us wanted to face the wrath of an angry god, and we really kept at it solidly.

By around 2330 hrs we were turning in and all listening intently to Timmy about the day's happenings.

Jake had approached Corporal of Horse Tighe for permission to go home. Tighe said he would require confirmation from home of the circumstances but that if matters got worse to let him know, and he would follow it up.

After this discussion Jake had told a few of us that Tighe was looking into him having some time at home. Later, while talking to Timmy at evening meal, Jake just carried on giving the impression it was not if, but how soon, so no one was too concerned.

When Corporal Fletcher had called back in that evening, and Jake went downstairs, he had only asked him if Corporal of Horse Tighe had mentioned his discussion from earlier. Corporal Fletcher had told him that if Corporal of Horse Tighe was dealing with the matter Jake would be the first to know.

Jake had very loudly replied, "Thank you Corporal, that sounds great," so to anyone in earshot, he sounded happy.

As soon as we left for the NAAFI, Jake had gone and knocked on the storeman's door, apologising and saying he had been given permission to go home immediately, and could he have his civvies. The storeman had heard his loud thank you to Corporal Fletcher so signed his civvies over to him.

Jake had briefly spoken to Jay on his way out, and Jay thought that Jake had been cleared to leave.

"Pretty smart, wasn't he?" said Timmy, and we all agreed that it took some balls to carry it through.

"The storeman was really pissed off to begin with," Timmy told us.

"Corporal of Horse Tighe told him he couldn't write in his statement, 'The devious little cunt knocked on my door.' But Corporal of Horse Tighe thought it was very funny at the time."

We were also missing Pete, who no doubt was regaling Room Four with his unique approach to the queen's English. We fell asleep listening to Ginger musing about how if Pete ever had kids and read them bedtime stories, their minds would be warped for the rest of their lives.

WEEK 5

MONDAY, DAY 29 – THURSDAY, DAY 32
A RUN IN THE PARK

Today began on a great note. Beginning tomorrow we were starting runs in Windsor Great Park. There was a buzz in the air as this would be the first time out of barracks since the course began.

We went into the gym on a high, and all we had to do was improve on our last assessment.

Corporal Kelly seemed in shock at first as half his super-fit recruits had vanished into thin air. The only things moving faster than us were the instructors' tongues and pens. A hard session of "Gimme more, another," and then the relief on hearing, "Warm down."

Two days later, we were in the gym again doing another circuit. By halfway I was breathing in air in ice cube-sized chunks.

"I know you are hurting but this is where it counts."

We had set off like greyhounds and finished like drunks in a dance hall.

Soon I went to the office for last Monday's assessment.

"Some improvement, but room for much more. Attitude and perseverance are good. Questions?"

"No, Corporal."

"Corporal Thomas, overall assessment.

"Green is more of a camel than a gazelle.

I glared at him and Corporal Kelly laughed saying, "It just means you are better on endurance than speed at the moment."

Me, a camel, it makes me want to spit.

When it was over, I went to the cookhouse and couldn't decide whether to eat lightly or store a big meal in my hump.

We began a new type of drill to us, the "Slow March." It's used mainly ceremoniously, for funerals or when a regiment is parading its colours. It's done with the body rigid, hands down by the sides, legs straight, feet parallel to the floor and toes pointed outwards. All done at half the speed of a, "Quick March."

Then began the difficult procedure of walking again…slowly. We went over and over it getting the correct body shape and positions, then for days mixed it with a "Quick March."

All with encouragement: "Hughes keep your arms down by your side, you look like a duck trying to take off."

"I'm trying, Corporal of Horse."

"Yes, my bloody patience. Keep your facking arms down."

Ah, now I've got it, Corporal of Horse."

We even managed an afternoon in the Lecture Room, learning the rank system, which apparently has turned grown men into quivering wrecks. It's a unique system to the British Army, having no sergeants, only corporals and horse-related ranks. This will definitely increase the press-up count during Q and A periods.

At least Pay Parade remained consistent. Trooper Bell was places farther down the line so that he could watch others do it. As he stepped forward, everyone behind the tables instinctively sat upright, but Ding Dong was on his game. He stepped back and saluted, and the WO, who was now relaxed, said, "Well done, Trooper."

"Thank you, sir," Ding Dong replied, then he promptly turned left instead of right and marched directly at the next man coming to the table.

Afterwards, Corporal of Horse Tighe came upstairs and asked Ding Dong if he was trying to, "…rectify a gene deficiency, or are you just bloody brain dead?"

On Tuesday we left the barracks and ran into Windsor Great Park. It is well named. It's a large royal park of about 5,000 acres.

After a couple of miles, we turned into a secluded field and were told to rest. It soon became apparent that these days would be a mix of running and outdoor exercises. We did leap frogging, shoulder carries, and piggy back carries with the losing team doing the ritual twenty press-ups.

We set off back and Arnold was bent double with stitch, so Corporal Jones dropped behind and accompanied him back.

As we approached the road, three young women were walking towards us. We stood upright with chests out, arms pumping, and in step. They smiled as we passed them then hopefully didn't look round as we folded back into our knackered selves. This became known as the "Peacock effect."

As we entered the block, Arnold came around the corner still impersonating a question mark, but soon got over it.

Thursday was an extension of Tuesday. A longer run but arriving in the same field. Today there were already sandwiches and drinks on site. For ninety minutes we exercised in our own outdoor gym.

This is what it is all about: fresh air, exercise, then get together and eat, drink, and banter.

We were slowly spreading our wings.

On the way back Tom Peters developed a sore, red, big toe and Jack Backhouse had a blister that popped.

As soon as we got back, Jack went to the MI room and got it dressed, and Tom spent five minutes with his foot in the sink, and a huge smile on his face.

The evenings were progressing well, as many of us were mixing more, especially with all the deals that were in operation. Still plenty to do but mainly we all just mucked in and got it done.

The NAAFI seemed to bring out the best in us. We looked forward to it and were able to relax totally in that hour. It was usually a lot of fun, but one evening I was sitting on a table next to Parkin (the Mouth), Bull Durham, and Paul Smith. Paul was telling them that his sister had been accepted at medical school to train as a doctor.

The Mouth said loudly, "If she wants a perfect specimen to play with, I'm available."

"No chance," said Paul, "she isn't training as a vet."

Parkin shot out of his seat, but Bull stopped him saying, "Don't think about it. If you can't take it, don't give it."

Another flash point averted, but it leaves a bad taste.

The following night was the opposite.

Jenny was a lot less shy by now. Keith was at the front of the queue and Jenny said, "You look as if you've had a hard day."

"It's a hard night I fancy, Jenny."

Then he shook as the voice from behind the pie rack said, "It's getting even harder now, get to the back of the queue and work out an apology."

A crestfallen Keith trudged to the back of the queue.

"He's got a one-track mind that lad, I think all his brains are in his trousers," she said loudly.

"Take it from me, Alice," boomed out Big Hippo, "I've seen him in the shower and he hasn't got a very big brain."

The NAAFI was reduced to laughter, and a red-faced Keith waving two fingers at us all, only made it funnier.

No problem getting to sleep tonight, after we wondered if Parkin was all there. Ginger said, "What does a Squadron Quarter Master Corporal wear?"

ZZZZZZZZZZ

FRIDAY, DAY 33 – SATURDAY, DAY 34
BILLY'S BOOTS

It was a fast run over to the cookhouse as the weather was cold, damp, and blustery, which prompted one or two not to go, as in Bob's case, who asked us to bring him something back.

"Yes Bob, we'll get pissed through so that you can eat," but we did, and Bob was really grateful for a moment. He took a huge bite out of his sausage sandwich and within five seconds was running to the washroom to cough up the hot curry powder that was mixed into his HP sauce. Strangely enough, he never asked us again, or maybe he just didn't like sausages. We were all finding this hilarious as we heard taps running, and then the toilet flushing, as the sandwich went off on the great sausage journey to the sea.

"Stand by your beds."

Bob quickly fell in as Corporal of Horse Tighe swept into the room, looked straight into Bob's locker, which was nearest the door, and then at Bob. "Are you alright McCann? You look flushed."

Of all the words to use "flushed" was a killer.

I saw Keith grinning and I grinned back and how Tighe saw us I don't know.

"You two, twenty press-ups, middle of the room."

As soon as Tighe had gone, Bob looked at us all and said loudly in his beautiful Scottish accent, "Ye's still aw a fuckin' bunch o' basterts though."

Before we could reply he had headed for the washrooms to have another mouth wash.

The morning was spent in the Lecture Room due to the poor weather. By midday the weather was much more amenable, so after lunch, we were out on the square dressed for drill.

"As you have not drilled for two days, and pea sized brains need constant attention, you will get that attention. Fall in." Then into basic left and right turns. "Brace your leg, you lazy prick, you look as if you've wet yourself."

"Oh, you have."

It was as if we were stuck in a crazy routine.

"If that knee is at ninety degrees, Green, I'll eat my hat." *And hopefully fucking choke on it, pillock* I screamed at him, but somehow, it got quietly stuck at the back of my mind.

It seemed Billy Jackson couldn't get the hang of about-turn on the march, so he was taken to one side by Corporal Wheeler, who about-turned him on his own for ages. Wheeler returned him to the squad as it was beginning to turn to dusk, and the Corporal of Horse wanted to do one last run through.

At the very first about-turn, a nervous Billy completely screwed up his timing, and turned too quickly. Like lightning, a visibly angry Corporal of Horse stormed over and prodded him in the chest with his riding whip.

"There's a fucking idiot on the end of this Jackson."

Without blinking or thinking Billy replied, "Well, it's not this end, sir."

The world fell into an uneasy silence, as twenty-seven recruits gulped in enough air to lower the cloud level by several feet, then not even daring to breath. We were transfixed, waiting for the inevitable explosion and the death of Billy Jackson.

We stood in total disbelief as Corporal of Horse Tighe turned away without saying a word, proceeded to drill for another ten minutes, and as darkness was closing in, bought us to a halt. "I do not have to tell you that today's performance was sub-standard and therefore we will be out on the square tomorrow. Next week your uniforms will be ready, and so tomorrow we will progress to drilling in ammo boots. Fall out."

He might as well as have hit us with a lump hammer.

Every one of us was in a state of shock, and Billy was still shaking, because of the bollocking that never was.

As the evening went on, Billy was still the talk of the squad but now was completely relaxed. He had us all laughing when he said. "As soon as I said it, I shit blue lights."

The following morning at 0915hrs we were on the square feeling very different in best boots as the studs made a distinct metallic sound as they hit the floor, which was good as they would help with the timing, or lack of it as the case may be.

"For inspection. Atten-shun."

The instructors inspected us with Corporal of Horse Tighe pointing out our failings in life, (which would have led to a serious tree shortage if they were all written down).

When Corporal of Horse Tighe stood in front of Billy and looked down at Billy's feet, he said, "You are stood at attention, are your toes forty-five degrees apart?"

Before Billy could glance down, Corporal of Horse Tighe slightly raised his right foot and slammed the sole and heel hard between Billy's toecaps. "That is forty-five degrees."

Billy looked down and saw his toecaps take on a mosaic pattern. Pieces of shiny black polish had fallen off, completely undoing his weeks of hard work.

"Anything to say, Jackson?"

In a kind of subdued voice, Billy said, "No, Corporal of Horse."

The rest of us looked on with a mixture of shock and dismay.

"I go to see a comedian if I want to laugh, he does not come to me." With that Tighe moved on and definitely had all of our unwavering attention from then.

There was a line not to cross, and through Billy we'd all been shown where it had been drawn.

"Upstairs, change boots, back on the square in three minutes."

We were off the square at the speed of light. It hadn't fully sunk in what had happened yet, but we had no wish to risk a repeat.

We went through our total repertoire to date, with only two very short breaks. But who was going to complain? Not me and definitely not Billy.

We tried to lift Billy's spirit at lunch, but he was really pissed off and not too receptive to anything.

On our way back from lunch we were met by Corporal of Horse Tighe and Corporal Wheeler, who were waiting in the foyer.

"Learn from today," said Tighe. "There will be a block inspection at 1500hrs tomorrow and personal inspection at 0930hrs." With that they turned and left us to begin our Saturday routines.

I had taken my boots to Don and chatted to him about Billy. He said that as the rest of us didn't have much to do in respect of bulling, he and one of the other guys were going to have a real good go at them. I remarked that Billy must be pleased with that and Don said he was sure Billy would have given him his first-born if he'd asked.

As the afternoon progressed, and the condition of the boots slowly improved, so did Billy's liver. By evening meal, Billy had got his sense of humour and his appetite back.

The cooks had heard about the escapade by now and were looking at Billy with a look normally only seen when someone had died. They were seemingly full of sympathy as he walked down the food line and one of the cooks said, "Try the sticky toffee pudding, it will keep them from bollocking you in the future."

Billy said inquisitively, "Will it? Why, how does that work?"

"It's very, very chewy," said the cook almost unable to speak for laughing. "It will help you keep you fucking mouth shut."

Even Billy found it funny, as we all burst out laughing.

There was a strangely funny mood set tonight, as everyone was having fun at Billy's expense, although by now he was enjoying it. To a man we agreed that this was a hell of a brave remark to make, bordering on suicidal. It was part of the constant reminder of a recruit's lot, knowing we'd definitely have more moments like this and they would appear out of the blue and strike any one of us at any time.

We all carried on with our cleaning of the windows, doors ledges, and whatever else we couldn't walk on.

It seemed a real relief to turn into bed that night and have a chat about Billy and the boot saga.

SUNDAY, DAY 35
"RISE AND SHINE!"

An easier start to the day, good food, everything looking up, and plenty of time to get ready, feeling up to scratch. What could possibly go wrong?

We were confidently standing by our beds.

He stormed through the door, marched to the top end of the room with the previous day's list in his hand, and started reading off it. "Green, show me your beret badge."

"There is a mark here," he shouted, pointing accusingly. "It looks like a fucking fingerprint to me.

*It should be, you absolute bell end, I just bloody well passed the thing to you…*which came out as "Sir?"

"Look at it, it's filthy. Don't show me this shit again." He dropped it as if it had suddenly become red hot.

My pleasure not to show it to you again, but I think you might weaken first, you prick. I could cheerfully not show it to you ever again.

"Get started on the block ready for inspection at 1500hrs. You've obviously done sweet FA to it yet."

It was instant noise as we all chatted about the inspection, and it was soon clear that all the rooms got the same going over. At least we were all the same degree of bad, which cheered us up, knowing that our consistency levels were still being maintained.

We really got into the floor cleaning, and as usual it became a very busy and chatty time with lots of laughs and banter.

Lockers and beds were moved into the centre of the floor and polish tossed over the floor. Then the Bumper made its entrance and was put through its cleaning and polishing routines. It then went next door to Room Two, at which point Tony Mahoney crossed himself, gave two fingers to the Bumper, and left the room.

By lunch time the moving around was finished. Everything was back in place and with only the corridors left, we went off to lunch.

We had only been back in the block a few minutes when someone called Tony Mahoney into the corridor, and we all went out to see what was going on.

In the middle of the corridor stood the Bumper.

Someone had fixed a great picture of a bull on a piece of cardboard and fixed it to the Bumper. It looked menacing with steam coming from its nostrils. It turned out John McGrath in Room Three had set it up after getting the picture from Alice. John was stood behind the Bumper, moving it slowly forward with all of Room Three following him. Arnold Moore had put a red T-shirt on a bit of wood.

Room Three were singing "Toreador" over and over again and we all joined in. John moved the Bumper towards Tony, who would dramatically wave the red T-shirt cape near to the bull as we all shouted "Ole." It was as if it had been rehearsed, and for ten minutes or so it was hilarious. Everyone was having a try with their own different matador spin. From the usual classical bum waving to a Scottish rock n' roll version by Bob McCann on how to "Ole" a mechanical bull. The cheering and fooling around was everywhere.

Suddenly the noise seemed to fade into a stutter from the back. As we looked at the top of the staircase, we saw Corporal Fletcher standing there.

He looked amazed. "I am sure I did not see this, and I will check for signs of bullshit later." He smiled. "I will be back at 1500hrs." Then he walked back down the staircase, shaking his head.

For the next hour we got totally stuck into the remainder of the floors, working really hard, but enjoying it. By 1455hrs the bull ring had disappeared completely to be replaced by a gleaming corridor floor.

The inspection, in our minds, was a success, as Corporal Fletcher seemed quite relaxed, with no real bollockings dished out.

By the time evening meal came around we were hungry and loud again.

The first impression was we were moving up a gear. We'd have real army uniforms from tomorrow, and already we had runs outside. An officer's inspection—looks as if we are on the next step of the ladder, and that was the main topic of conversation during the period leading to our nightly hour in the NAAFI.

The whole time in there was great fun and we were soon back into the bull fighting story. Alice knew it had been happening and she came over with Jenny and spoke to everyone, but especially John McGrath, asking him how it all went.

"Terrific Alice, better than we had hoped. Watch this." With no further ado he stood up, put his hands on his head, extended a finger on each side, and bent over as if to charge. Tony immediately jumped up and grabbed his jacket, waving it like a cape. All the rest of us started singing "Toreador" and then shouted a huge "Ole" as John pretended to charge past Tony, who swung his jacket to one side. It had all of us singing and laughing, so they did a couple more charges.

On our return, the joking and piss taking just carried on, even after the Mouth remarked to four of us sitting in the cleaning room laughing, that we had the mentality of "fucking school kids."

I replied, "That may be true, coming from one with inside knowledge."

He slammed a chair under a table and stormed out.

WEEK 6

MONDAY, DAY 36
UNIFORMS AND NECK TORPEDOS

I was wondering to myself how the family was as I shuffled down to the washroom, thinking of Dad hogging the only toilet reading the newspaper, while the rest were tying themselves in knots banging on the door.

As soon as we got back from breakfast, Timmy proudly pointed to his belt. "Look at this Jimmy, when he walks in, I will get the light to bounce straight into his eyes and blind him.

"Yes, they look good, Timmy," I told him.

"Good? *Good?* These are the dog's bollocks of the brasses world," he said proudly.

"Stand by your beds." Corporal of Horse Tighe was straight in and when he picked up Timmy's belt said, "Why is this Blanco cracking?"

Timmy looked, saw something akin to an ant's whisker, and decided to say nothing as Corporal of Horse Tighe threw the belt onto the bed, without even looking at the brasses, and moved on.

When Tighe had left I looked quizzically at Timmy. "The dog's bollocks of brasses?" I can't repeat Timmy's reply, but it caused us all to go into fits of laughter, as for once he completely "out-facked" Pete.

We fell in at 0905hrs on the square to be told, "You will be taken to the tailor's shop throughout the day in pairs for final fittings. Then go to the stores and draw up accessories."

We went in room order, so Timmy and Keith were marched across to the tailor's shop by Corporal Fletcher and fifteen minutes or so later were marched to the storeroom carrying some clothing.

I was marched across with Ginger. The tailor put our forage caps on our heads, moved them around, and put them back on the table. He gave us a pair of braces, two pairs of trousers and a tunic. He checked the fit, marking the excess length with white chalk. Any for altering were given to his assistant. We were then handed a three-quarter-length great coat and tried a couple on until the tailor was happy with the fit.

We were looking in the full-length mirror when he placed our caps on our heads again, which immediately made us stand up with our shoulders back, in order to see under the peak. It was a strange realisation that this was me, beginning to actually look like a soldier, and that the transformation was really under way. We went across to our block with the good fitting items and stopped at the storeroom.

Shirts —Khaki—no collars—two

Collars — Detached—three

Ties — Khaki —two

Collar Studs—Front/rear—two pairs

We went upstairs, laid it all on our beds and joined the squad on the square. This procedure was repeated all through the day, with the assistant working flat out, and joined by the tailor when all the fittings were over. By the late afternoon it was all completed except for four tunics, which were completed early next morning.

It was a weird kind of day. Drill carried on, even though at any given time there were at least four of us on the move.

In spite of all this, nothing could really dampen our spirits today, as we were all itching to try on these new super-smart uniforms.

It appears that when Dave Marx was in the tailor's he saw a "Hoffman Press." This was a large, electrical contraption used for pressing large pieces of clothing, such as suits and trousers, and wonder of wonders, army uniforms or great coats. He remarked to the tailor that he had operated one of these before joining the army, and this was noted down.

The tailor worked through, and by the end of our evening meal all alterations had been completed.

We couldn't wait to get back to the block and try on our uniforms. By the time I did, it was full of bodies marching around in various degrees of undress.

Everyone would probably have been fully dressed up by now, but we had just encountered the collar studs—easily the smallest and most awkward piece of subtle torture, which must have been designed by someone with a pure sadistic streak. To put your detached collar on your shirt, the smaller back stud went through a slit in the back of the collar and through the back of the shirt before you put the shirt on, and then the front one went through slits on either side of the collar and the two slits on the shirt neck. A tie was put on and then the starched, cardboard-like collar folded over, hiding the stud from view, and leaving it free to seek out your Adam's apple completely unnoticed.

Until completely familiar with them, this was a two-man job. At the moment, it was the excitement of putting on the uniform and forage caps that overtook all else.

I got on the phone around 1830hrs and spoke with Mum. Suddenly Dad was on the phone, "Hi son, Mum tells me you are settling in now."

"Yes Dad, just got our new uniforms today."

"Good. Anything else you need?"

"A couple of pints in six weeks or so."

"That I can arrange. Keep batting, and I'll speak to you soon."

"Hi John, it's Mum. Dad had a big smile when he gave me the phone back."

"Are you sure it wasn't wind?"

I heard his voice say, "I am not that far away from the phone."

After I hung up, I wandered back upstairs feeling quite melancholy.

I walked back into the room thinking the circus had come to town. I was just in time to see Big Hippo parading down the room naked, wearing only his new tunic. He threw back his head, raised his arms skyward, and shouted, "It's time to meet my best friend again."

Timmy came from the side again, boot polished Hippo's best friend again, legged it again, and Big Hippo went and showered his best friend again.

The evening was spent trying on uniforms and forage caps, marching up to the mirrors and saluting, again realising how the forage caps made us straighten our backs and hold our heads up.

Around 1900hrs, Corporal Fletcher came in and showed everyone how to prepare the caps for inspections: remove chin strap and badge, run damp hand along crown of cap and lightly brush, hoping with time it would always go this way. Cover the gold braid, highly polish the peak and chin strap with a little boot polish until gleaming, and replace chin strap and badge. Little wonder after all this, it took pride of place in the centre of the top shelf in the locker.

Most of us had a shorter NAAFI break tonight and didn't mind the extra cleaning that was happening. We were beginning to look more like soldiers than very clean car mechanics.

The remainder of the evening was spent on our personal gear plus revamping lockers as per diagram. I remember just standing there staring at it, thinking that they must want me to stay or they wouldn't be doing all this, then realising that the army doesn't work that way for recruits, and permanency was a fine line to begin with.

Eventually, as we were dozing off, Keith's voice drifted up the room, asking Alex if he was dreaming, or just trying to get the polish off his best friend.

I heard Timmy sniggering as Alex warned us all that his day would come.

TUESDAY, DAY 37
"HAND OFF COCKS!"

It was a routine wash morning until Alex came out of the shower with a penis that had all the shades of a box of Liquorice Allsorts.

"You may laugh now," and we took that as an order. "But you will be laughing on the other side of your face soon." He looked mainly at Timmy, who had assumed prime position for a sprint out of the door.

Soon it was out on the yard dressed in T-shirts, combat suits, and boots; it was a bit chilly and a relief to get going. A long jog up the road, across into the park through the trees, around another field. A quick break, then off again. We ran and jogged at varying paces. Whenever the paths were fairly straight, the back two men sprinted to the front, the loser getting a sore ear, but all of us getting a lesson in heavy breathing.

By the next break we were feeling it and after flopping down, the hardest thing was getting up again. We went back on another route, and it seemed as if it was all uphill. I developed a limp caused by some grit in my boot but no chance of a stop—kind of like it or limp it. We were a mile from the main road when we saw a young family coming towards us. We went into single file with bodies upright, adopting the peacock effect and smiling and waving to them all. Then we did our impression of a deflating balloon as we got back into twos.

Off we went again and were back in barracks fifteen minutes later. We dashed upstairs for a quick shower before lunch.

I had a bright red sore area on my right heel where a hole in my sock had let my heel rub against the boot. There were four of us needing some kind of running repairs, (puns are us) magic powder or plasters. No blisters, so it looked as if our feet were toughening up.

We had lunch and were out on the square for another drill session, still in our car mechanics coveralls, and after a brief inspection were ready for off. Although much better than a month ago, we were still prone to cocking things up, and it was rarely the same man involved. Some of the mistakes were technical such as the saluting positions of hands or arms to shoulder height, but on other occasions someone just would have a brain fart.

After about an hour we got the command "About-turn."

The entire squad did an about-turn except Joe Walters who was in the middle of the squad. He executed a beautiful right turn, went to move off, and was marched into by the guy alongside him. This caused a knock-on effect as three more guys tried to march off and got tangled up. There was no hiding this one; it had all the finesse of a motorway pile up.

"Walters, get out here now, you pea-brained balloon. Are you trying to win the tit of the week award?"

Although Joe's body appeared to be in the right place, his brain was obviously not functioning at full capacity.

"No Corporal of Horse, Yes Corporal of Horse, err, no Corporal of Horse."

Joe twitched as Tighe shouted at him, "You have the smallest brain I have ever come across. How the fuck can you have trouble making it up? Trooper Walters is going to demonstrate left-right and about-turns on the march."

Joe was off at speed, a left turn, about-turn, right turn, about-turn, about-turn. Right in front of us he was doing it so quickly that he looked as if he was on hot coal.

"Halt. McGrath, you are smiling. Do you find this funny?"

"I wasn't aware that I was, Corporal of Horse."

"Round the square, doing ten press-ups in each corner, and report back to me."

He gave us a quick general talk on how he needed to reach a standard with us, which could only be reached by an IQ above that of a mouse, and that at this moment the mouse is winning. "Any more of you finding this funny? Good. We will carry on."

At this moment, John arrived back only to be told go round and do it again, as he'd only done nine press-ups on the second corner, which was totally impressive, as Tighe had his back to that area the entire time.

At approximately 1515hrs we were finished drilling, were marching across to the education room for more progress in our thirst for knowledge, and were truly not unhappy to be going for a sit down.

We went over everything that we had covered previously, and then a Q and A session took place with wrong answers bringing on a crawl across the floor and back and correct answers only a crawl one way. Before finishing we were told there would be an officer's inspection on Friday.

We went straight across to the cookhouse for evening meal and of course Joe and John took a lot of ribbing from the rest of us. It was especially funny after we thanked John for taking the pressure off the rest of us and we kept hearing him repeating, "I didn't fucking smile, that's what pisses me off."

As always, we got into a heavy cleaning session, and I got a chance to make a good job of mine and Don's white belts. We started again on how to starch collars and on practicing how to get the bloody collar studs in place, but they seemed to have a mind of their own. By the time they were in, all we wanted to do was get them out again.

There had been a power failure in the NAAFI, or so we were informed, and no one went down there tonight. We were all hard at it when around 2200hrs we heard a commotion in Room Two and Bull, Danny, and Paul Smith ran into the room to see Parkin threatening Joe Walters. They said Joe looked really frightened and they took him outside, while Bull told the Mouth, "No more, I've just about had it with you."

Parkin said, "And you will do what?" as they did eye daggers at twenty paces.

"You really don't want to find out," Bull told him, and Parkin sneered and strolled off.

Parkin had just gone off at Joe for no apparent reason, so they all agreed that he would not be left alone in the room in the future.

There was an uneasy feeling in the room due to this, and other outbursts. Danny said he'd keep an eye on Joe as he was in the next bed, which made Joe feel better. Danny was about fifteen pounds lighter than Joe, and twenty pounds lighter than the Mouth, but he had a confident air about him.

By midnight we were getting into bed and all our lockers had a gleaming array of boots and belts, forage caps, and uniforms laid out in our lockers as per diagrams.

We chatted in our room about the tension next door and again agreed that it must be lousy being in a room with that kind of atmosphere. We were pleased we got on so well together. Life was tough enough at the moment without putting up roadblocks.

Keith gave us one of his deep psychological utterings: "It only takes one drop of poison to contaminate the deepest well."

It was so psychological we all immediately fell into a deep sleep.

WEDNESDAY, DAY 38 – THURSDAY, DAY 39
"WIDE AWAKE AND VIRGINIA LAKE!"

B*lood and sand, that's too loud for this time of day. I don't care, this is the day he gets his.*

I fell out of bed as soon as he switched the lights on, but I must have been sleeping on a nerve and my leg was numb, resulting in my doing a great impression of a live flounder on a fish slab. This got the loud one off the hook again and caused much amusement as I limped to the washroom.

We were marching back from the cookhouse in the dark and could see and hear the thunder and lightning rumbling and flashing in the distance. Within ten minutes it was absolutely pelting down.

First though, a pre-inspection to build on for the officer's inspection on Friday.

"Stand by your beds." Corporal of Horse Tighe came straight to the far end of the room. "Why is this ring two different shades?"

"Is it the light, Corporal of Horse?"

"I'll shine a light up your nose and watch it come out of your ears, you idiot; there's nothing in there to stop it."

I stood rigidly to attention, staring straight ahead, thinking, *Shit, here we go,* when he said, "Boots may be acceptable by Friday, with a lot of hard work."

Thinking this was nearly a compliment I almost fell over, but he'd already moved on.

All our kit had varying degrees of disdain heaped on it, in the cause of consistency.

One tunic and greatcoat had been pressed in the tailor's previously, and they looked very smart. One was to be our number-one uniform, which was for special inspections, and number two for more general use, especially when drilling. They were difficult to iron, but we had a secret weapon in the shape of Dave Marx to use in the future.

"Corridor ten minutes, number-two uniform, white belts, forage caps, and DMS boots."

It took about one minute to be ready, but five minutes to put the collars on. Most of us helped each other to get the stud through, almost choking when fingers were behind, trying to get the stud through the last slit in the shirt. They lined us up in the corridor in two lines and inspected us front and back, mainly to make sure everything fitted correctly.

We were no longer raw recruits in baggy coveralls but very smart in our new uniforms, and it was defining what was to be our new way of life. The NCO's continued to move along the line checking trouser heights, belt tightness, ties, and space left in collar when it was fastened up. All the time we were trying to gulp studs off Adam's apples.

The real heart stopper came when Corporal of Horse Tighe stood in front of Billy. "Are those feet supposed to be at forty-five degrees?"

The guys nearest to Billy thought he was going to pass out as Corporal of Horse Tighe arched his back, and Billy instinctively twitched and slightly moved one foot backwards. Corporal of Horse Tighe then gave him a knowing smile and moved on, mission accomplished.

Bill Allen, who was next to Billy, said he could have blown up a car tyre with the air that escaped from Billy's body.

"This is the worst you will ever look in uniform, each day will be progressively better. If it doesn't, your life will go rapidly downhill. You are now wearing the uniform of Her Majesty the Queen, don't ever forget it."

"Her Majesty the Queen," and I felt a sudden burst of pride. The Queen, who as a child I had always viewed as a mystical figure, and the country boy now had a connection, however tenuous.

As soon as the inspection was done, we changed into our jogging gear and ten minutes later were sitting in the back of a Bedford and leaving the barracks.

After a short drive we got out alongside a lake.

"This is Virginia Lake, and we will jog the five miles around it," said Corporal Miles, "and stop at some of the attractions."

We had a really relaxing jog, admiring the various sights, along with a commentary from Corporal Miles.

There was a hundred-foot totem pole (a gift from Canada to the queen), which was only erected six years previously. We saw the glorious Cascade Waterfalls rebuilt after storms in the 1790s, plus the Leptis Magna ruins (a gift from Libya in 1816 and rebuilt in situ in 1826). This was a terrific break in a sea of relentless encouragement.

On our return, we marched pretty happily over to the education block, thinking how good it would be to sit and bone up on our knowledge.

This lasted until we were ushered into the room to see four tables along the wall with rifles on them, and a chair opposite each table twenty feet away. We were a bit taken aback as we hadn't seen guns for about twelve days, but as usual there was no time to dwell on it—straight in with the spiel.

"Line-up in your rooms behind the chairs. To get your minds working again, the first person will strip the weapon, second one will reassemble it. Keep going until you have all done both."

No pressure then, and it was going well with just a couple of nervous fingers resulting in a piston on the floor.

"Do that again, and I will ram it in the vacant space between your ears," was as bad as it got for most of us.

"Parkin, lie face down on the floor."

Corporal Fletcher moved his arms into position, bent his legs, and lay a rifle across his arms. "This is the position for crawling with a rifle. Now using elbows and knees move forward."

Parkin glared at Corporal Fletcher, made one half-hearted attempt, and started to get up.

"Did I tell you to get up? Get on your belly and crawl."

Parkin did it slowly, almost arrogantly.

Corporal Fletcher shouted, "Get up, lie down, get up, lie down" and after five or six times, while Parkin was standing up, Corporal Fletcher got right in his face.

"You have an attitude problem, improve it or I will get rid of it for you, do you understand?"

Parkin glared at him and said nothing.

"Stand to attention when you speak to me, and address me as corporal, do you understand?"

"Yes, Corporal," the Mouth said begrudgingly.

"You better had. I will remove the attitude, or I will remove you. Now get on the floor and crawl."

And he did.

"Next, number one run to table, take the rifle and crawl back, hand it to number two and repeat until everyone has done it. Last team twenty press-ups. Go."

Off we went with lots of shouting, but it's not easy to crawl on hard carpet with rifles waving around a bit.

"Peters, if that rifle touches the floor, where it goes next will seriously impede your ability to walk. Coleman, use your elbows and keep a straight line—you look like a slug on a piss up, do it again."

Eventually we all finished, and Team Three did twenty press-ups.

After a ten-minute break, the room was blacked out and the lights were on as they placed a rifle under each table.

"This time, number one crawl to the rifle, slide off cover and remove the breech block, and crawl back. Number two crawl forward and reassemble it. Repeat this until you've all done it twice."

This is easy, I thought. *They must be weakening.*

"Go!" and number one and the lights went off at the same time, torches were flashing all over the floor, there were loud shouts of "Get a move on!" and it was bedlam. Some of us were just shouting encouragement to stay involved, others were more serious, but that was the whole idea, to see how we would react to the pressure and noise. By the time we finished and got over to the cookhouse we felt as if we'd been through a sausage-making machine.

The evening was all about tomorrow's inspection, as Corporal of Horse Tighe and Corporal Miles delivered expectancy speeches. "Pure perfection is the minimum. Get this wrong and you will think a full body rash is not invasive. I will not have my instructors or myself looking inept."

Looking in where? I thought.

"Start now, and there will be another inspection tomorrow at 0800hrs."

We cleaned the place inside out, doing every inch of the floors, walls, windows, the washrooms, and cleaning rooms.

Four hours later we stood back and admired our work, and then started on our personal gear.

I went and saw Don, as I'd had a bollocking over my belt. "Sorry Don, but they nailed me as well, but thanks again, as I got almost complimented for my boots."

Then Don told me, "I was told my belt was coming along but my boots needed more work," which had everyone in earshot laughing at the irony of it all.

By the time we were lying in bed we chatted about Parkin's bollocking, but for now sleep was a priority.

FRIDAY, DAY 40
IT'S A DOG'S LIFE

For crying out loud, he must be early it can't be that time already. But it is, the lights are on and I can hear Reveille playing.

We had a wash and cleaned the washrooms again, then over to breakfast, and back in time to be ready for inspection.

"Stand by your beds." Tighe strode around, frowning, gulping, raising eyebrows, doing everything, except get a round in. "Am I missing something, or is the inspection not today?"

The silence was almost deafening.

"You have just over two hours to get this place ready. At the moment I would not let his dog in here, now get a move on."

We repeated most of what we had done last night with instructors wandering in and out, poking and prodding at things to be done. By 1040hrs it smelled and looked like the cleanest hardware store in town.

"Dress in berets, coveralls, web belts, and plimsolls, then stand by your beds at 1059hrs."

They marched to the top of the staircase.

"Good morning, sir, block present and ready for your inspection."

"Room atten-shun!"

Seven pairs of plimsolls plopped to attention, holding up seven very nervous recruits. In came Captain Forbes-Hart looking immaculate, followed by Corporal of Horse Tighe, and Corporal Miles, with the obligatory clip board. Tiber, with a real hangdog look, just flopped against the wall, and never moved again until they left.

We were all asked basic stuff by Captain Forbes-Hart. "How are you progressing? Can you think of a way to improve things?"

I was asked if the instructors were looking after us. With Corporal of Horse Tighe two feet away staring over his shoulder, a *bunch of sadistic arseholes* went through my head, but left my mouth as, "Yes sir, they are."

He smiled and moved on, and Corporal of Horse Tighe gave me a half grimace, mainly because of the delay in answering. Captain Forbes-Hart didn't really disturb much, just made occasional comments to Corporal Miles.

They then went into Room Two, same procedure, after which we were lined up in the washrooms around the walls, as if it was a practice run for a firing squad. More poking around and scribbling, then into the cleaning room. Tiber expressed most of our feelings, as he lay against the cleaning room wall, and treated us all to a noisy yawn.

The highlight of the inspection was when Captain Forbes-Hart pointed to the Bumper and asked Corporal of Horse Tighe what it was.

"It's a buffing machine, sir."

"A buffing machine?"

"Yes sir, it cleans, scrubs, and polishes the floors."

"It looks lethal."

"Yes sir, Corporal Miles can testify to that."

We all smiled as Corporal Miles said, "Easier to shoot a fly with a machine gun, than tame the Bumper, sir."

After another loud yawn from Tiber, they all went down the other end of the block to begin again.

Not long after they had entered Room Four, we heard Corporal of Horse Tighe shouting at someone, and more shouting when Forbes-Hart left.

"Parade ground-ready for inspection at 1345hrs in number one uniform, forage caps, white belts, best boots, collar, and tie. It had better be good or..." and he was gone.

We felt so far it had gone pretty well, nobody hung, drawn, or quartered, but as we had found in the past our pretty well, and that of an instructor, were more often pretty well different.

At lunch we discovered what all the shouting had been about. Tiber had settled next to Chris Pratley and Chris suddenly began sneezing a lot.

"What's the matter with you?"

"I'm allergic to dogs. Ahchoo, Corporal of Horse."

"You will be when I ram one up your arse, you idiot. Get out, I will see you afterwards."

When the inspection was over and Forbes-Hart and Tiber had gone, Tighe came back upstairs, got Room Four together and went to Chris, getting straight in his face. "That is the last time you screw up in front of an officer. Next time you either choke, or you fucking well die. You do not complain about his dog or anything else in his earshot. You come and see me, then I will slowly choke you myself." He looked at Chris, then round the rest of the room, and slowly walked out.

After lunch we got back in the block and changed. The collar studs were still being a complete nightmare, and we were all having to help each other to put them in. The effort seemed worthwhile, as we all agreed we felt the part in our new uniforms.

"Fall in on the square."

"Squad Attennn-shun."

"Squad present, and ready for inspection, sir."

Captain Forbes-Hart returned the salute and walked over to inspect us. He would point out little or vague things, and Corporal Miles would diligently write it all down.

These were obviously earth-shattering moments for a recruit, but if Captain Forbes-Hart said it was something, then it was indeed something—no second opinion needed or sought. We fully accepted this was the way forward. It did lead to some lighter moments though.

"When he reached a very nervous Trooper Moore the captain said, "What's your name?"

Arnold replied, "Sir, Moore, sir."

Captain Forbes-Hart looked at Corporal of Horse Tighe and said, "Do we have a knight of the realm in our midst?"

Chuckling, Corporal of Horse Tighe stepped forward, and touched Moore on the shoulder with his whip. "Arise, Sir Moore."

We all enjoyed that, except Arnold, whose face went as red as his cap band.

We drilled for fifteen minutes, and when the inspection was over, not one slip or slide. Eventually we were brought to a halt in front of Captain Forbes-Hart, who proceeded to give us a pep talk. "It is almost six weeks since I addressed you all, and there has been a noticeable change. Although you have improved, you have still a long way to go to being good, excellent, and then onto the standards of the Household Division, so we will need to work you harder. To achieve these standards, we are going to increase your work rate, add more pressure."

He saluted Corporal of Horse Tighe. "Thank you, Corporal of Horse," and he marched off the square.

We drilled for another thirty minutes then Corporal of Horse Tighe halted us outside the block. He informed us that the address was "Captain Forbes-Hart's words, not mine," but a slight smile had formed. He told us to be in the foyer at 1515hrs in coveralls and we ran upstairs and changed.

By 1530hrs we had been marched over to the Lecture Room and were all seated.

Tighe proceeded to move along in the theme of "just." It was *just* up to standard in the rooms, *just* passable on the square inspection, and *just* bearable on the drill.

He seemed to be drawing it out, when there was an explosive crack as his riding whip smashed down on the table, and twenty-eight bodies sat bolt upright, eyes wide open with shock.

"You don't fall asleep in my time, get on the drill yard."

We never knew who was asleep, if anyone; he had probably *just* run out of conversation and decided to freshen us up.

Within minutes we were in a hectic session of effin/ights until we were breathing like the old proverbial bull dogs in heat.

We finished and went straight in for our evening meal after being told, "We will be in your rooms at 1830hrs."

Corporal of Horse Tighe and Corporal Wheeler arrived at exactly 1830hrs in a block still looking good from the inspection. Obviously only *just,* as the first thing that was said involved digging it out properly over the weekend. Then a few eye openers.

"Acceptable is the bad side of poor."

"We will tell you what is clean; you will not assume anything, and we do not give an officer any problem, only solutions." This was obviously referring to Chris, but clearly laying out the ground rules for the rest of us.

They left at 1930hrs and we trooped off down to the NAAFI, chatting about the day. We'd had a warning that things would heat up and more pressure would get put on, but we had also shown improvement.

Pete, being positive, said, "What will be, will be. I'd still like to know why Tighe always has a facking fly up his arse."

"There is no need for that kind of talk in here Peter," Alice said.

Pete said in all seriousness, "Sorry Alice, I meant a facking fly up his bottom."

Alice smiled, shook her head, and walked off.

We soon moved on to Sir Arnold, Earl of Combermere, third in line for the toilet, which was a joint effort at keeping us all amused.

Tonight, getting to sleep did not take long. I said, "You will not fall asleep in my time," and they did.

SATURDAY, DAY 41
"HANDS OFF COCKS!"

I'm going to booby trap that effing door. No, I'll booby trap Room Two's door and look suitably amazed when he gets his comeuppance. Better still, booby trap the washroom with odds at fourteen to one on who did it.

I trundled off to the washroom just in time to hear Bob groaning. It sounded as if an orchestra had started up, mainly the wind section, and his relief was obvious to the entire washroom.

After breakfast we had an inspection by Corporals Wheeler and Fletcher. They had obviously been briefed as they lined us up in the corridor afterwards.

"Everything looks reasonable this morning, agreed?"

"Yes, Corporal," shouted twenty-eight voices in unison.

"Right. Lecture room."

Corporals Wheeler and Fletcher then took us in the Lecture Room and amongst other things informed us we would be begin guard duties on Thursday. Room One first, then in room order.

It would run from 1800hrs–0600hrs with an inspection at 1755hrs outside the guardroom.

It consisted of two periods of two hours each, called "stags."

First: 1800–2000hrs. Second: 2000–2200hrs. Third: 2200–2400hrs.
First: 2400–0200hrs. Second: 0200–0400hrs. Third: 0400–0600hrs.

"We will go into it in more detail nearer the time."

We were buzzing at lunch when a cook said, "I don't know much, but in the future, you will be pissed off with guard duties."

Someone said, "Wow, not many people admit to not knowing much."

The cook's reply was unprintable, but it turned out to be correct many times over.

We were all busy cleaning, when Corporals Wheeler and Fletcher were spotted heading for the block.

"Get the washrooms cleaned; they are wet, we are not bloody fish. Clean this place out and work on your personal gear, we will be back later today or tomorrow."

By the time we went over to evening meal we agreed the block had been scrubbed so often recently, it could probably scrub itself.

I talked with Joe Walters and asked him how things were with him.

"Ok," he said after looking around. "It's been a bit better now that Bull spoke to Parkin, and Danny is in the next bed."

"It's a bad environment, Joe, why don't you ask for a room change?"

"I don't want to fight with him, but I would always be the guy he frightened off," he said, and he shrugged his shoulders.

SUNDAY, DAY 42
BOXED IN

The day turned into another huge cleaning day, with lots of the usual piss taking and practical jokes, but none of us knew what was just around the corner.

I was in the cleaning room around 2115hrs. As I was walking out of the door with Tony Mahoney, we heard a brief shout come from Room Two, followed by a louder bang, as if something had collapsed.

We raced into the room and saw Tom Peters and Joe Walters staring at Parkin lying semi-conscious on the floor, with blood coming from his nose and mouth. Danny Williams was to one side holding his left hand in his right. We were followed by Bull, who stopped anyone else from coming in, ushering most of them back to the cleaning room.

The first thing I noticed, apart from Parkin, was the contents of a locker spread over the floor. A bed had moved sideways away from the locker and Parkin was lying in the space between. We had a quick look at him, and Tony held a towel against his face. I told Tom Peters to run to the MI room and get the medic.

Within minutes the medic took over. He had managed to stem the bleeding from Parkin's nose, but this began again, as Parkin started to vomit. All in all, he seemed pretty much out of it.

The medic sent me to the Guard Room to get the duty driver, as he was going to take Parkin to the hospital, which was right across from the barracks. Within fifteen minutes of it occurring, Parkin had been placed in the vehicle and was at the casualty department with the medic.

A short time after this, Corporal Miles arrived, followed five minutes later by Corporal of Horse Tighe in civilian clothes. After a quick chat, Corporal Miles ran across to the hospital.

Room Two was still in disarray. Corporal of Horse Tighe looked around and then took Tom, Joe, and Danny downstairs to another room.

Everyone was trying to have a look at the mess, and trying to take in what had happened, as so much had taken place in such a short time.

It seemed fairly apparent that Danny had punched Parkin, but none of us had a clue about the full story, and speculation was rife.

It was cut short around 2230hrs when Corporal Miles returned from the hospital. He came back into the block and told everyone not to discuss it, and he would bring us up to date as soon as possible.

"Don't discuss it." He might as well have asked a fish to stop swimming.

He asked, "Who were the first people into the room?"

I told him it was Tony and me, and he took us downstairs.

Corporal of Horse Tighe was there with Joe and Tom, (who were still a bit shaken up), and Danny Williams, who seemed much more composed.

Corporal of Horse Tighe asked us what we had seen, wrote it down, and we signed it. While this was going on, the medic appeared at the door, and Corporal Miles went out to speak to him. When we were all finished Tighe told us to go back, and they would be up shortly.

Shortly after, Corporal of Horse Tighe gathered everyone into a cleaning room. "There has been a minor altercation, nothing for you to worry about. Trooper Parkin is being kept in hospital overnight due to a concussion and will be out tomorrow. Clean up the area. I don't want to see any blood stains on the floor. Go to your rooms for tonight as normal, and we will keep you up to date tomorrow."

Tighe and Miles hung around for fifteen minutes and then left. We went straight into Room Two and sat on the beds.

There was no way we could settle down now, until we had talked to the main guys. It was as if a cork had been pulled from a bottle. It's amazing the three of them could breathe.

It appeared Parkin had suddenly taken it into his head to have a go at Joe, who was talking to Tom Peters. He grabbed Joe by his lapels and flung him against the wall. Danny Williams, who was at the other end of the room, ran down and said to Parkin, "If you lay a hand on him again, I'll smack you one."

Tom and Joe then told us what happened next.

Parkin spun around and said to Danny, "Fuck you, you cocky little twat," and swung at him.

They both said Danny hit Parkin twice in the head, then really hard in the ribs, and as he bent forward, punched him in the head again. This caused him to spin into the open locker, and bounce into the bed, moving it sideways. Both of them agreed that it was over very quickly.

It then transpired that in his statement to Corporal of Horse Tighe, Danny told him that from the age of eight to eighteen he'd been taught to box, and when he was seventeen was an amateur boxing champion. When asked why he hadn't talked about this before, he stated that he had quit a year earlier, and didn't want type casting.

We were all looking at Danny differently now, realising why he had this quiet confidence about him, and he explained it from his point of view. "I'm not happy this happened, but Parkin couldn't carry on like this with Joe, especially after his behaviour with Banjo. I was worried for Joe."

After a short while Timmy stood up and said, "The lengths some fuckers will go to avoid cleaning," and we knew it was getting back to business as usual.

We lay in bed with all of us remembering different aspects of Parkin. His behaviour with Banjo, his attitude in the Lecture Room, and the remarks about Paul's sister.

There was so much of it when it was all put together. The only impression I gathered from the tone of the room, was that we wouldn't require grief counselling.

WEEK 7

MONDAY, DAY 43
"HANDS OFF COCKS, GET A MOVE ON!"

I don't care this morning, you noisy, light-flicking pain in the arse, I want to see what is going to happen today, so let's get cracking.

The conversation in the washrooms was about the fracas and carried on during breakfast. The cooks had even heard that there was a fight in the block, and we told them some of the story.

Danny was halfway through his breakfast when one of the cooks, with a plate full of sausage and bacon and a cloth over his arm, asked if, "sir, would like "building up."

We were enjoying the moment; it's a great life if you don't weaken.

"Stand by your beds."

We had everything laid out and Tighe's inspection was more of a push and prod Q and A session with no correct answers on our side.

On a more positive note, we were becoming aware that the air mail aspect of the inspections was decreasing; nothing had been thrown for a long time, so we must be doing something right at last.

By 0850hrs we were in the gym and wind milling.

We got into our routines and it was always "More, more, gimme another, harder, faster, speed up, more, more. We exercised individually and as a group, and then the circuit equipment was laid out.

Plenty of shouting and yelling, except for the team that had just finished, who were allowed a short period of pretending that life could be maintained in short heavy breathing gulps, while writhing on the floor.

There was no sign of Danny or Parkin at lunch, and we were at our inquisitive best.

As soon as we reached the block, Corporal Fletcher was in the foyer saying we had to be back down in five minutes with coveralls, web belts, boots, and berets.

We had a non-stop drill session to keep us occupied but there was a little buzz of awareness around 1330hrs as Corporal Miles and Danny Williams marched back into the block. Having got changed, Danny joined in the drill session.

It's amazing that there weren't more cockups during the afternoon. Every time we saw Danny, we began wondering what was going on. Corporal Fletcher was probably aware of this, which is no doubt why we went all afternoon non-stop.

We finished drilling at about 1620hrs, ready to go to evening meal. A large number of us got into the foyer at the same time as Corporal of Horse Tighe was entering with Parkin, and we were told to go straight over to the cookhouse.

Parkin looked a bit the worse for wear with bruising around the face and an obviously swollen jaw, plus he was walking fairly stiffly. As he also had a seriously damaged ego, he didn't look directly at us.

At evening meal, most of us pulled a couple of tables together and were on pins and needles to get Danny's version going. It was to the quietest bunch of recruits imaginable when Danny began his story.

It transpired that at 1300hrs he and Parkin were marched into an office by Tighe and Miles. Behind a large table were Captain Forbes-Hart and another warrant officer Danny hadn't seen before. They were told to salute, which caused Parkin a bit of pain, so they were stood at ease.

Then, in Danny's words, they received an "absolutely perfect bollocking" from Forbes-Hart, who barely raised his voice. He let them have both barrels, leaving them in no doubt that they were, "ill-disciplined and idiotic people." He said he was seriously considering long and hard if there was a place for them in the regiment.

He asked if they had anything to say and they both said, "No sir."

He told them that they were to have two days stoppage of pay and then said,

"Corporal of Horse, get them out of my sight."

Once outside, Danny was marched back to the block to join the squad, but Parkin was told to remain behind with Corporal of Horse Tighe.

At this point, Danny shrugged his shoulders and said, "I haven't a clue what's going on now, you know as much as me."

Around 1800hrs Corporal of Horse Tighe appeared in the block and got everyone together. "Just to keep you updated and stop the obvious rumour mongering that you will not be able to resist, Trooper Parkin is staying in the MI room tonight for further observation. Carry on with your work and stop jumping to conclusions, as inevitably, you will be wrong." He hung around until we were all cleaning, and then silently left.

As soon as he was out of the block, I legged it straight to the phone, and was quickly talking to Mum. I told her about guard duties beginning, Virginia Waters, and the tour around the lake, and how I had always wanted to see the world, but had not envisaged it being on foot. There was always so much to talk about, but I never mentioned the fight and in what seemed no time at all I was back in the block.

I don't know about dispelling any rumours. Corporal of Horse Tighe had lit the blue touch paper and retired. It didn't matter who I joined, there was only one topic of conversation.

The main positive was Room Two could have an evening of peace and quiet, without wondering what was going to happen next.

We had eased off the theories by the time we went to the NAAFI, but as we lined up it was obvious that Alice and Jenny knew there was something in the air. As Keith was at the front, Jenny asked him what was going on.

"There's a lot, Jenny," he said quietly, "We'll need a quiet corner for me to get it out in the open."

He immediately realised that Alice's hearing was far superior to his, as she walked back and said, "Get to the back of the line, randy little sod."

"Oh hell, Alice give me a break," he whined.

"Certainly, my pleasure, arm or leg?"

Keith sloped off to the back. He secretly enjoyed all this by now, as he smiled and contorted his face to the guys he was passing, and Alice did save him one of the better-looking pies.

When they were told the whole story about Parkin, Alice said simply, "He needs help that lad."

Jenny said nothing, just shook her head.

By the time we turned in, it was not mentioned, except towards the very end of some laughing and joking around. We had just turned off the lights and somebody said, "Has anybody been to see Parkin?"

"Don't know, does anybody want to?"

"Doesn't look like it."

"Speaks volumes, does it not?"

TUESDAY DAY 44
"HANDS OFF COCKS!"

The first fifteen minutes or so were always taken up with washing and shaving, and the usual wait for the toilets. If by a minor miracle Bob had got up early and blocked one off for ten minutes, mayhem could ensue.

"Stand by your beds." Corporal of Horse Tighe launched a full-scale assault on our ears and personal gear, which was treated as if it had attacked him personally.

In our room that morning we had, "...two wankers, three pricks, and a couple of mental cripples," to throw into the mix.

He was good at this, though, as none of us felt any form of favouritism, more of a screwed-up squad syndrome, with a high degree of togetherness.

The good thing was he didn't say anything resembling "well done," or I think we might not have been able to cope with it. It's a fair bet he wouldn't though, as this did not appear to be in the early days recruit development manual.

"Be on the square at 0900hrs: coveralls, berets, plus web belts."

There were still occasional cockups, not normally big, but we saved one of them for this morning, when we had been drilling about forty-five minutes and were covering a lot of ground around the square.

We were given the command "right wheel," and Tony Mahoney, who was on the right corner, had a total brain fart and instead of shortening his pace carried on, turning full stride. This led to everyone else having to run to try to catch up with him and realising they couldn't, start jumping around like a corral full of wild horses.

We stopped and stared at Tony, who had a look of *please ground open up and swallow me* on his face. Although there had been many, this had to rate in the top five of all bollockings.

When Corporal of Horse Tighe had done his best to break nearby windows, we thought all had calmed down, but then came a backup bollocking from Corporal Wheeler. "What a total load of dickheads. I promise you if this happens again, I will beat you over your heads with your own bollocks."

On a more positive note, this was the last big train wreck.

The cooks were also on form, asking us if we could drill correctly every now and then, as this morning's bollocking nearly broke *their* windows.

I said, "A bit like those rock-hard, soft-boiled eggs maybe," which drew comments of "very touchy," and "nerve hit there then."

After lunch, we were told by Corporals Fletcher and Wheeler to be on the parade ground at 1315hrs in number-one dress, best boots, white belts, and forage caps.

As we stood on the square, we saw Corporal of Horse Tighe, Corporal Miles, and Parkin, who was in coveralls, march in through the main doors of our block, and thought Parkin would join us as soon he had changed.

After about an hour, Corporal Miles came out of the block and spoke to the instructors, then marched off again. They marched us over towards the block facing the main doors, but a little farther back than usual and stood us at ease.

We had been standing at ease waiting for the next command, but that was given by Corporal Miles as he marched across from the block again and came to attention in front of us.

The next move shook us all.

We saw Parkin in civvies, with his holdall, walk out of the block with Corporal of Horse Tighe, stop, then quickly turn, and go straight towards the Guard Room.

This was the last time we saw him.

Later, we all thought it was done so we could see him go, and he could see us in our finery watching him. As soon as they were out of sight, just to re-focus us, we immediately got into another thirty minutes of more gentle type drilling.

We were then told to change into coveralls and be on the square at 1530hrs.

In Room Two, Parkin's bed was now bare of bedding, and his locker completely empty. The only trace of him were two uniforms, a forage cap, and great coat lying across the mattress.

We were then marched to the Lecture Room.

"Sit down and shut up." Corporal of Horse Tighe carried on, "To put a quick stop to the rumours that are flying around, I will explain the events of the last couple of days to you."

He went through the Sunday evening events, and Monday's follow up, and soon bought us to the time that Danny and Parkin went into the office on orders. After Danny was taken back to the block, Parkin was marched back into the office.

"His general attitude was that he did not want to return to this squad, so we offered him the option of back-squadding or leaving altogether. This morning, after calling home again, he informed us that he wanted to be discharged. He has now completely finished. There is no more to be said on the matter." Tighe then proceeded to give us a general procedural ear bashing on accepted practices, teamwork, and respect for ourselves and others, finishing in his own inimitable way: "If any of you have even the slightest doubt, get out now. There is no room in this man's army for any of you who have no balls, and I have no time to waste on wankers."

(*Ouch, he certainly has a way with the queen's English.*)

On arrival back in the block, we found all remaining traces of Parkin were removed, including locker and bed, and it was evening meal as usual.

It was as if none of us had spoken since birth, the volume level being really high, with a kind of surprised excitement. None of us had considered him leaving, and we were finding it hard to take in.

The cooks were just as surprised but soon recovered saying, "He must have some sense, given a choice we'd leave you fuckers behind if we could," and then they just kept walking around grinning.

There was a lightness tonight about the conversations, and it was apparent that not only Room Two was glad to see the back of him—his negative presence was no longer a problem.

We were all doing our own thing when around 1915hrs Bull came to Timmy and me and asked us to follow him back to Room Two.

We went in and saw three beds spaced neatly down each wall, and the floor was gleaming. The guys were all in there and looking really pleased with themselves, especially Joe, who looked a lot more relaxed. Bull said, "Even though it's dark outside, the room feels much brighter."

I nodded at Tony "Did you take the bumpering beast to this?"

"Piss off, Jimmy," he said in mock horror. "I'd rather slide down a razor blade using my balls as a brake, than go near that thing."

"Ok everyone, let's do it," I said, and we all piled into Tony, laughing and clowning around, as a rugby scrum took place.

The room was already on the mend, as it seemed to them that a weight had been lifted off their shoulders, and we all headed off down to the NAAFI in high spirits.

After Alice and Jenny had been told the whole story, it soon got lighter and drifted into the more necessary aspects of a recruit's life.

This carried on into the block-cleaning session, as Parkin began to drift further back in our thoughts. The conversations were definitely in a lighter vein, as many people's frustrations with him had been put to rest.

We worked until midnight and turned in, having seen Room Two more together as a group than for many weeks. The one thing they all agreed on, was looking forward to a good night's sleep.

We lay in bed not saying much, thinking our own thoughts when Dave said out loud, "As an afterthought, is there another course scheduled after we finish?"

"Not that I know of," Bob replied.

"Then it would have been pretty hard to back squad him, wouldn't it?"

We fell asleep, realising that this was exactly the way the army works.

WEDNESDAY, DAY 45
AN ORANGUTAN'S BALLS

I was at the sinks opposite Joe and asked him how he slept.

"I've got to admit it, Jimmy, that's my best night's sleep since I got here."

"Looks like you're buying the pies tonight," Keith said.

"My pleasure," said Joe.

It's a strange life that's measured in meat pie sales.

After a heart-warming run, we were ready for Pay Parade, which went off without a hitch—almost.

Paul Smith confidently marched out, slamming his right foot down, and not respecting the god of boot studs, his foot shot forward. He did a beautiful half pirouette, waved his arms around for balance, and stood back to attention as if nothing had happened.

The warrant officer remarked that it would have done a ballet dancer proud.

"Thank you, sir," Tighe said smiling, "I will work on his pirouette, or place my boot firmly up his tutu."

Gym assessments were worked out and this led to a move around, including Ding Dong into Team Three, and Bull came up into Team Two, probably to see if our strength was at the level of carrying a bulldozer.

In the office Corporal Kelly told me that they were pleased with my extra effort and then he said, "Any questions?

"Yes, Corporal, do camels get extra pay?"

He looked baffled. "Where did you get that from?"

"An orangutan in Team Three."

We were all laughing as I walked back into the gym.

During a later drill session which went very well, with no big cockups, came a Tighe-type backhanded compliment. "So, no more should I see you pissing about, with your thumb up your bum, and your mind in neutral."

That evening in the NAAFI, the atmosphere was really light-hearted. I was sitting with about eight of us around a table.

Alex asked what "Ticker" and I had been laughing about when we came out of the office, so I told them the story."

"Was I the orangutan?" Alex asked.

"No."

"Are you sure?"

"Yes Alex, orangutans don't have shiny best friends."

Timmy shouted across to Alice. "Alice have you any boot polish remover?"

"Who for?"

"Big Hippo."

"For his hands?"

"No, his John Thomas."

"Without skipping a beat Alice replied, "Oh, you'll only want a small tin then?"

This carried on right through until lights out. As we were lying in bed, Timmy shouted, "Jimmy, have you got a tiny bit of cloth for removing an orangutan's ball polish?"

"I've got feelings you know," Alex shouted back.

"Only very tiny ones according to Alice," I reminded him.

Alex went full on Geordie saying something in the area of, "Awae man, you'se aw ganna get it up yawse. (Rough translation: I'll sort you lot out soon.)

Timmy burst out laughing, as he was probably the only one who had a clue what was being said.

THURSDAY, DAY 46
ON GUARD

At evening meal, we all chatted about the up-coming guard and put on our best *no-big-deal* faces in front of everyone else. On return, looking at our uniforms laid out on our beds, we got an attack of being all fingers and thumbs, with nerves beginning to set in. Fortunately, the other guys were on hand to help with the neck chokehold and stiff collars, plus brushing off clothing.

At 1740hrs we were all dressed up with somewhere to go, and with shouts of good luck ringing in our ears, we made our way to the foyer.

Corporal Fletcher arrived and said, "Just relax, do as we tell you, and there will not be a problem." He marched us down to the Guard Room and inside into the corridor.

The Guard Room was situated roughly twelve yards from the main gate, which in turn was about ten yards from a main road. There was a perimeter wall around nine feet high along the edge of the pavement (sidewalk) and the gate was fairly central in it. The gates themselves were two big, black, wrought iron ones. They were hinged on the wall side with a wheel on the bottom corner, which ran along a metal floor plate so they could be opened for vehicles to go in or out. There was also a smaller wrought iron gate to the side of them for foot traffic. The Guard Room building roof overhung the path that passed the main Guard Room window. At night it was brightly lit up by overhead lights, and the light from the Guard Room itself.

The Guard Room itself had two big, glass entry doors into a short corridor and on the left was the main room about twenty-five feet by fifteen feet, all open. Through the main room another door led into a room with no windows, just small glass blocks at ceiling level on one side. This was the inaptly named sleeping quarters.

The front of the main room had a sliding window about three feet off the floor. This opened to the pathway outside. Inside, next to the window, a desk contained a book, which anyone going in or out had to sign. It was also very bright during the day due to its large glass frontage. If you went straight on through the main doors, another corridor ran across the top, which contained the cells and washrooms.

The Regimental Police left, and we lined up outside. The Corporal of Horse did a brief inspection, straightened a tie or two, then stepped back. "Numbers one, three, five—main gate. Numbers two, four, six—patrolling. Number seven will take up any slack. Main gates are closed from 1800–0600hrs. Check all drivers' ID cards; if there is any problem at all send them to the Guard Room or we will come out to you. Only when you are completely satisfied, will you open one gate to let them in or out.

"Those patrolling—you will walk around the barracks and check all building exteriors. Do not enter any blocks or the mess, and report back here every forty minutes. If you are overdue, we will come look for you. The only excuse permitted for this is death. Fall out."

I was number four, so no walkabout until 2000hrs. I watched Corporal Fletcher go out to the main gate with Bob McCann and go through it all again. Meanwhile, the Corporal of Horse gave Ginger a pick-axe handle and off he went. At least he wouldn't need a map as we were not a big barracks, and we had run around it often enough recently.

On his return, Corporal Fletcher took us into the sleeping quarters where there were eight beds, four on each wall, with a chair beside each one. On each bed was a one-inch-thick mattress made of pure itch, a pillow, and one blanket.

"After 2200hrs you can keep a restful watch. While you are in the sleeping quarters, remove boots and collars, keep on shirts, trousers, and socks. If you leave you will be dressed properly. We will wake you ten minutes before your stag. Be quiet, and use the corridor mirror to make sure you look respectable."

We were back in the main Guard Room as a soldier was booking out. The Corporal of Horse pushed him a book to sign, and he leaned in to sign it.

"This is how anyone leaving must look on leaving and entering, collar and tie, smart jacket and trousers or overcoat, no tie-no go," said the Corporal of Horse.

The soldier waved his hand in the universal sign of going for a beer, smiled, and walked out.

The Corporal of Horse took over and Corporal Fletcher disappeared. He chatted to us about how this was a good time to learn the ropes as it is quieter with the regiment being away.

As he was talking, Ginger walked to the window, waved, and went off again.

In no time at all it was 1955hrs and Dave went to relieve Bob at the gate. I took Ginger's piece of modern warfare off him and strolled off into the barracks. It was not too chilly, and I was enjoying walking around checking doors and windows.

It was a bit different around the garage and vehicle park areas, though. Lots of trees and not much light, which made it all pretty spooky. In what seemed double-quick time, I was doing my first Guard Room check, then off again. I went the other way round the blocks, feeling more confident by now, and walked at my pace trying more doors and windows. Soon I was back at the Guard Room with only thirty minutes left, so I went around the office area again making sure I could see the clock on the square. When I saw them changing the main gate, I walked into view.

It was perfectly timed to give Keith the hallowed pick-axe handle, tell him I thought there were strange spooky goings on in the garage area, and leave him with it.

When I got inside the main Guard Room, I saw a table that had appeared since I'd left that was full of sandwiches, tea and coffee urns, fruit, sugar, and milk. I went and threw my greatcoat on a bed, poured myself a brew, and grabbed a door-step sized corned beef sandwich. Then

I joined the rest of them listening to the Corporal of Horse telling them about the realities of army life and really feeling a part of all this now.

Timmy, who was number seven, was having a laugh at our expense, as after he had helped the duty driver bring all the food down, there was nothing else to do. He would sleep from midnight to 0600hrs, "So would you be quiet?"

I saw the Corporal of Horse look sideways at him and smile.

With last orders in the pubs being 2230hrs, by 2300hrs onwards there were a few guys drifting back in, definitely more boisterous and ties slackened off, no doubt fuelled by an amber nectar or five, and for a moment I was envious.

It was roughly 2330hrs when Corporal Fletcher reappeared, chatted with the Corporal of Horse for a few minutes, and then took over as the Corporal of Horse walked off in the direction of the mess.

Soon Bob was doing his second stag on the gate and Ginger had left with his new best friend under his arm as Keith and Alex came in and ate some sandwiches.

As this was going on, Timmy stood up smiling, saying he was going for a good sleep and I decided to have a lie-down before my 0200hr stag. I don't know whether I slept at all, but the next thing I remember Corporal Fletcher was there, and I went outside to the mirror, just as Timmy came out.

Corporal Fletcher was behind him smiling, "The guard commander thought you might benefit more from tonight if you accompanied Trooper Green on his stag; we don't want you to feel left out."

Timmy muttered a long sentence, in which the only word I could make out rhymed with "prat," as Corporal Fletcher went and sat down laughing at Timmy's response.

It was a lot colder than earlier. Once we got walking, Timmy settled down and we had a good chat and then did a check in.

Corporal Fletcher started to laugh at Timmy's face, which made all three of us laugh. Before we set off again, Fletcher asked us to check the gate at the far corner of the vehicle park, probably to make sure we did a full walk, so we set off down there.

On the way, I told Timmy I thought that weird things were going on in that area. The gate was in a really dark spot surrounded by trees and led outside the barracks, to a very dark back alley behind some houses.

We were just walking by some bushes approaching the gate when there was a large squealing sound, the bush came alive, and some kind of an animal ran from it across the front of us and vanished into the night.

I turned to Timmy. "What the fuck was that?" and realised he was twenty yards up the vehicle park.

I quickly joined him. "I hope it was just a fucking cat."

"It frightened the shit out of me," he said.

"Shall we go back and check the gate?"

We both walked away from the gate to a well-lit area and then had a slow walk taking the long way back, which was very well lit, and reported back to the Guard Room.

Corporal Fletcher told us to get a quick brew and warm up before going out again. I told him about the animal, which by now was the size of a wolf.

Corporal Fletcher was still chuckling when he told us to carry on.

We wandered around, checking that all the lamppost lights were working, and avoided anywhere a Hound of the Baskervilles could be lurking. We went over to the admin block as it had a good view of the Guard Room and waited for the main gate to begin changing.

When we got to the Guard Room I handed a bleary-eyed Keith the semi-automatic pick axe handle, and went for a lie down. As it wasn't too warm, I used my blanket with a greatcoat over it. Just as I got warm, the lights came on at 0530hrs.

"Right, get dressed, clean the sleeping quarters, main room and corridors and be ready to leave at 0559hrs."

By 0550hrs the duty driver had picked up a tired-looking Timmy and all the mugs were taken to the cookhouse. The Regimental Police were back at 0555hrs and we were dismissed and marched back to the block. As we meandered up the staircase, we heard the time-honoured shout from Corporal Fletcher.

FRIDAY, DAY 47
"HANDS OFF COCKS!"

It was strange watching Room Two staggering into the washroom, half asleep, realising that we also looked like this most mornings. We went into the toilet cubicles, closed the doors, and listened to their groans.

Soon we got into our normal routine and marched across to the cookhouse feeling smug and confident, now that our guard was over. Everyone was talking at once, especially Room Two, and we all gave them slightly different versions.

"Stand by your beds."

We only just made it when he bounded through the door. "Apparently last night went without a hitch," he said as if it was incredulous.

As he was finishing, he saw Keith's number-two uniform on a coat hanger with the tunic unbuttoned, as the inspection had started a bit early. Giving Keith a look of *I dare you,* he said, "Don't let me see trousers so bad again, they look as if they have been slept in."

Keith just glared at him.

"Oh, so you obviously agree, do twenty press-ups, saying this will not happen again."

When Keith was halfway through, Corporal of Horse Tighe gave a wry smile and went off down the corridor.

Keith stood up and kept counting, while waving his two informative fingers in the direction that Tighe had gone. We all chanted "This will not happen again," and waved our fingers in support, but Keith was still pissed off.

"How the fuck am I supposed to press these? He knows I've just come off guard."

"Listen Keith," Bob said. "He didn't say press them; he said don't let me see them like this, meaning button up your tunic and hide your problem."

There was that army logic in play—you are only guilty if you get caught.

Keith nodded and smiled. "He's still a prick though."

The rest of us totally agreed.

We were soon out on the square getting another inspection for our troubles. It was one of those *I dare you* ones where berets were removed because the badge was not over the eye, and then they were jammed back on our head with an *I dare you to make it comfortable* look. Next was a bollocking for it not being on straight.

The session was spent on more simple stuff. The whole morning was spent on improving personal movement, mainly small things. We would salute and invariably felt a helping hand pushing an elbow up a little or a hand into place.

"You are at least one inch short over your eye. There are times in life when an inch is very important and where your fingers are is also very important."

"If you think that was an inch, you'd better prepare your wife for a big disappointment."

That was funnier and we all had a smile over it, then realised we had fallen into the ever-present danger.

"Two laps of the square to re-focus."

But sometimes a run was welcomed when doing static drills. We drilled through to lunch time with only one short break for a rest and treatment for earache.

At lunch I was with Timmy, Joe, and Tony Mahoney, who asked us again what to expect tonight, when they were on guard duty. I gave them a rundown, and then a little gremlin popped into my head. I looked at

Timmy. "I'll have to mention it." Then I looked at them as if I was making a solemn statement. "If you are on patrol, they will ask you on each stag to go down to the rear gate, which gets really dark, be very careful."

I looked back at Timmy. "Luckily there were two of us but you don't have a spare man so you will be alone."

"So what?" Joe said.

"There's a large animal there and it's fast moving," Timmy told him.

Tony spoke up. "It's probably only a cat."

"No, no," Timmy said heatedly. "We thought that, until we saw its outline dash out of the shadows."

"It was bigger than a fox, but smaller than a wolf, and it's definitely fast," I said.

Timmy then told them, "When you go on patrol, they give you a pick-axe handle, but don't tell you why. I think it's for when you go to the rear gate. Anyway, it doesn't matter—you may get the main gate."

By 1310hrs we were back on the square and went straight over to the gym, paying our customary entrance fee before falling into our three teams.

We worked in teams and I was still working on my no-arm forward somersault. I had definitely achieved a better class of splat when I hit the mat.

They would move us around the equipment, often thinking up new or more strenuous exercises, and with one or two short stops two hours quickly passed.

After a longer rest we raced against each other in teams. A lot of energy went into these races and they were extremely competitive.

During the evening meal I sat with Danny, Paul Smith, and Tom Peters.

Tom said "Jimmy, Joe was telling us before we came over, about the rear gate?"

I thought, *I'll lead in gracefully,* and told them about our inspection, patrolling, sleeping quarters, and main gate. Then, quite seriously, I said, "I've got to say, whoever is on patrol, be aware of whatever is in the bushes near the back gate. There were two of us and we were lucky, or God knows what may have happened."

"It has to be a cat," Paul said.

"No mate, I know a cat when I see one and this was way too big, but it was fast, so take care."

After they had gone, we settled down to our cleaning routine, chatting to the rest about what the guard would be doing. We were still chatting around 1900hrs when Dave Marx came to the door and said, "Be quiet and come and see this."

We followed him to our room and Alex and Bob put their fingers on their lips and pointed at Keith. He was sitting on the edge of his bed with a boot on one hand, and a duster over a finger on the other one, which would move a little. Then his head would jerk back as he fought to stay awake. Soon there were about ten of us watching Keith, when Alex went up behind him and shouted in his ear,

"Hands off cocks!"

Keith leapt off his bed and knocked over his polish lid full of water. His boot skidded across the floor, and then he saw us all laughing and his face went bright red. "You lousy bastards!"

This rendered us totally useless, and Keith had to start all over again with his boot.

We were still taking the mickey out of him when we got to the NAAFI.

As he felt warmer, he began to nod off again.

Jenny, not knowing about earlier, said to him, "Are you feeling tired, had a rough night last night?"

"I did Jenny, would you like to come and put me in bed?"

"No chance, I haven't got a spade, and what would we do with all the other weeds I'd have to dig up?"

This was deep and we all started beating the tables and making even more noise when it seemed he hadn't got it, but it didn't matter as within minutes he was nodding off again.

There was more work to do when we got back and we got on with the more physical stuff, as it became apparent over the next hour or two that most of us who had been on guard were feeling the lack of sleep.

By 2300hrs there were more of us nodding off and violently jerking around trying to stay awake. As soon as we could, we went to bed and fell asleep listening to Keith snoring.

SATURDAY, DAY 48
"WAKEY, WAKEY!"

Wakey-fucking-Wakey, *what the hell is this all about?* I didn't recognise the voice at all, as he switched on the lights and woke us.

By the time we got to the washroom, Room Two were in there and on a noisy high, having completed their first guard duty.

The one thing all of us enjoyed was watching Bob doing his muted Highland fling. "Go to the other bogs, Bob," Room Two were urging him, but Bob didn't have the confidence to open his legs, let alone run.

We went across to breakfast and the guys in Room Two were still full of it and couldn't wait to wind up Room Three before they went on guard tonight. I was sitting with Timmy and we were silently smirking at each other as we heard part of a conversation. Tony was saying to John McGrath, "I'm telling you...it's big...back gate."

I thought, *This is going to be as big as a horse by tomorrow night.*

Back to the present and it's another Saturday.

"Stand by your beds." He marched straight into Room Two and gave them a similar spiel as ours yesterday, then came into our room.

We got a fairly quick awakening, probably to show that you don't need to come off guard for him to be a pain in the arse as he got among our gear as well.

Around mid-morning we were heading to the square, and the thunder and lightning seemed to be coming our way. Corporal of Horse Tighe ran us to the Lecture Room.

We spent the morning learning the phonetic alphabet, which clarified letters with their own word, and was used through all different parts of the army.

A-Alpha, B-Bravo through to Z-Zulu, and from early on we had heard a lot of them. Tango Sierra was most commonly used. We enjoyed learning the rest, until they were firmly embedded in our heads.

By the time we got over to lunch we were still trying them out. At lunch we quickly learned to listen carefully to what we had been told as Billy, showing off, said to some of us behind him, "This looks a bit like Sierra Hotel India Tango."

Virtually all the cookhouse fell apart laughing as a cook said to him, "And you are a stupid Tango Whiskey Alpha Tango," as Billy realised the instructors had said, "all different branches of the army." He went a bright shade of Romeo Echo Delta.

All through lunch, Room Three were trying not to appear over-anxious about guard, so nobody took them on, but when we got back and began the big clean, they were all questions.

Timmy and I decided to stay close together, so if there was the slightest whiff of a "Hound," we would be happy to accommodate. If it wasn't mentioned for any length of time, one of us would just make a passing comment. "At least you have two men to go down to the rear gate," or "You are lucky, you've been warned, nobody said a word to us."

One burning question had been answered, though. Who were the occasional 0600hr wakeup callers?" Now we knew; it was one of the Guard NCOs giving our instructors a later start.

When we got back from lunch, Room Three finished getting their gear ready, then joined the rest of us, who got on with what was now becoming a pretty well organised cleaning routine.

Saturdays were cleaning above floor level, including windows and walls throughout the block, drill permitting, and Sundays was moving lockers and polishing floors. Evenings were spent ironing uniforms after sleeping in them, (sleeping being a bad word in this context), and any other personal stuff. The iron was red-hot most evenings, pressing shirts, collars, and getting creases out of trousers, using a damp white cloth.

As soon as we got back, one or two guys helped Room Three who were going on guard to get ready. As usual, to nervous fingers the throat torpedo was like trying to play a piano while riding a bucking bronco.

We heard a strange voice telling them to fall in, and then their footsteps fading as they marched off into the night.

We got stuck into the remainder of the washrooms and cleaning room then made a start on our own personal gear until we all went off to the NAAFI at 1930hrs.

Halfway through the evening Jenny asked Keith, "Have you got over your falling asleep all over the place?"

"You know, I wasn't sleeping Jenny. I was just dreaming of you."

Jenny looked at him. "I dreamt of you too last night."

Keith sat bolt upright and made sure we could all hear. "Did you Jenny?"

Then he slumped back down as he proved he had learned nothing as Jenny replied, "Yes, well, actually it was more of a nightmare."

The place erupted as Jenny turned and winked at Alice.

At 2030hrs we were just getting close to the block when a voice from the shadows said, "Be quiet, have some respect for the people who are giving up their night to keep you safe." Then Billy appeared with his modern warfare on his shoulder.

"I see you got the short straw Billy," I said to him. "Keep your swinging arm supple when you get down near the back gate, and be quiet when you come in the block tomorrow morning."

Billy wandered off saying something that rhymed with "pluck it."

We got on with the work on hand and making sure that when Room Four were with us, the topic got around to guard duty, as they had still to do it.

We would mention how rough the night was. Little or no sleep, cold, and the animal in the dark near the rear gate.

We had our usual chat between ourselves on all kinds of things until Bob said, "Keith, be quiet. I don't want you giving me nightmares."

"You can laugh," Keith said, "But one day…"

He never got to finish, as we all obeyed the last order and laughed out loud.

SUNDAY, DAY 49
SWAHILI BAZ

In the distance, I heard a kind of strange noise and then fell asleep again until around 0630hrs when I heard Billy Jackson's dulcet tones.

"Right, out of your smelly pits, you lazy fuckers." He flicked the lights and went off laughing.

At least we had managed some kind of a lie-in.

Over at breakfast it turns out that the strange noise was Room Three trying to shut up Billy, who was just a pain in the arse, but they were wide awake after Billy's antics.

"You have a shite bedside manner, Billy," Big Hippo told him.

"One up all up," said Billy.

Big Hippo stared at him. "OK, I get it."

It was obvious this was not over.

While cleaning, Room Three told us about an interesting incident last night, when Baz, a guy returning after a liquid night out, was well pissed. He was quite funny and trying to tell jokes, but couldn't get the punch lines right, and just laughed at himself. The Guard corporal asked Al Hopkins to accompany him to his block and then come back.

"You were gone a while," the corporal said, when he returned.

Al laughed. "He didn't have a straight line in him and I had to keep holding him up, but when we were coming up the staircase in the block two other guys appeared. They asked what the fuck was going on and then they saw me holding this guy up and burst out laughing. 'Fucking hell Baz, you've had a good night,' they said. Baz said something in what sounded like Swahili. They took him off me as another guy came to help as well."

Apparently, Al mentioned to the corporal how the guys were all easy going and that they had thanked him for doing all this. "Are they always like that?"

The corporal smiled. "When you are doing their guard duty for them, definitely."

Back to the block and immediately into auto-cleaning mode, the place looking as if a bomb had hit it. Everything was pulled into the middle of the room, then put back together again, when floors had been bumpered and backs of lockers wiped down.

It was also a fun time in many respects, with lots of leg pulling, hiding of equipment, and ongoing jokes. This part took most of the day with a thirty-minute break in the morning and a good lunch thrown in.

The lunch was good and as long as we ignored the remarks from the cooks about the cookhouse smelling like a cleaning woman's nylons, it went well.

I managed to get in a couple of remarks about the Hound, for the ears of Room Four. This was greatly helped by a couple of guys from Room Three having what seemed a serious discussion about the eerie feel as soon as they went near that area.

The afternoon was more of the same and by evening meal there were only the walking paths left to polish up later, but we'd had a good clean up and enjoyed setting people up.

The best part was when John McGrath was bumpering the corridor and someone unplugged the Bumper. We heard him saying, "It's like being in a fucking nursery." As he pushed the door open to walk to the plug, a bucket of water came off the top, absolutely soaking him. The rest of his summing up certainly would not have been heard in a nursery, as he cursed his way past everyone. By the time he got back into the corridor he was lost for words until a voice shouted.

"Hey John, you're not leaving water all over the floor, are you? It's dangerous."

All we heard was, "It's you sick fucks who are dangerous."

And we folded up laughing again.

We were really looking forward to going over for evening meal and another winding up session with Room Four before they went on guard duties. They totally ignored any of our "honest endeavours" to enlighten them.

They had just got near the top of the staircase to leave when Bill Allen tried the subtle approach. "I'm glad it's not me outside on this cold, dark, scary night, not knowing what's going to happen."

Pete said, "Fack off, it has to be facking simple."

"Why?"

"You facking did it, didn't you?"

Bill was wishing he'd not said anything now as he went quiet, and the rest of us nodded and agreed with Pete. Room Four went down to the foyer, and yet another strange voice came in and marched them off.

I went to see Don and we had a good chat while we cleaned each other's gear. It worked well as Don was an interesting character, very unassuming but not afraid to speak out when necessary. Like me, he had a big family. He told me that he was one of ten kids so, "It's not much different from here."

As NAAFI was approaching, we finished boots and belts and feeling a good evening's work underway, decided to go down to the NAAFI. Don told me that four of his sisters slept in the same bed, and the three youngest brothers shared a bed.

Timmy, who had walked in to see if I was going to the NAAFI, overheard him. "Bet it was exciting when you had beans for supper," and subject back to normal went off to the NAAFI.

On the way back from the NAAFI, everyone in front of us was still in the foyer and sounding very excited. We went and looked at routine orders that had been put up while we were in the NAAFI.

Monday —Drill, Gym, Weapon Training

Tuesday —Outside Run and Field Work

Wednesday—Live Firing at Pirbright Ranges

Thursday —Debrief, Cleaning, Drill,
Friday —Road Work, Field and Fitness Training
Saturday —As Normal
Sunday —As Normal (This was to remind us that the only thing normal about weekends was the spelling of the word.)

But who at the moment gave a damn? There, leaping off routine orders in what seemed gigantic writing, was what we had been waiting for. Now we were moving onwards and upwards. We were actually going to fire a rifle. It was as if we had been injected with a *don't believe it* serum.

As the shock wore off the excitement built up, and there was no other topic on the menu for the rest of the evening. The whole squad was buzzing and it was like a question and no answer session, as we all got onto a high. *Holy shit*—it has arrived.

The talk carried on through the big Bumper session with recruits jumping from behind doors shouting, "Bang! Bang!" like kids coming out of a Saturday-morning film.

We went to bed wanting to get the days out of the way ready for Wednesday.

It was then that Timmy told us he had been to a firing range in his Territorial Army days.

When Dave asked him if it was exciting and Timmy replied, "You bet your sweet bollocks it was." We all fell into a satisfying sleep of anticipation.

WEEK 8

MONDAY, DAY 50–TUESDAY, DAY 51
LOGGING IN

The ranges were still the main talking point, but we also had a promise of a different type of day, if all went well.

It didn't seem to be much different initially, as we lined up on the square and ran off into the park, eventually arriving in our "field." We did a nice, relaxed morning doing all our usual field exercising and by lunch time sandwiches and drinks were there. We enjoyed another good chat and everyone was in a relaxed frame of mind.

Smiling, Corporal of Horse Tighe said, "Take everything back to the Bedford and line-up behind it."

This was looking good; if we were leaving, maybe it was Virginia Lake again.

Tighe stood facing us as the driver dropped the tailboard to reveal three big-arsed logs lying there. The silence was deafening as we stared at him.

Still smiling he said, "Well, this is different, isn't it? Each team take a log back to the field and stand alongside it."

Easier said than done; the logs bumped and banged off our shoulders and by the time we put them down it felt as if we'd been mauled by a bear.

We were put in height order and then practised picking them up and putting them down, first on left shoulders, then on right shoulders.

When the NCOs were satisfied, we had a gentle walk around with them, to "get the feel." Now a walk down the slight slope and back up, which was much tougher, what with weight balance shifting. Tempers were getting a bit frayed.

After a short break, the logs were placed about fifteen feet apart and Corporal Fletcher and Corporal Kelly walked about sixty feet away. We ran round them and back, then picked up the logs to go round them again. This led to a lot of cursing and swearing as we were picking them up, and tempers were fraying again.

Teams One and Two were halfway down when we heard a shout.

"Stop all of you, you dozy arseholes! You are a total embarrassment."

We put our logs down and looked back to see Arnold, Ding Dong, and two others on the floor. The rest were looking at the log about six feet away. As Arnold and Ding Dong were helped up, it was obvious they were suffering from a shortage of breath, heavy legs, and acute anxiety over what was coming next.

"The pair of you fuck off out of my sight, before I lose my temper."

I glanced at Timmy as if to say *If this is under control, I'd hate to see him lose it.*

Tighe tore into everyone again and then told us to load the logs back up and run back. "Except those two wankers. Corporal Fletcher take them with you, and keep them out of my sight."

By 1600hrs we were gathered in the Lecture Room, and the Corporal of Horse still had a large arse full of itch to scratch.

"After today's debacle I'm wondering if the ranges are a good idea. If I can't trust you with a lump of wood, how can I trust you with live ammunition? If the others hadn't reacted quickly, we could be looking at some serious injuries."

Listening to the story back in the block, we learned that Arnold and Ding Dong had both slipped on the damp grass and knocked the other two guys' legs from under them. Big Hippo and the rest of the guys managed to throw the log sideways.

Tighe's fear was that if the log had dropped straight down it could have landed on the guys on the ground, causing a lot more damage.

He came to see us later, after having mellowed out, and asked if everyone was alright. Then he gave us a more constructive bollocking and told us what to wear for the ranges.

In the NAAFI the log incident soon became background news as the ranges were taking over. In my world I couldn't believe my luck when Jack Backhouse came over and said, "I had middle stag on guard with Chris Pratley and we were walking towards the back gate when the bushes shook and something ran round the back of them."

"Did you see it?"

"No, we both turned and legged it at the same time."

Other guys were listening to this, unsure what to make of it.

I looked at Timmy with a very serious face, and he shook his head as if he was worried. My stomach was aching from trying not to laugh, and on our return to the block we had to stay away from the rest as we couldn't stop laughing.

When we had turned in that night, I was telling them all in the room about what Jack had said, thinking they were all in on it, when Bob said, "If I get patrol, I'm not going anywhere near that gate at night."

We hadn't a clue whether he was serious or not.

WEDNESDAY, DAY 52
LIVE FIRING

In spite of all the talking, we managed to put away a large breakfast in preparation for a long day. At 0745hrs we were marched straight to the armoury.

One at a time, we were allotted a self-loading rifle, magazine, and sling. As this was going on, a Land Rover pulled up, driven by Corporal Fletcher, and was loaded with boxes of ammunition.

When we had collected rifles, it was into the Lecture Room for a final briefing. They reiterated, "Cock, hook, and look," for making sure there was nothing in the chamber. Then other golden rules: "Don't point it at anyone unless you mean it," and "Don't let it out of your possession." At this point, with all the flair of a man gifted with a command of the English language, Corporal Wheeler said, "Fuck up any of these, I will ram it so far up your arse your fillings will wobble."

Ok, point taken.

We arrived at Pirbright Guards Depot around 1030hrs, and then drove another ten minutes until the vehicle came to a halt.

After parking near a smallish, flat building where we saw Corporal of Horse Tighe and Corporal Fletcher, we were told to fall in. A tall, swarthy Scots Guards sergeant with a manicured, walrus-type moustache, who was the range NCO, took over and went through range etiquette.

Soon we were in two ranks, rifles slung over our shoulders, marching the quarter-mile or so to the ranges, along a track that opened up on the right to show the full range.

We lined up on a raised mound made for a large number of people to lie on when firing. This looked over a sloping field to other man-made mounds, with plywood boards resembling enemy soldiers, standing in front of them. These mounds would absorb the rounds being fired and stop ricochets from flying around. Almost hidden away to the right was a brick building for observation and replacing targets.

We went through how to lie, kneel, and stand when holding a weapon, and how to move forward to the hundred-yard and fifty-yard positions. By the time we had gone through all this, it was around lunch time, so they decided to eat first, and marched us back to the Bedford.

We all sat around in the open, eating and having a good chat while holding onto our weapons as if glued to them.

By the time we had the rifles over our shoulders and marched back, we were really up for it. Red flags had been put out to denote live firing. We took our magazines out and loaded them with seventeen rounds. After removing the slings, we were split into three groups. I was in the first group to go and shoot, and we went to the raised firing area, as everyone else stayed behind us to watch. We lay on the mound and inserted our magazines.

"Fire two warming rounds into the banking at two hundred yards."

This was the first time I had ever fired a rifle, except on a fairground, and what a shock it was. I didn't pull it too tightly to my shoulder, and as I squeezed the trigger it let my shoulder know. This was the first and last time I ever treated it lightly, and from conversations afterwards, we had all learned a good lesson today.

"In your own time, at your target in front. Five rounds. Fire."

It was an exciting, exhilarating, and emotionally powerful experience all at the same time, with the expelled rounds clanging out of the breech and the power of the rifle evident. The range officer moved up and down, telling us how to spread our feet and grip the weapon. Then he indicated safety catch back on, and he checked it.

"Keep the rifle pointing down range, walk to the hundred-yard marker, onto one knee, safety catch off. In your own time at your target in front. Five rounds. Fire."

It felt very different from lying down. More control was needed and the rifle felt bigger and more powerful. Then it was the same procedure down to the fifty-yard marker, and into the standing position.

"Standing position, safety catch off, at your target in front. Five rounds. Fire."

This must have been done for effect as the closeness to the targets brought home the true power I was holding. I leaned in to steady the weapon and heard the heavy thud as the rounds thumped into the mound. Spurts of soil and sand leapt up and bits of wood splintered off the targets. With the noise that accompanied a metallic clang as rounds were ejected, it was a completely unreal experience.

Suddenly all was quiet except for the instructor's voice. "Safety catch on."

We cleared weapons to the instructor to show the rifle was empty, then went to look at the "enemy."

From the number of rounds fired they looked pretty healthy, but really it was all about the rifle and us. I'm still convinced that with the number of "hits" I had, some went through the same holes. Even if I didn't see many in the centre of the target, he would definitely have gone home deaf.

We spread a canvas on the ground and started a quick clean of the inside of the rifle, before watching the other two groups as they moved along the range. The seriousness as they went down range firing, and the smiles as they came back, suggested a day to always remember.

We did a range declaration of, "No live rounds or empty shells in my possession, sir" and he double checked. As group three returned, a loud klaxon horn sounded, denoting the end of live firing and the red flags were removed.

While group three were cleaning their weapons, the rest of us did another sweep of the ranges, picking up empties and generally tidying up. We replaced slings on rifles, put magazines in pockets, and marched back to the Bedford.

There was a lot of inter-regimental rivalry between the Guards regiments and the Scots Guards sergeant got a remark in about it being an ok day for "donkey wallopers," but a bit behind the expectation for a "foot guard." It went clean over our heads as no one had explained this rivalry to us. He was more gracious in finishing saying, "In all honesty, I have seen far worse for a first shoot."

At this remark, Corporal of Horse Tighe smiled, and thanked him on our behalf for his well-organised range day, and for not feeling too overwhelmed in the presence of the Household Cavalry.

We left the ranges and headed back to Windsor with Corporal Miles in the back, answering a thousand and one questions thrown at him. Sitting in the dark with recently fired weapons between our knees, we were becoming real soldiers.

We were taken straight back to the Lecture Room, put sheets on the floor, and then stripped the rifles down. We gave all parts a thorough cleaning and oiling and showed them to an instructor, who either said "Good" or "Do it again." Eventually, we returned the weapons to the armoury where we signed them back in.

We went to the block, cleaned up and changed, by which time it was 1930hrs and off to the NAAFI. With Room Two fitting in phone calls, it was almost as normal.

The NAAFI ladies must have been warned that there would be a pie fest, as the minimum order was two.

The place was just alive with stories of the day with everyone becoming a bit of a legend in their own lunch time. It really got back to normal when we overheard Keith telling Jenny that Corporal Wheeler had told him, as he climbed into the back of the Bedford, that he was a "natural crack shot."

Tony who was right behind him said, "Is that when you mixed your feet up and slipped?"

"Yes," Keith said, looking at Jenny proudly.

Then Tony told us all loudly, "No, he said you're a natural crack-pot."

Normal serviced was resumed.

Back in the block, the whole place was still buzzing with what was really total bullshit on a large scale. In no time at all we began to sound like seasoned war veterans—average age, nineteen.

THURSDAY, DAY 53
DEBRIEFS AND ARMOURED CARS

In the washroom I was opposite Tom Peters, who was in his T-shirt, where the rest of us were naked from the waist up. As he bent over the sink, I noticed a dark area just under his neckline, and pointed to it.

Tom put his finger to his lips so I wouldn't say anything. We strolled into the corridor and he quickly showed me a large bruise on his right collar bone, and quickly covered it again.

"Fucking hell, Tom. That looks fierce, are you going to get it looked at?"

"Don't mention it to anyone, Jimmy. I'm sure it's not broken, as it's a lot better today. I've got full use; it's just a bit bloody sore, and I've come too far to risk getting back-squadded."

He saluted and smiled. "I couldn't do that yesterday."

"When did you bang it?"

"Remember that fucking log, when Ding Dong and Arnold slipped? I had my hand under it, and it slid across my shoulder as we threw it. Looking on the bright side, I'm left-handed."

"Be careful mate. If it gets really bad, who knows?"

"If it gets worse, I'm screwed, but it's a day and a half old now, so fingers crossed."

I walked back in the room and Bob looked at me. "Had a good long shit this morning?"

"It's better than standing here and listening to it."

"Very touchy today, aren't we?" He carried on making his bedpack.

At 0905hrs we were in the Lecture Room for a debrief on yesterday. The debrief is mainly either a time for collective reasoning or a bollocking or a bit of both. This was our first one, just to get us into the swing of things. I discovered at a later date that the army loves de-briefs. If we hadn't had one for a while, we would have a de-brief about not having a de-brief, in case withdrawal symptoms set in.

We were given one of Corporal of Horse Tighe's Shakespearian-type dramas about his great apprehension leading up to yesterday and the relief when it was all over, but he felt it had been an interesting and productive day.

Tighe then told us that there was a night-exercise next week in Pirbright, where a team has to set up a defensive area, and that Sergeant McMoody would like us to be the attacking force.

The room immediately began to fill with an excited buzz, quickly nipped in the bud by Corporal of Horse Tighe saying, "Shut up, I initially questioned his sanity, but then realised this could be a great opportunity for you all, and so agreed. We will have a briefing nearer to the time."

Corporal Miles marched us down to the NAAFI and let us blow off steam for half an hour, then lined us up outside and without a word marched us down to the vehicle yard.

There in all their glory were two light-armoured vehicles. Corporal Miles thanked the crew for deviating on their way through, to show them to us.

"For those of you who elect to join the armoured regiment, instead of the Household Cavalry in London, you will soon become very familiar with these."

We spent over an hour and a half looking over them, getting in them, and discussing all aspects of their role in warfare. They had with them a two-man crew, a four-wheeled Ferret scout car, and a Saladin six-wheeled larger vehicle, which carried a three-man crew. The ferret weight was about three to four tons with a top speed of ninety km/hour with a browning .30 machine gun mounted on it. The Saladin was a little slower at seventy km/hour but with a larger 76mm main armament. Both vehicles had smoke launchers on each side at the front, to provide cover if required.

As we were going to join a light reconnaissance regiment, whose main role was not engagement but feeding information back to troops behind us, speed was necessary. We were shown the inside of the vehicles, with banks of radio and ammunition stowage. There was a pre-select gearbox, with a transfer lever for forward and reverse, so it was capable of going as fast in reverse as forward. We sat in the commander's seats and looked out through the cupolas on the top, and then closed down inside and looked through periscopes, which was a bit claustrophobic.

There was only a Junior NCO and two privates and when we finished, they drove to the edge of the square and joined us for lunch.

In the last couple of days, we had upped our combat training with logs, been live firing, were going to take part in a night attack, and had seen the vehicles up close. Life was getting better…well almost.

"Downstairs number-two uniforms, forage caps, white belts, and best boots. Parade on edge of square 1315hrs."

Ah well, life goes on, some things don't change. It was an all-in afternoon drill session that with a couple of breaks, went on until dusk.

During the first break I chatted to Tom about his shoulder and he said, "I don't know which is worse, the bruise or this fucking collar stud."

The rest of the afternoon went off relatively smoothly without any earth-shattering mishaps. We always felt more a part of a drill squad when we were in our uniforms; looking the part also helped in being the part.

Later that evening, Tom told me that he had been to see the medic in the MI room and got cream to rub in. Thankfully he didn't use it until we got back from the NAAFI, as it stunk to high heaven and he became a bit of a no-go zone for a while.

The evening went really quickly, as we just kept talking about the day's events. There was a lot of speculation about the night attack, mainly centred around the fact that they had no chance, as they didn't know who they were up against. We were always the dog's bollocks when we were in our rooms.

We were not too late getting into our "pits." Midnight was the hour we strived for and if we made it by then we were happy. After turning in, we had our usual nightly chat for a long time, as we were all feeling upbeat about what was happening. We fell into a decent sleep after convincing each other that the night attack would be a piece of cake.

FRIDAY, DAY 54
WINDSOR CASTLE

We had another "surprise" today, but this was more exciting than the last one.

"Be on the square at 0900hrs ready for a run; we will go and see Windsor Castle."

I was immediately on a high. *The* Windsor Castle, and we were getting a close up of it.

We'd been jogging for a while when we came to a huge statue known as the Copper Horse. It is on Snow Hill at one end of the Long Walk, and is a statue of George III on horseback, looking down the Long Walk to Windsor Castle. It was commissioned by his son George IV. The long walk is approximately three to four kilometres long, and as Corporal Wheeler enjoyed telling us, "That little building at the other end is Windsor Castle."

We looked at it in the distance, thinking it always looked bigger than that.

"Soon we will run down to it and stop at George's Gate. There you can appreciate it in all its magnificent splendour."

We didn't have much time to dwell on it.

"Fall in, in twos, jog trot."

Bloody jog trot, I think he's confusing us with horses. No that can't be true, as the horses are well looked after.

There is something disheartening about running in a dead straight line, and this was no different until we were halfway down. I can hardly remember the rest of the run, as the castle began to get bigger and bigger in front of our eyes. When we reached George's Gate the castle was huge, and it was breath-taking just to gaze at it.

"See that flag flying over there? That denotes a member of the royal family is in residence," said Corporal of Horse Tighe. He smiled. "If you are going to sweat, then today you will perspire, and perspire reverently."

After a long time of us admiring the castle, he said, "We have confused the royal family enough today, seeing you lot and wondering if you are human. We will jog off in style."

On the way back I remember thinking that not many people have a boss with a house like that.

We went for a shower, then lunch, all completely knocked out by having got so close to the castle. I couldn't get over the fact that it seemed bigger than the village I was brought up in.

After lunch we were in the gym doing our usual warm up. I glanced over at Tom and it was hard to believe he had any injury.

We spent a fairly relaxed afternoon on our personal achievement work, doing a lot of groundwork and exercising on what we believed would personally benefit us most.

Corporals Kelly and Jones left after the first hour and Corporal Thomas took over and put Al looking after the mat work again. Corporal Thomas kept it all at an even pace. If we decided we had overworked something, we just went on the mats and did mild stuff until we were ready to go again.

After only a few minutes, those in the know about Tom, which was most of us by now, were totally impressed with Al. He went to Corporal Thomas saying he needed to work on his personal goals, and had put Tom Peters in charge of the mats, which Corporal Thomas was fine with.

This gave Tom an easy hour, as all he really needed to do was count and encourage or hold onto ankles when guys were doing sit-ups.

After a good evening meal, we got down to our usual cleaning routines knowing that the weekend would bring a major increase in block cleaning.

I got to the NAAFI with Keith, Timmy, and Bob. As Alice was nowhere to be seen, Keith zeroed straight in on Jenny, who was behind the counter. "We've been in the park today, Jenny."

"Yes, I heard."

"I found a secluded spot for us when I have a weekend off."

He suddenly jumped back as Alice's head appeared from below the counter. "And I've a secluded spot for you as well. It's twenty-feet deep in Virginia Lake."

I don't know why he bothered, but full marks for perseverance.

Back in the block the cleaning carried on as if every day was new and our equipment had to look as if it was too.

In bed the nightly summing up finished when I asked Keith, "Do you think it's cold and dark at twenty feet in Vir–"

I never got to finish as he advised me to go away in a two-word statement ending in…off. I fell asleep listening to some of the others sniggering.

SATURDAY, DAY 55–SUNDAY, DAY 56
FRUIT AND CHOCOLATE

I don't know about block cleaning all weekend, there was also plenty of room for other things.

Corporal of Horse Tighe appeared at 0900hrs and at 0905 we were drilling. This took us through to lunch, but he still had one on him. "Be back at 1305hrs in Number twos, white belt, forage caps, and DMS boots. This will be your drill wear from now, unless told differently."

Someone commented on his still having "a weasel up his arse," or as a cook put it, "a toad in his hole."

The break must have treated him kindly as the other, more amenable Tighe showed up. We had drilled another hour when he must have remembered he hadn't taken his medicine and sent us back to clean.

Because we had more freedom during block cleaning, a lot of banter and fooling around took place. During one conversation we were discussing Tighe's direct method of bollocking us.

"Yes, it's tunnel vision," Timmy said.

"No, I think it's tunnel tongue," Alex offered.

I said, "No, I think he's a tongue in torment, or a TIT for short."

By the time we hit the NAAFI the subject got back to the tit. Alice heard the last bit and said, "I hope I misheard that."

Keith was in like a shot. "No Alice, they've been discussing tits all evening."

Alice looked at us saying, "I hope it's the bluebird type and not the ones in his tiny mind?"

"Oh Alice," said Keith feigning amazement, "we are discussing tongues in torment. What on earth was in your mind?"

Alice smile and wagged her finger at him, and walked off, probably Keith's only real victory.

But the night wasn't over yet.

We were turning the lights out as we got into bed when Timmy threw off his bedding shouting, "What dirty bastard did this?"

At the bottom of his bed was a turd in a plastic bag.

He was absolutely furious. "I'll kill the fucking twat when I find out who it was."

Alex calmly walked across to his bed, picked up the turd, took a bite out of it and said, "This chocolate log is absolutely delicious." Then he strolled back to his bed.

He looked back at Timmy, who looked stunned.

"On behalf of my best friend and myself, our day has come."

Just as Alice had done earlier, Timmy smiled, and wagged his finger, as Alex got back in bed.

The last word went to Alex as he said to Timmy. "I hope you sleep like a log tonight."

At breakfast, as the other rooms were learning about it, the number of sausages waved at Timmy for comparison kept everyone amused.

We were left to ourselves later, and we really got into our cleaning routine. Tighe called in mid-morning, chatted pleasantly, pointed out a couple of fleas' left balls, and left.

At lunch we collected some apples, oranges, and one banana. Back in the block we rolled the apples and oranges at the banana; the two nearest got to pick who was on the Bumper. Everyone had a go, and it was always competitive and great fun.

At evening meal, a cook remarked that, no one was taking bananas.

Bananas don't roll," Jack told him.

The cook just stared into space.

At 1830hrs Corporal Wheeler called in and had a chat with some of us. Then, as he was leaving, he said, "What the hell is that awful smell?"

We all looked vague, as Tom Peters slid out of the room and headed for the NAAFI.

"Alice, did you know that bananas don't roll?" said Jay.

"Oh boy, dare I ask where this is going?"

Keith couldn't resist and jumped in, "A banana is a very versatile fruit," and looking at Jenny he pretended to stroke one.

"Correct," said Alice, "and if you do that again, you will need medical help, in removing it from where I shove it."

As we were getting in bed, Keith had his nightly bout with Alex shouting, "Goodnight, tunnel tongue."

Alex said, "One more tunnel tongue from you, and I'll stuff a banana in the same place as Alice would.

"Ah, you want to be friends," said Keith, as Alex grunted and rolled over.

WEEK 9

MONDAY, DAY 57– WEDNESDAY, DAY 59
THE BEAT GOES ON

The next few days were all about assessments and results, drilling, and monitoring fitness levels, but all other niceties still had to be observed.

First, a daily room inspection that didn't happen, as we heard Corporal of Horse Tighe's voice shout from the washroom. "Get in here."

"Whose are these?" he said, pointing to a clothes hanger in the shower with a pair of undershorts—white-baggy-stained—pairs one.

Silence.

"Once more, whose is it?"

"Mine, Corporal of Horse, sir, said a very nervous Paul Smith.

"What's this shit on them?"

"A scorch mark from the iron, Corporal of Horse."

"I said it's shit, are you arguing with me? Explain to me why this is not shit."

"It's on the front, Corporal of Horse."

"That just shows me how bloody dysfunctional you are." He then moved his bollocking up a notch to include all of us. "Don't be smart arses because of recent events. It doesn't make you John 'fucking' Wayne. He said, "You are still near the bottom of a big ladder," and he strode off.

We looked in amazement at each other trying to fathom where this came from, and Paul seemed as if he had been hit with a cattle prod.

Timmy jokingly said to Paul, "That *is* a funny place to have a skid mark; have you had your arsehole relocated?"

Quick as a flash Alex said, "Yes, he has, and it's just left the building."

We all relaxed, enjoying this moment.

The beat goes on and we spent a lot of time in the gym. It was our fourth assessment and the tempo was definitely raised.

The PTIs were all over us, and the noise of tortured bodies rebounded around the gym. It was a hectic, frantic, seething mass of human exertion, amid an increasing sea of sweat, and the smell of sweat filled the air.

Suddenly, "Stop!"

We collapsed onto the mats, the sense of relief was palpable, and the warm down was a pleasure. Slowly the gym was a bright area of recreation again and not an instrument of pain.

Two days later and the results were in, but that didn't mean we couldn't have a workout while interviews were carried out. Afterwards I practised my personal goals, with two guys helping me with a lift under my shoulders, after I'd tried it alone and flattened the gym floor with my more mature type of splat. It helped my confidence levels, and I was landing better by doing a couple of forward rolls.

Soon I was in the office with Corporal Kelly. "Keep up this effort," he said, "and we will see more improvement in the future. Questions?"

"No, Corporal."

"By the way, did you speak to the orangutan?"

"Yes, Corporal, he went totally bananas."

Corporal Kelly laughed and pointed to the door again.

It seemed to go well as there was no movement between teams, although Ding Dong was in for a while, and looked a bit sheepish when he came out.

Drill was always on the menu. We were definitely improving, in our minds anyway, as we were going longer and longer with no mishaps, but encouragement still flowed. "Backhouse, you are prancing around like a fairy, your parents must have paid us to take you off their hands."

We were doing our two laps and were on the other side of the square when Jack whispered loud enough for us to hear, "What a wanker."

Good job Tighe didn't hear it too, or we would still be running. No one was wound up by this anymore, though, the greater shock would be if he said, "Well done." Then we might need medication.

I talked to Mum and my sisters Celia and Barbara and brother Len, about live firing, Windsor Castle, the pending night attack and losing twelve pounds. The girls only wanted to talk about the weight loss. Soon, according to Ginger's middle finger, it was time to hang up.

For some crazy reason the next day they decided to take us out into our "field" in the park again, with the logs.

During the morning it was exercising as usual, and as we stopped for lunch, we heard a ripple of applause from the edge of the field. We put the "peacock effect" into operation. The people moved on, hopefully not seeing what can only be described as a load of balloons with the air draining out of them.

The log control was better; the grass was dry and we were more focussed, but it was hard graft.

No racing this time, we concentrated on carrying the logs and overcoming obstacles. As we worked in our teams, we had to carry the logs down the side of a hedgerow, go through a narrow stile, then turn around and come back to the start. It was a hard process, as the log was bouncing up and down, and was tough on the shoulders, thighs, backs, and temperaments, and Team Three took quite a while.

On our returning Corporal of Horse Tighe said, "Right, you look half asleep, we'll do it again."

Half asleep, with a fucking big tree on our shoulders—what a pillock.

"Throw it over the hedgerow, walk around and then throw it back," and Team Three were off.

A bit different now, and tiring bodies took over as they were coming back, and the log landed half at an angle, in the middle of the hedge. An argument broke out as they tried to pull it off, and as it got louder, we heard Corporal Fletcher's voice: "Somebody had better take over, or the fucking hedge will grow over it."

Eventually, Alex took over, and they returned to hear Corporal of Horse Tighe say to the rest of us, "Do you think if we paint their faces white, and put red noses on them, we can charge circus fees?"

They were soon smiling again, as we were told to load the logs back on the Bedford.

In a weird way the evenings were getting more relaxing, as our gear was getting easier to clean, and we were better at it. Later, without fail, there was always Keith to brighten up the NAAFI.

"I heard you've been in the park all day," Alice said to him.

"Yes, Alice, we've been playing with our logs in the woods."

"I believe in your case it would be more a twig," and the place erupted into laughter, as Jenny walked past him waving her little finger.

There wasn't a lot of talk tonight as it had been a heavy physical day, but Alex couldn't resist winding Keith up about Alice's remark. "I'm guessing by the size of your twig, not many birds have landed on it?" Alex sniggered.

"Up yours too," Keith said to him.

"Ah, so tonight *you* want to be friends," said Alex.

THURSDAY, DAY 60–FRIDAY, DAY 61
THE NIGHT ATTACK

Into auto mode, clean and over to breakfast then back to our rooms.
"Stand by your beds."

This was definitely different as he shouted, "Show me your winter underwear."

Well I never, so you do have a dark side. But we unfolded our vests and long johns, and laid them out. He went to each of our beds, using his whip as a disinfectant barrier, as he kept his distance.

Another minor success though, even if the beds looked a mess everything was still on them.

Today was straight into effin/ights with no preamble. It was a blustery, chilly morning and the movement helped us to keep warm, but hot, cold, or indifferent some things never change.

Corporal of Horse Tighe at top pitch yelled, "Ladd, straighten your arms at the elbows—they look like a dog's back legs."

Quick as a flash Corporal Miles said, "There's a prick in between those as well."

Tighe could hardly speak as he began to smile, then laugh. They were both still laughing as we completed our second lap.

We stayed out there until 1215hrs, then changed and went to lunch, but on the way back the heavens opened. We got into our coveralls and combat jackets, sprinted across to the Lecture Room, and removed our boots as it was carpeted, albeit industrial.

"Sit still, shut up, and listen."

Corporal of Horse Tighe and Corporal Fletcher proceeded to give us an insight into what to expect tonight. Pointing to a blackboard Tighe said, "This is a rough diagram, and there will be another update in situ tonight."

Rough diagram it was, as the spider that had done it must have had a serious drinking problem.

"Questions?"

There were none, as by now there were so many arrows on the diagram, it looked as if we were in imminent danger of an Indian attack.

They put us into three teams and for the rest of the afternoon we practiced belly crawling, signalling to each other, and if firing, immediately moving.

By the time the afternoon was over we knew it all and couldn't wait to get at them. What no one bothered to tell us was the "enemy" had a couple of days to dig in, and they knew that sometime tonight we were coming.

At 1805hrs we were at the armoury drawing up our rifles and magazines. The rifles had all been fitted with bright-yellow blank adaptors for use with blank ammunition, and we went back to the Lecture Room for a final debrief.

"These rifles have all been fitted with blank adaptors; they reduce some flash. Do not fire them close to someone's face as they can still do damage."

We clamoured into the back of the Bedford with Corporal Wheeler and sat with the rifles between our legs, feeling like real soldiers, impatient for it all to begin.

On arrival we were driven to some outbuildings on the edge of a large vehicle park and ushered into a garage-like room in one of the buildings, where we sat on the floor.

Corporal of Horse Tighe and Corporal Miles were already there with Sergeant McMoody, and Corporals Fletcher and Wheeler joined them at the front. There was a large diagram on a blackboard similar to the one earlier, but the spider had sobered up, and no death by arrows yet.

When we were settled, Sergeant McMoody went straight into the night's events. "You will begin by silently approaching the enemy positions, led by an instructor with each team; he will accompany you until you are in position and then withdraw. Do not engage the enemy until a red flare is fired and then only when you can see them. The whole idea is to get in as close as possible, before they are aware of you. Two rapid red flares mean stop exactly where you are. Do not move until we tell you. A green flare is exercise ends. Questions? None, good." He left.

Our instructors gave us a final briefing. I was in Team Two, who would take the centre position. "No rush, as you have an hour to get into position. Team Two down the middle. Team One on their left tree line and Team Three their right tree line. Follow hand signals at all times. The attack is timed to begin at 2353hrs. Load your magazines and keep the safety catch on until the red flare goes up. If at any time you become disorientated, stay down until you are back on track. Remember, do not open fire, until you are completely sure who you are firing at."

We got on the Bedford and for about fifteen minutes were taken very slowly with no lights to within one mile of the zone. There we were told to cease any talking and prepare to approach on foot.

A voice whispered, "Team Two with Corporal Fletcher."

We followed him for about three-quarters of a mile then saw the clearing with the trees on each side and he signalled us to get down and crawl for the last two hundred yards. Then he moved away.

This was our first shock as the grass was still wet from the earlier rain, and within a few minutes we were decidedly damp. But as long as the weapons were dry, that was all that mattered. It took over an hour to crawl into our starting positions. All we could do now was to lie there and shiver until the flare went up. It was pitch-black—so much for hand signals, we could barely make out the person on either side of us.

All at once there was a whoosh and an overhead thud, and the whole area was lit up by a red flare. We hugged the ground until it had all gone dark again. I remember thinking, if they didn't know we were here before, they fucking did now. At first it seemed a bit of an anti-climax as we slowly began to crawl forward, and we weren't sure that the flare hadn't gone off by mistake.

Suddenly all holy hell let loose with the team on our right in silhouette, as huge bangs briefly lit up the area. The air stank of smoke as it drifted across our positions. We had no time to think. As soon as we moved forward, it began again. What did they say, if disorientated or confused hit the ground?

I saw muzzle flashes and fired a couple of rounds at them, then moved to one side, and lay hugging the ground so tight, I must have been tangled in the grass roots. I lay trying to get my breathing and thoughts in order. There were huge bangs again from my left, and I saw vague shadows of Team One getting back into the trees for cover.

The explosions were irregular, and they made Team One look like puppets, dancing in strange jerky movements. Then there was this cold, eerie silence, as the smoke just hung over the area, amid the strong stench of gunpowder. I had rolled over a couple of times, thinking *What the fuck just happened?*

I ended up lying right next to Jack Backhouse, who was shaking as he whispered, "What the fuck was that?"

"Total fucking chaos," I replied, "and my ears are ringing." We lay there and thirty seconds later Corporal Fletcher crawled from behind us.

"Where are the—" was as far as I got as he put his fingers to his lips and told us to regroup and press forward and engage the enemy. No point grovelling through the mud and shit now.

We advanced, crouching right down, looking left and right as the whole world must have been woken up. I saw flashes from a couple of rifle barrels in front and to the left, and it made me feel better, as I let rip in their direction. I hit the ground, rolled over in a load of mud, and then crouched, ran, and fired again.

We had made about twenty yards over the ground when the rest of the country's ordinance kicked in, and the noise and chaos were incredible, as the whole area beyond the tree lines was exploding.

Men could just be made out firing, diving to the ground, and vanishing again. As we went to ground, a line of bangs and flashes occurred fifteen yards in front of us right across the clearing, and we hugged the ground again. It was absolute mayhem. I was dirty, wet, and exhausted. It was hard to know which way to run—as soon as we got up there were more bangs and flashes. We'd run the other way and another lot went off, and so we'd dive any fucking way, until we were totally disorientated.

It stopped as quickly as it started.

We lay flat out, sucking on lumps of the smoke-filled air, wondering what the fuck had just happened. There was an almost audible sigh of relief as a green flare lit up the smoky sky.

We heard voices and there appeared a number of guys, including our instructors, walking out of the smoke holding torches.

They cleared our weapons and then took us over our own areas, followed by the other team's areas. They pointed out where the double layer of trip wires, about thirty yards apart had been installed, where the thunder flashes and smoke canisters were set, and where we went after they had been tripped.

The Bedford was waiting for us, and ran everyone back to the outbuilding, where they hosed the mud off us.

At the front of the room Sergeant McMoody was standing with four NCOs. "These were your entire enemy to-night. They are on an instructor's course and would like to thank you for your participation."

We stared at them thinking, *You are taking the piss—just the four of them?* But they weren't.

"It was an interesting experience for us all, one I'm sure you will never forget. You can discuss it on debrief tomorrow with your instructors," said Sergeant McMoody. He stood there smiling, obviously enjoying every minute of it and said, "Any questions?"

We were cold, tired, and hungry but to a man shouted, "No, Corporal of Horse."

Our instructors and the other NCOs burst out laughing, and Sergeant McMoody said, "Touché" as he left.

A pile of sandwiches had arrived. We hung up our wet jackets and spent the next thirty minutes eating, drinking, and trying to make some sense of it all.

We were decidedly more subdued on the way back, sitting in the dark thinking about what had just happened. We arrived back in barracks around 0300hrs, went upstairs and finished cleaning our rifles, and around 0330hrs we signed them back in.

We had an absolutely brilliant shower, hung combat gear in the washroom, and were fast asleep by 0415hrs.

At 0600hrs I sleep-walked into the washroom. It looked like a zombie apocalypse convention: conversation nil, movement slow, and an occasional grunt. It was over to breakfast and ready for inspection as usual.

"Stand by your beds." In breezed Corporal of Horse Tighe looking bright-eyed and bushy tailed and full of energy. He went through all the rooms inferring standards had dropped today— not good enough. "Outside, gym at 0900hrs."

We put everything away, enviously looked at our beds, and went outside at 0900hrs, where for the first time there were no instructors except Corporal Jones to take us to the gym. The official story was a meeting in the WO's and NCO's mess, but we speculated they were having a lie in this morning.

It turned into an enjoyable morning with nothing at flat-out speed and plenty of team games and personal time. Corporal Thomas spent a lot of time with Ding Dong urging him along.

At lunch the cooks were in good form and having a ball, because we had not had much sleep. One of them was waving his watch. "Look into my eyes—you feel drowsy. You all look fucked, except you Cassius. More bangers?"

After this we were marched into the Lecture Room for a debrief. Corporal Fletcher was standing with his drunken-spider plan of attack. "As you are fully aware by now, the enemy consisted of only four men. Last night was to show them how effective their defences were, and to show you how quickly an attack can go downhill, in the noise and confusion of war. At no time was anyone dug in on the hill directly in front of you. Your instructors were just behind you all night and the course NCOs were watching from the side.

"Observations:

1) Up to the red flare being fired, your approach work was good, especially Team Two, who had a long difficult crawl in poor conditions, but all teams acquitted themselves well.

2) The first set of trip wires led to total chaos. At this point all teams fired a large number of rounds at the enemy ahead. This would have been good, had there been any enemy ahead, but there was never any enemy there."

It went very quiet as we all looked a bit sheepish, and he held the silence for a while.

3) "You regrouped and advanced again, and the reaction was very similar. Team One hit the trip wires, set off the first bank of thunder flashes, and opened fire. They were assisted almost immediately by Teams Two and Three, who were running, ducking, and diving. They set off another two banks of thunder flashes while laying down a withering amount of fire power. At this point we fired the green flare before the British army completely ran out of ordnance."

He then amended his blackboard by drawing a semi-circle showing where we had started out, and where we had finished up. "Anyone who fired from this angle fired into a big nothingness, and this was most of you. The remainder then helped them to completely shoot the shit out of a big nothingness." This was followed by a dramatic pause. "At no time during the attack did the enemy ever fire a weapon, and at no time once it started were they in front of you. Questions?"

We did ask a lot of questions. It became apparent that most of us had seen things differently, due to where we had ended up, or where the gun flashes came from. We agreed that the explosions were very disorientating.

Eventually Tighe did a summing up. "For a first time under difficult night conditions, you will now understand more clearly what the noise and confusion can do to a person. From the questions, I know that you realise only constant training and discipline is the way to improve your skills. The chaos and noise can only be mastered by training and discipline, which is why we will up your training schedule. Not to be arseholes, but to prepare you for what lies ahead."

Yes, bang on Corporal of Horse; you can be a complete tit for our own good.

It was a loud evening meal as we realised that although none of us came out looking like John "fucking" Wayne, at least we had come out of it and would have a better idea of what to expect next time.

Back in the block after the debrief, we had stopped pretending that we were perfect, as we all knew that wasn't the case. I chatted to Don about the night attack and joined in with most of the rest of the squad in doing the head-roll fandango, jerking around violently to keep awake.

We all went to the NAAFI that night just to keep awake and were finding it doesn't always follow that noise keeps a tired man awake.

Just to prove a point, Bob did a head roll and grabbed onto the edge of the table. Then he looked blearily back at the rest of us laughing at him.

We got back in the block and carried on with our cleaning and head rolling and by 2230 hours no one had shown up. By 2300 hours the block was fast asleep.

SATURDAY, DAY 62–SUNDAY, DAY 63
COW TURDS AND COLD WATER

We dropped into our weekend "anything goes" routine, but an impromptu run in the park led to an all-day long theme. Chris had gone to the MI room because of a blister and the rest of us to our "field."

We'd lined up to leave when Corporal Wheeler said to Tom Peters, "What's that shit on your boot?"

"Looks like a cow turd, Corporal."

"It is, Peters. Did you know I'm an expert on turds? "There are three kinds of turds: there is musturd, custurd, and you, you little shit, wipe it in the grass."

Within thirty seconds we were in step chanting, "Musturd, custurd, and you, you little shit," which fitted in nicely.

During cleaning, a drill session was thrown in. We noticed Captain Forbes-Hart and two warrant officers watching for a long period of time, which is probably why we were there. Later, Tighe told us that Captain Forbes-Hart had asked him to tell us he had seen an improvement in our drill and bearing. Being Corporal of Horse Tighe, it ended with, "His words, not mine." But he smiled and we felt pleased about it.

In between all this, the god of fruit decided that Joe Walters and Chris (by default) were seeded one and two and given job selection. We had been getting on with it when someone asked where Bob was.

"I think he went for a tomtit (rhyming slang) but that was ages ago."

We quietly went to the washroom door and could hear Bob in a stall, tunelessly whistling to himself. We quietly went and filled two buckets with cold water. I went and pushed a mop under the door with a note on it saying, 'You will need this.'

As he read it, he shouted, "You bast—" and the water came over the door.

The door opened with Bob, wet through, his soaked trousers around his ankles. Despite his promises of a Scottish fate worse than death to "Fucking sassenachs," it's impossible to take a man seriously with his pants around his ankles, and man bits like a chipolata sausage and two garden peas, shrivelled due to the freezing water.

The NAAFI was given back over to Tom, though, as Timmy said to Alice, "Tom really put his foot in it today."

"Why, what did he say?"

"No, he put it in a huge cow turd." He pointed at Tom and said, "Musturd," and we said, "Custurd, and you, you little shit," doing it twice more and pointing at Tom, who stood up and bowed.

Alice shook her head saying, "You are the first group I have ever come across, who enjoys being in the shit."

On the way back in we saw routine orders,

Monday. —Room Inspection-Lecture Room-Gym-Drill
Tuesday —10 Mile Run-Field Work
Wednesday—Visit Hyde Park Barracks/Knightsbridge Barracks
Thursday —Drill-Gym-Run
Friday —Drill—Lecture Room—Guard Duty
Saturday —Normal—Guard Duty
Sunday. —Normal—Guard Duty

Plenty to chew on here. A second round of guard duties, a ten-mile run and what looks a great day out in London with the Household Cavalry at the Knightsbridge barracks. The day's beginning to look a little different—plenty of exercise and re-visit the Hound of the Baskervilles.

There was not much left to talk about, but Alex had to keep Bob on his toes. "Hey Bob, I hope it *was* the cold water that shrank your wedding tackle?"

Bob's reply of "Fuck awf awa bastert. Ahm gonna gie youse freid on a fuckin' skewer," (You'll stop laughing when I serve yours up fried on a metal rod) only led to more raucous laughter.

WEEK 10

MONDAY, DAY 64
"HANDS OFF COCKS!"

It's that noisy gobshite again. Nail him Dave, you are nearest. I looked at Dave moving at the speed of a two-legged tortoise with a hernia and realised Corporal Wheeler was free to piss us off for another day.

Off we went for a wash, looking like an Indian scouting party walking in each other's footsteps. Then we gave everything a last good polish, and by the time we went to breakfast, it looked immaculate.

We marched over to the Lecture Room and were seated when the other instructors marched in. In keeping with the improving movements, not a single chair went flying as we stood up.

"Sit down, we will run out what is happening this week. Today you will be issued with a harness that goes over your shoulders and attaches to your web belt with a pouch fitted on each side at the front, this will aid in your ten-mile run tomorrow. On Wednesday the Household Cavalry in London have kindly allowed us a rare visit, so make the most of it. We will leave no later than 0800hrs dressed in pullovers, number-two trousers, forage caps, and DMS boots, carrying a combat jacket in case of rain. Your turnout will be immaculate."

He then gave us a crooked grin. "By popular demand we will do another set of guard duties from Friday to Monday. If you patrolled last time, you will do main gate this time, and vice versa, Questions? None, good. Corporal Wheeler, march them back to the block and over to the gym by 1000hrs."

At 1010hrs we were in the gym and frantically waving bits of our bodies in all directions. It was very much a repeat of last Wednesday. My forward-spring somersault was still on track. With my body overtaking my feet at landing and rolling forward, this was feeling better now. Still aided, but with no ugly back splats, I was determined to get to the completely unaided stage.

The instructors took it in turns to help out with Ding Dong, who always managed to look knackered, so they would try to pep him up a bit. It was a good morning as we topped it off with a game of touch rugby that ended up in a brawl, but mainly we enjoyed it.

We were in the stores by 1305hrs, where we were issued with harnesses and two pouches each. We put the pouches on each shoulder strap and adjusted them, and then it was back in the block and dressed for drill at 1430hrs.

"We will begin to drill in earnest starting from now, and anyone who does not reach our standards will not go on the long weekend. You look as if you need a rest so we will take pity on you. In future you will be expected to stand still for long periods of time without moving. Fix your eyes on a distant object and control your breathing. To keep alert, change the focus of the eye without moving the eye, do slight finger movement inside a clenched fist, and wiggle your toes in your boots. We will hold this position for fifteen minutes and the first person to waver, wobble, cough, fart, or pass out will wish for a quick death."

Piece of cake, do nothing for fifteen minutes, except stare at that window. I eventually thought that must be close to fifteen minutes when a voice said, "Halfway there."

You must be kidding, but this was as if a signal had activated something in my brain. My cap began to feel tighter on my head, and the dreaded collar stud seemed to be trying to force its way through my Adam's apple. Another three or four minutes and my toes were wiggling fast enough to play a boogie on a piano's pedals. I looked at the guys in front of me and noticed they had gone from looking completely in control, to a face-twitching, eyebrow-raising, zombie-like trance.

"Stand at ease, stand easy."

There was a noticeable feeling of relief.

The instructors were all smiling, as Corporal of Horse Tighe told us to fall out and change for evening meal.

As soon as we got in the block, caps were off. I went into the washroom wrestling to remove my stud in front of the mirror, looking at two red marks on my forehead from my cap, and a flat Adams apple.

I was on the phone talking to Mum by 1845hrs and she said, "Not long before your weekend home."

"Hopefully. They are still saying if any of us screw up we won't get it off, but I don't really think that would happen."

I told her about the trip to London on Wednesday to Hyde Park Barracks, which is close to Buckingham Palace. "Who knows? We may see that as well."

"That sounds really exciting, Celia and Barbara will be so envious," she said.

"I know, sometimes I have to pinch myself.

I chatted about guard duties, then the night attack, and she asked me if I was still truly happy with my choice.

"Yes, it's harder than I first imagined, but it won't always be like this, and I'm doing things I never thought I would do." By now my time was up and I walked back to the block.

I had a shower, then sat relaxing, and we were playing guess-the-pouches, which to us were obviously for magazines, or more hopefully our sandwiches. There was a lurking feeling that if there were magazines, would we be carrying rifles? The next day would show us how green we all were, and only the bookmaker would benefit from our guesses.

Within ten minutes of being in the NAAFI, Keith was at it telling Jenny about standing rigidly to attention this afternoon. Then very subtly he said, "I think I could keep it up for hours, given the right circumstances."

But it wasn't too subtle for Alice. "Small things in small minds Jenny, and this mind is tiny."

Keith furrowed his eyebrows, and Alice and Jenny waved their little fingers at him as they walked off laughing.

We returned to the block in good spirits and soon had everything ready for tomorrow, followed by an early night.

TUESDAY, DAY 65
TEN MILE RUN

After a good breakfast, we lined up outside the block at 0900hrs in combat trousers, pullovers, webbing, and DMS with full water bottles hung on belts.

"Bring combat jackets as the weather looks in limbo. Put them in the back of the Bedford that will be waiting there."

At 0900hrs we were on the square ready to go.

"Follow me." Corporal Fletcher jogged off to the rear of the blocks to the boundary wall and stopped facing a pile of bricks, which we thought was for a wall repair.

"Take two bricks and put one in each pouch."

(Crafty bastards, none of us won the pouch bets last night.)

We were only in the Bedford a short time before we pulled onto a large, rough-looking car park. We got off and formed two ranks.

"Anyone who does not complete it has failed and will not need to worry about being on the next one. If you die on route, do it gracefully, as the public may be watching."

It was a good pace to begin with, and for the first couple of miles everything was as it should be: all in step and cruising. We ran through a short woodland path and up a fairly steep incline for a half mile and by the top the legs were just feeling it. A little respite on a short level bit then downhill for another mile.

It was beginning to get a bit irritating by now as the water bottles bounced around on the belt, and the bricks were in a perfect position to rub across our nipples, plus sweat was starting to be a nuisance. We were constantly having to put our hands between the pouch and our nipples or shove our water bottles around to stop their rhythmic bouncing on the same area.

I was running alongside Timmy and as we were about six miles into it, the run was beginning to take its toll. Breathing was getting heavier with nowhere near as much conversation going on, just the constant drone of the instructors urging us on. I was reasonably comfortable and then suddenly felt a pain in my side and bent over, grabbing it. Timmy, who was on my right side said, "Are you ok?"

"No, I've got a stitch on my right side, and it hurts like fuck."

As I said this, Corporal Wheeler came level with me. "Don't stop, keep hydrated, stamp your left foot down and stretch to your left a bit," and he was gone.

I took my water bottle and had a drink, and then Timmy took it off me and put his hand under my armpit saying, "It will go, but concentrate on running it off."

For a while I was doing a half bent, foot stomping, deep breathing shuffle with Timmy's help.

"Give me the bricks if it gets worse," he said.

I managed to slowly, over the next five minutes, straighten up more, and then eventually with a little pain got back into it. I could feel it improving; it was still sore but not tugging as much. "Thanks Timmy," I said. "It's much better now. I can manage."

"Good on you Jimmy, now take a look behind you."

I turned to look and saw a group of four were way back off the main troop with two instructors yelling encouragement at them. They were running, but in a disjointed kind of way. It was a slow, methodical jog along with the constant shouts of, "Keep going, don't stop, keep running, good, good." I noticed Ding Dong was one of them.

Our main group was in a good rhythm, and as we turned at the edge of some tree's we realised that we must have run in a semi-circle. We got some welcome relief as we knew it was the reverse. Now we knew what we had to do, all that remained was to do it. We were soaking in sweat in every nook and cranny and holding onto our thighs, as we struggled and grunted our way up the hill and then onto a welcome, short, level stretch. I looked back and saw the four stragglers were now five and were being pushed and cajoled as they came up the hill. We could hear the encouragement from two hundred yards away as they fought to get up the incline.

Now we were on the downhill stretch and having to readjust to downhill, and it was a relief to get back to fairly level, and jog the last stretch to the start point.

We heard loud voices and looking back again saw two guys half-sliding and half-rolling down the grassy side of the hill to the vocal encouragement of the instructors. "Get up, move, nearly there, keep moving," as another body joined in the new national sport of hill rolling.

Total relief as we reached the Bedford.

"Squad halt, fall out."

We totally relaxed, feeling pleased with ourselves. Some were bent double, sucking in large amounts of air, some were sitting heads in hands, and some were just plain flat out on the floor. All of us were visibly steaming and sweating profusely. We removed our water bottles and harnesses and saw Corporal Fletcher behind three of the guys. "Keep going, you are there," he said. "Well done, well done," as they sank to their knees.

Soon after, we heard another voice, which was Corporal Wheeler driving in the last two. "Yes, one last big effort—you can see the finish, don't stop now!"

We all got up and started to shout and applaud as they neared.

"Well done, great effort, now relax."

Before Wheeler had said the last words, they were spread-eagled out on their backs, looking skywards, and gulping in lumps of air.

Twenty minutes later it was one big happy squad, as we had eaten our sandwiches, rehydrated, and were busy bullshitting about the day so far.

The truth was, almost everyone had experienced some difficulty at some point, but we were pleased with our performances.

I was chatting to Keith, who had also developed the stitch, and it had never really left him. He'd felt on the last uphill stretch it was improving, and he'd tried to speed up a little coming down, but his legs gave way and he was one of the three high rollers. He was absolutely over the moon that he had completed it, and showed he hadn't lost his sense of humour, when Corporal Wheeler shouted over to him. "Are you still aching all over, Durban?"

Keith replied, "No Corporal, just my ears."

Wheeler sat back smiling: job done so far.

Eventually we heard, "Fall in, harnesses and water bottles in the back of the Bedford."

We fell in our three teams and Corporal of Horse Tighe said, "We'll do some field training as some of you look a bit tired and stiff, although after a nice quiet morning, I don't understand why."

I just love this sense of humour, and we were all getting used to it by now. It was mainly a fun afternoon, and by 1530hrs we were on the Bedford and heading back, feeling tired but happy with how the day had gone.

After a shower and a good meal, we were back in the block and preparing for tomorrow's day out. The whole chatter was about the day out in London.

The irons were used flat out and bulling and gear cleaning were in full swing. The atmosphere was upbeat, and we all went off to the NAAFI to carry on the banter.

Almost immediately, Bob set up Keith, who could never resist saying something. Seeing Jenny behind Keith he said, "Hey Jenny, Keith went for a roll in the park today, but he couldn't keep it up, and just wilted very quickly."

Keith winked at Jenny and said, "You know that wouldn't happen if you were in the park."

Jenny said, "Sorry, I wouldn't have twenty seconds to spare."

Keith didn't even look round as he dropped his head, but it was a great moment for the rest of us.

We talked in bed for a short while, which ended when Alex, determined to get the last word in tonight said, "Pervy Durban your twenty seconds begins *now,*" which was followed by a long guttural growl from Keith.

WEDNESDAY, DAY 66
IN LONDON WITH ALEXANDER THE GREAT

Not as stiff as I thought this morning and getting over it fairly quickly. Off to the washroom and then over for a good breakfast, which would have to last for a few hours, then back to our rooms.

At 0745hrs a voice boomed out, "Be on the square at 0800hrs, ready to leave," and we lined up, feeling very smart.

After a brief inspection, we were loaded into the Bedford with Corporal Fletcher, having drawn the short straw, in the back, and Tighe and Corporal Miles in a Land Rover in front.

We set off down the M4 and headed for London. When we got close it was a job holding on, as we slid up and down the benches, due to the truck swerving in and out of traffic.

Suddenly Corporal Fletcher said, "We are very close now, so get ready to disembark."

I looked out the back thinking how could anywhere be so big, busy and alive, but there was no time to fully take it in as the truck stopped.

Corporal Fletcher shouted, "Dismount quickly," and we all piled out and lined up at the railings and gazed at Buckingham Palace.

"You have fifteen minutes, enjoy it."

I stood totally amazed, looking at a building I had only ever seen on television, or a postcard. It was already busy with lots of people all the way along the railings. This was a blur to me, as all I could think of was, this is what our training is about.

I took in the sheer size of the palace, and the realisation that the "balcony" where the royal family often appeared, was in front of me. This was the queen's residence, and it had a magic all of its own. I looked at the faces of other people, from all nations, looking on with the same excitement as I was.

Three months ago, I never thought in my wildest dreams, I would be here today, becoming a part of this huge national and worldwide institution. It was beginning to fall into place: *This is why we are here.*

In no time at all, the Bedford was back, and we quickly jumped in the back and left, still seeing huge numbers of people making their way to the palace.

In minutes we were at Hyde Park/ Knightsbridge barracks. My first impression was of a large building reminiscent of a First World War hospital. It looked a bit austere, and inside it had a feel of times gone by: large, imposing buildings with outside metal staircases, overlooking central open areas. I hadn't expected it to look like this.

We went first to the stables and saw some of the guys cleaning out and brushing the absolutely beautiful, black Irish horses. We had a great time talking to the guys and hearing their stories. They were all friendly and enjoying showing us the horses. It was immediately obvious how strong the affection was between them and their mounts. The most common statement was, "The horses always come first." The heady smell of the stables and the hay was a reminder of home, when we worked helping the local farmers with hay making.

We went to the farrier's forge, where we watched two of them at work in a very hot forge, shoeing a horse. There was a truly interesting and informative discussion. They told us how they rode at the back of ceremonial parades carrying large axes, with a curved blade on the front and a spike on the back, and both wore dark-coloured tunics under their breastplates. The Life Guards farrier wore a black plume and Royal Horse Guards a red one.

In bygone times in battle, the farriers came through after the fighting and used the spike to put any seriously injured horses out of their misery.

The axe was to remove a hoof, which had a number on it to prove the horse had died in battle and was accounted for. The horses still had a number on their hooves, but thankfully the axe was now purely ceremonial.

It was a fascinating morning, which passed all too quickly. The magic word was said, and we all made our way up an outside metal stair, to a cookhouse on an upper floor where we met more of the guys. We sat mixed up with some of the regulars, and it became apparent why they were upbeat.

The barracks, built around the 1880s, was scheduled to be demolished, and a new one would be built on the same spot.

"Anyone who opts to come here will only have a short time in temporary accommodation, and then back into a bright, new barracks." I thought afterwards that this may have been the main reason for the visit. Whatever the reason, though, it was certainly turning into a great day out.

We finished eating and marched off to another large room on the other side of the square. It had a long table full of equipment and immediately Corporal Fletcher said, "Keep your grubby little hands off everything. Touch anything and I will chop your fingers off at the elbow."

Got it, point taken.

Lying on the table was an assortment of items including white sheepskin, sword, slings and sword knot, scabbard, white gauntlets, spurs and fasteners, gold-coloured braids (aiguillettes) and a white cross belt.

"Form a semi-circle around the table."

As we settled down, two troopers in ceremonial dress came in through a side door and stood behind the table.

The Life Guard was in his scarlet tunic and white helmet plume, and the Royal Horse Guard was in his blue tunic and red plume. They both had a gleaming metal breastplate (cuirass) covering the upper body, with a white cross belt diagonally across it, and a cartouche pouch on the back. Both were carrying swords. They stood at attention, and we saw the white gauntlets and buckskin trousers plus an absolutely immaculate pair of jackboots, of which the back reached the back of the knee and the front went over halfway up the thigh, plus a pair of spurs.

The room was totally silent for a minute as we took in the moment, thinking that all the pictures we had seen didn't do them justice. We realised why there was so much emphasis put on the cleaning.

In answer to a question, one of them said that once it was up to standard, it didn't take too long to do. I liked that. One of the instructors took us through the various parts again, how they had evolved over the centuries, why they were there, and the tradition behind it. The two troopers left to a rousing send-off, and then the instructor explained other bits more fully.

The sheepskins were for under the saddles and the spurs were blunt and only ever used for direction. He showed us the sword and attachments. Then, as he was talking, The Life Guard returned in a more relaxed dress.

He was wearing his forage cap and white belt over his red tunic with blue trousers and shorter riding boots and spurs. Corporal Fletcher had just finished the rank system using aiguillettes and brought the soldier to the table and removed his belt. They fitted sword slings, a scabbard, and the sword knot on the hilt of the sword and replaced the belt. The soldier then stood at attention, with the scabbard by his left side, and the sword sloped on his right shoulder.

The room was totally quiet, as we all seemed to be taking in the fact this was what the future could have in store—that we could one day soon, form the Sovereign's Escort. It was beginning to sink in that there were numerous options to consider, with the main one being a small matter of six more weeks training to finish.

They took us back to the courtyard ready to leave when Corporal of Horse Tighe appeared, told us to get into two ranks, and marched us back towards the stables. "You are extremely privileged today," he said, and with that, amid a clattering of hooves, a huge piebald horse was led out to our front. He looked absolutely massive as his handler turned to us and said, "Meet Alexander the Great, drum horse of the Household Cavalry."

We formed a semi-circle around him, and once he had looked us over, seemed quite happy to be there. The handler gave us a potted history of the horses. He told us that on ceremonial parades, Alexander carried kettle drums on either side and a drummer in heavy ceremonial golden braid with a combined weight of over three hundred pounds. We realised why he had to be so big. Also, all drum horses have the rank of major.

Someone asked, "If you are drumming how do you control him?"

"We have reins fixed to our feet and use those."

I was again struck by the huge amount of training undertaken between man and horse, and the great amount of affection that they had for each other.

Unfortunately, like all good things the day had to end, and we climbed back into the Bedford for our journey back.

We left Knightsbridge and were treated to another episode of 'spot the space' or how to get a large vehicle into a fast-moving space, or no space at all. Eventually, we stopped sliding up and down the seats and began our excited chatter about the day's events. We arrived back around 1815hrs, went straight into the cookhouse and ate the sandwiches left out for us, and then returned to the block.

It was not long after that Corporal of Horse Tighe came in and got us all together for a kind of debrief. "Now you know why we will increase intensity in drilling and cleaning to reach the standard for a weekend off, and to progress to the last weeks. Remember today, some of it will be inserted into your training in the near future."

He looked fairly relaxed and whatever devious plan he had in mind would involve us all, so enjoy the moment. Most of us didn't go to the NAAFI as we had eaten only an hour ago, one exception being Keith, who probably needed his nightly ration of insults, to keep him on his normal path.

The cleaning tonight was done with a renewed vigour, and according to some of the squad, they would be seriously considering going to the mounted section. I sat with Don for a while, and he asked me if I was considering the Household Cavalry.

"Are you?" I asked him.

"No not really, why?"

"In that case then I've no choice. I've no chance of bulling those bloody big boots if you are not there."

It was a night that a lot of cleaning and talking got done, with all of us having opened a thought process that until today we'd had no real idea what it was about.

It must have been a good day as before midnight we were all in bed and asleep.

THURSDAY, DAY 67–MONDAY, DAY 71
SATURDAY'S CHILD

This period revolved around guard duties with everything else fitting in around them. We were not as worried this time round as we knew what to expect. Some funny things occurred during this time, caused mainly by lack of sleep.

They can say what they want (and they usually did), but we were improving daily now, especially on the drill front. We were drilling in uniform and feeling much smarter within ourselves. Still getting plenty of encouragement though.

"Jones, pull your shoulders back; you look like a stand-in for the hunchback of Notre Dame."

"Green, if that arm is straight, the rest of you is a total fuck up."

It's unbelievable how they kept it up.

"That white belt is loose at the front."

Well, it will be if you keep pulling on it, you pillock.

"Look at the hairs on your tunic, I can see them from an upstairs window."

Don't go upstairs then, we can't see either of them from here.

We were totally into this drilling and had a count meter in our heads that would switch on subconsciously. We would do left or right turns out of the blue, or march to a mirror and salute in two/three time. It was completely normal for it to happen to anyone, at any moment, and no-one thought it at all strange.

The gym was still a bit random, except for Monday assessments and Wednesday results, so along with drill it was sometimes slotted in with weekend block cleaning.

The Monday assessment was in the same format as the others, but with a higher number than last time. The end result was just the same; we were absolutely knackered at the end of it. On the positive side, we had increased our stamina and fitness. Now we had to wait until Wednesday for the results.'

The guard duties were the main topic of discussion and along with Timmy I felt that, in the interest of safety, we should keep everyone aware of the "Hound."

While on guard we had a new corporal. When he marched us back to the foyer, Alex asked him if he could do the wake-up calls. The corporal agreed and left.

Alex went quietly to Billy's bed, switched on his bedside light, and tipped him onto the floor.

Billy shot bolt upright saying, "What the fuck, who the f—?" and then saw Big Hippo smiling at him as the main lights came on.

"You stupid twat, I could have had a fucking heart attack."

"Well, I was up, so I thought everyone was up."

Al Hopkins couldn't stop laughing as he said to Billy, "I told you not to do it," but there was no pacifying Billy as he ranted on and on. Al reminded him that not only was Alex built like an elephant, but also had the memory of one.

During lunch, Keith and Alex, who were on the 0200hr–0400hr stag, were telling guys around them that about 0300hrs they were heading towards the back gate when Alex suddenly shouted, "Fucking hell," and ran back up the yard. Keith said he immediately followed him.

"Did you see the size of that?" said Alex.

"How could I? I was right behind you, but I heard the awful noise."

The "Hound" was successfully rejuvenated ahead of the others coming on guard.

It was obvious from some comments that the back gate was not getting much attention. It had gained so much traction that for a while, even Timmy and me were beginning to believe it.

The block cleaning was crazy. As soon as everything was pulled out, we would end up in the gym or drilling, and then we'd come back and have to start again as floor polish had dried, or walls were smeared. But it had a good side: when we were all together there was always lots of joking or funny stories, which would spring up from nothing.

Don said, "Hell, Tighe had a right one on him today, why is he like this every Saturday?"

"It's not his fault," I told them. "He's a Saturday's child." I had their attention. "Do you know the rhyme that says that Wednesday's child is full of woe, and Thursday's child has far to go? Well, he's Saturday's child."

"Saturday's child?" said John McGrath.

"Yes, it says Friday's child is full of wit, and Saturday's child is full of shit."

We started to laugh as Alan Ladd said, "Does it really say that?"

Pete chimed in with, "It facking does now."

On Monday morning I walked into the washroom with Alex saying, "It looks as if Billy has learned his lesson; he was noticeable by his silence this morning."

Alex laughed, "Maybe, but I'm never sure with that cunning little turd, but we'll see."

Time would prove what a prophetic remark that was, but for now it was business as usual.

At around 0830hrs the nation's entire supply of water for a month seemed to drop in a big downfall and we raced across to the Lecture Room.

We were very attentive as Corporal Wheeler went through the history of the UN peace keeping force in Cyprus and talked about other countries.

The warm room was proving too much for Billy, and Corporal Miles must have seen his head rolling. He kept on talking until he was next to Billy then yelled in his ear, "Wake up you dozy pillock."

Billy jumped bolt upright and said, "Nyasaland, Corporal."

Corporal Miles stepped back in surprise and said, "What are you babbling about, you idiot, that was ten minutes ago."

By now Billy was wide awake but hadn't a clue what he had said.

Miles said, "Go to the front, and tell us all you know about Nyasaland."

Billy said, "I don't know anything about it."

"I know, you slept through it. Shake hands with everyone and tell them what an arsehole you are."

Billy entered right into the spirit of it all and went along the front row. "Shake hands with a complete arsehole," then he turned around, bent over, and put his hand between his legs.

Corporal Miles was nearly crying with laughing, and just told him to sit down.

Later, in the cookhouse, Tony, who was in front of Billy at the counter said to a cook, "What do they eat in Nyasaland?"

"Nyasa who, where the hell is that?"

Tony pointed at Billy and said, "Ask him, he's the expert at this."

"Ok Professor, where is it?"

"Abroad," and Billy used up his entire knowledge in one word.

I was on the phone later and Mum said, "John, the girls want to know if you saw Buckingham Palace."

"Yes, it was brilliant, the queen was on the balcony and waved, so I waved back, and she said good morning.

Barbara said, "I wish—"

Mum said, "He's pulling your leg again," and then pulled them apart as Celia started teasing Barbara.

I told Mum about all we'd done, especially Alexander the huge drum horse, who was a bit slower than the smaller ones, so Dad would probably put a bet on him.

I got back in the block and joined in the wrestling match that was going on.

We got to the NAAFI a bit red and sweaty, and Alice asked what we had been up to.

"We've been checking if any bits fell off while we were wrestling," Dave told her.

"Ask a silly question. Ok what bits?"

Keith sat back, opened his legs, and stroked his thighs.

Alice looked at him and said, "Did someone bring a magnifying glass to help you find your twig for you?"

Keith just looked at us blankly and tried to smile.

It was a good finish to the day, and as soon as possible we were all in bed.

WEEK 11

TUESDAY, DAY 72–THURSDAY, DAY 74
THE SWORD OF DAMOCLES

"There will be an officer's inspection on Friday. We will increase the drill sessions beginning today. Also, your personal gear will be immaculate. Corporal of Horse Tighe smiled. "If you do not reach the required standard, you can forget next weekend."

Increase drill periods, has someone invented the thirty-hour day?

Within ten minutes he proved he meant every word he said. During the inspection, we were pulled and prodded around, followed by a full morning's session.

"After lunch be in the gym for assessment results."

Like many of the guys I was beginning to enjoy pre-assessment days done at a reasonable pace. The first part was doing the exercise correctly, plus personal goals, team-style games, and the assessment itself. The end result this time was Ding Dong, Arnold, and Joe Walters were put together in Team Three to help motivate each other. They were quite a comical trio and became known as "The Three Stooges." Arnold especially worked hard and had lost a load of weight, but all in all they were a popular bunch.

Later, Corporal Jones decided to have a boxing afternoon. The only rule was no hitting low. If this happened, that person received a free hit from his opponent. The first time it happened, Chris Pratley had to punch Jim Jones and gave him a love tap.

Corporal Jones, having put gloves on said, "No, like this," and hit Chris hard in the ribs knocking him onto one knee. Chris leapt up, eyes blazing, and took a God Almighty swing and missed by a mile. Bull held on to him.

Jones said, "If you think it can't get any worse, do that again."

But Chris's anger had subsided and the moment passed.

In the cookhouse, trying to save face Chris said, "He's lucky I didn't knock him out cold."

Bull laughed and said he was the lucky one not to dislocate his shoulder.

This may have led to another altercation later. I was in our washroom and heard a loud shout from the other end and ran down.

It was chaotic as about six guys were pulling John McGrath off Jack Backhouse.

Jack had bumped a table, knocking John's polish and a boot onto the floor. He immediately apologised, but John exploded and launched himself at Jack. The others were holding John before it got really going.

It did bring home the stress that was just below the surface as such a trivial thing could set off such a violent reaction. Ten minutes later, it was purely a handbag at five paces moment, and all was forgotten.

Next morning after Dave had gone to breakfast, we moved his bed to the other end of the room, and he was pissed off when we wouldn't put it back. Suddenly there was a shout of "Stand by your beds," and Dave went into headless chicken mode, as we heard boot studs coming up the corridor.

We all stood to attention as Billy Jackson stood at the door in his underwear and best boots and said, "Stand at ease."

The whole room collapsed laughing, except Dave, who just collapsed. We had arranged the whole thing before breakfast, and even though we put the bed back it took Dave a while to see the funny side of it.

Today was all about drill, round the square, round the barracks, and round the bend.

At one point we marched close to the back gate and with the number of us looking at it, it could have been a drill movement. It was too early for the "Hound" to be lurking, but Timmy and I made sure that everyone could see us looking at it.

We carried on all afternoon going round and round the square, practising everything we had learned. Corporal of Horse Tighe went up to a window in the block for an aerial view. I thought this must be a good sight, but when he returned, he said we looked, "...like a dysfunctional spider vanishing up its own arse, but I will make it functional."

His summing up was that it was passable, but if we don't keep showing improvement there would be no weekend off. This was now the Sword of Damocles that would be hanging over our heads, until we actually left.

The NAAFI was humming tonight as so much was happening, what with Chris attempting to give Corporal Jones a head cold with the draft from his haymaker, and Billy's morning parade. As soon as there was a quiet moment, Dave began telling Alice and Jenny about the bed incident. All evening, every time they looked at Billy, they would burst out laughing.

After a short while, not to be outdone Keith said, "You wouldn't laugh if you saw him in his underwear; it would make you cry."

Jenny said loudly, "I guess you are the expert on little things in men's underwear making women cry."

Keith, having lost again, sat back in his chair.

We spent another three hours on cleaning and were happy to get into bed with our own thoughts, until Ginger said, "Eight days to go. That's longer than the life span of a butterfly."

We all turned over, as the knowledge of what butterflies got up to in their own time didn't amount to a hill of beans.

FRIDAY, DAY 75–SUNDAY, DAY 77
"HANDS OFF COCKS!"

I'm going to shoot this prick, right through his vocal cords. Better still, get Bob to do it, he's nearer. On waking I saw Bob hanging half out of his bed and knew it was a bad idea; he'd probably shoot himself—not at his best yet.

A voice shouted, "Outside, dressed for drill at 0900hrs for your last practice before officer's inspection at 1300hrs."

We drilled and we drilled and we drilled, in ranks of twos and fours. In effect, we could fit in anywhere. But for big inspections or special displays, we would always be in our height uniformity.

By the time we finished at lunch time, it was obvious we were streets ahead of even two weeks ago.

At 1255hrs, in number-one uniform and best boots, we paraded on the square, and in a strange way looked forward to strutting our stuff in front of Captain Forbes-Hart.

At exactly 1300hrs, our warrant officer from the pay table marched across to us.

Nice one, Corporal of Horse, we fell for this one hook, line, and sinker. As it was only a preliminary, the warrant officer would fill in until the full inspection next week. He was very good though and gave positive and instructional observations. He told me my boots were excellent and said I must have spent a lot of time on them. I told him I had (and hoped my nose wouldn't grow too quickly). He told Don his boots were getting there.

As he stood in front of Arnold he said, "Stand up straight, don't stoop over, was your father a bellringer at Notre Dame Cathedral?" He was smiling with Tighe, but quickly moved on when quite seriously, Arnold replied, "No sir, he's not musical."

After watching us drill for thirty minutes he addressed us. "This is a big improvement from the squad that appeared to have a vendetta against my pay table, it is obvious for all to see. I would like to thank you for your effort and enthusiasm. Keep up the good work," and he marched off.

Corporal of Horse Tighe stood in front of us and said, "His words, not mine," but was smiling.

Tighe left after this, and Corporal Miles took over. "If this next drill is good, we will finish early."

It was, and we didn't.

This carried on until evening meal, after which we went to the Lecture Room. Corporal of Horse Tighe gave us another list of expectations or, wait for it, wait for it: "You will not go home at the weekend."

In order to leave we had to say our name in the phonetic alphabet, I got away with Juliet-India-Mike-Mike-Yabba dabba doo.

That evening, sitting with a bunch of other guys, I jokingly asked Don if he would like me to do his boots. The sad picture of me trying to outshine Don led to a long discussion on all we had been through. The one thing that stuck in my mind was how many people had forgotten Banjo's name, and Parkin wasn't mentioned at all—there was too much to take in.

The next day started with good news. Dave had been cleared to use the Hoffman press, and through the day would do all our uniforms. This would happen during our block cleaning today.

After the ceremonial rolling of the fruit, we really got stuck into it, while enjoying the banter. Someone mentioned to Alex about Billy winding him up and he said, "Yes, I've still got that little turd to deal with."

This started us shouting down the corridor, "Look out Billy, Big Hippo is coming to get you."

Even Alex burst out laughing as Billy replied. "It's ok, I'm over in the tailor's shop."

We were admiring our hard work when Corporal of Horse Tighe came in and said, "As the block is almost done, you will be pleased to hear I have been able to arrange another ten-mile bash tomorrow at 0900hrs, so that we can gauge your progress with the last one." With that he gave us a cheery wave and left.

This wasn't the shock he'd expected, as many of us preferred to be out and about rather than cleaning.

When we got up in the morning it felt a bit different, and it wasn't until a cook apologised for the bacon and eggs being late because Hard-boiled had forgotten to put his clock forward, that we realised why it felt different. It didn't matter to us, because we had our own alarms.

There was no inspection this morning. "No harnesses, bring combat jackets, and get in the Bedford.

Twenty minutes later we were in a new area, with Tighe and Miles alongside their long wheel-based Land Rover. Tighe smiled as Corporal Miles pulled back the canvas cover to reveal a mass of rucksacks.

"Shut up, put your jackets inside the rucksacks, and to help with the balance, we have put a brick in each side pocket. Take a water bottle each."

We were soon underway and all was good for the first half hour until Arnold, who was in front of Timmy and me, had turned bright red and was slowing down.

Corporal Miles ran alongside and said, "Don't forget this is a team effort."

We took a brick each from Arnold, and Timmy also grabbed his jacket. Al took his water bottle and stayed with him.

I looked behind and there was a small group forming. One of them was Alex, who had a lot of body to move, but would keep going at his own pace.

Eventually we saw the Bedford, dressed Arnold, and all ran in together. Corporal of Horse Tighe checked our rucksacks, and this was our signal to collapse.

Soon Alex arrived and fell on his back, making a noise as if his throat had slipped into his stomach. He could only manage to raise his arms upwards and say, "Come and get me."

I hadn't realised he was religious, but then neither did whoever he was talking to, and fortunately no-one came for him.

On our return we tweaked the cleaning and relaxed in the NAAFI, then as soon as was reasonable turned in.

Alex was still talking to Keith, who said something we couldn't understand, but Alex said, "Are you all going to let him say that?"

I said, "Well thanks Alex, after I stood up for you earlier."

"How?"

"On the way back from NAAFI, someone said you weren't fit to sleep with a pig."

"Which fucker said that?"

"It doesn't matter. I stood up for you."

"Thanks Jimmy, what did you say?"

"I told him I thought you were."

With that Alex grunted and turned over.

WEEK 12

MONDAY, DAY 78
A CARNIVAL ATMOSPHERE

We hadn't expected to spend much time in the gym today as hopefully we were leaving on Thursday, but no-one had confirmed this yet.

Corporal Kelly informed us that this was our last gym day before Thursday. "Fail it and you may not go home...or return." (Even he'd caught the tell-them-nothing bug).

"Today is to see if you have maintained expectancies."

It soon became obvious that Ding Dong, Arnold, and Joe were being appraised more than the rest of us.

We all did one circuit and then personal goals, while these three were monitored more closely. I was improving as much as I could at spinning through the air. I just couldn't land on my feet yet. I either ended up diving forward into a splat, or doing forward rolls.

Later, we were in the Lecture Room with Corporal of Horse Tighe, and Corporal Kelly took the "Three Stooges" next door.

Five minutes after this Corporal of Horse Tighe joined them.

Another five minutes and they all came back in, and the Stooges looked pretty upbeat. Corporal of Horse Tighe told them that he would accept Corporal Kelly's recommendation and looked forward to their improvement on their return. This cheered all of us up as they were trying hard and were a popular part of the squad.

Tighe said, "Make quick phone calls for the next two nights and let you parents know you will be home this weekend." He waited until the room calmed down and then smiled and said, "Remember, only if we are satisfied with the next three days."

Back in the block it sounded like a chicken coop, with everyone jumping around.

I went to the phone, waited for 1800hrs and immediately called Mum. "I will be home late on Thursday night." She was as excited as I was. I spoke quickly to Dad who said, "First pints on me, son."

I floated back to the block.

The excitement was still high the following morning and a shout of, "Hands off cocks!" only awakened a happy mind.

Do your worst, dickhead, today is a great day. Play with your light switches, play with yourself, play on the motorway, I don't care.

We did nothing for the next two days except drill and clean the block and our personal gear.

A couple of bits of information that slipped out in the cookhouse, only added to our happy state. A junior cook told some of us at the hotplate that they'd been told to order less food for the weekend, as we would be away.

He saw our faces light up and said, "Oh fuck, don't let on I mentioned it." But before anyone could say they wouldn't, it had spread through the rest of us like dysentery in a hot curry house. He was off the hook by evening meal, as two other cooks said they had a long weekend off, as we wouldn't be here.

During a lot of this time, we were enjoying drill and cleaning; nothing was too much trouble, even when Tighe called in, pointing out various areas of "concern." To us it was more of an eyesight concern as we couldn't see them. It was hard enough seeing a flea's left ball without having to find a pimple on it.

We saved our best for drill. This would have to be special in order to showcase all we had learned, and we put our whole selves into it. Our own pride was urging us to show that we were no longer the guys from eleven weeks ago who couldn't walk in a straight line, and we had a great incentive to do well.

I went for a chat with Don and overheard Jay, who had no family, say to Pete, "That's great, I'd love to."

They had got on really well since Pete changed rooms and it wasn't hard to guess what had happened. In the NAAFI I made a beeline for Jay.

He had a smile like a Cheshire cat and said Pete's parents had said they would be pleased to have him stay, and he looked over at Pete quite emotionally. Pete's family lived in east London, and I thought these guys will be in their local pub having a sing-song before we get off the train.

I talked to Danny and Don later and we were all really pleased for Jay and agreed what a super family Pete had.

Another minor miracle occurred when we got through Pay Parade unscathed. It took longer as we were getting the extra pay for the weekend off: two and a half week's pay for three days and no train fares. As soon as I got it, I went upstairs and guys had theirs spread over their beds, just to make sure they weren't dreaming.

It was an infectious time and even the instructors seemed to have caught it, and called in on Wednesday for a chat, to mention that the room inspection would be at 1000hrs and drill at 1115hrs.

Corporal Miles asked me if I had any plans. I told him I'd arranged for my Dad to shout "hands off cocks" at 0600hrs and flick the lights on and off.

"Good, so long as it's not your mother."

It was a relaxed visit…but then a touch of reality. "I expect nothing but the best tomorrow. If you fuck up, I can still accommodate you."

Not if our cooks have a say in it, you won't.

The last three nights in the NAAFI were in a carnival atmosphere with everyone on a high. Alice and Jenny were enjoying the fooling around, but said it was going to be awful quiet over the weekend.

The last night was really funny as Keith was trying to get close to Jenny for a chat. Every time he got close, Alice would appear, and after the fourth time it was so obvious that even Alice was laughing. We all went and wished Alice and Jenny goodnight.

Around midnight, as usual, Alex was winding Keith up. "You know what, Keith, I think Alice fancies you. I noticed tonight she followed you everywhere you went."

In Keith's measured and beautifully selected words he said, "Piss off."

THURSDAY, DAY 81
"RISE AND SHINE"

This was a very easy awakening today as Corporal Miles didn't even play with the lights. He just switched them on and we were already getting up.

The washrooms were noisy as we were in great spirits right from the get-go. There were guys singing and whistling and the mood was brilliant.

We got all our personal kit laid out and went to breakfast, and by the amount of food put away, nerves had not yet set in.

Corporal Miles called in at 0745hrs and told us to change sheets and pillowcases, so they would be clean when we returned.

He left and the magic template appeared, and soon the bed packs were all looking the same. It looked like a treasure trove of shine: clothing pressed, brasses catching the light, boots gleaming, and locker layout perfect. He returned at 0830hrs with Corporal of Horse Tighe and then the doors to the washrooms and cleaning rooms were closed.

"You will have to tie a knot in it."

We got changed into number ones, white belts, best boots, and forage caps and waited for the arrival of Captain Forbes-Hart. At exactly 1000hrs we heard Corporal of Horse Tighe downstairs welcoming him into the block. "Block and squad present and ready for your inspection, sir."

"Thank you, Corporal of Horse, lead on."

They came upstairs and we heard them go into the washroom and cleaning room and then heard "Room Atten-shun."

It was like watching a military caterpillar moving around. Captain Forbes-Hart, Corporal of Horse Tighe then Corporals Miles, Wheeler, and Fletcher following in each other's footsteps. Tiber wisely stayed by the door. I'm sure if Captain Forbes-Hart had fallen through the window the rest would have stacked up on him.

It was fairly informal as Captain Forbes-Hart asked us basic questions as he looked over our layouts. "Are your instructors looking after you?"

No, they are a bunch of schizophrenic fucking nutcases, who are led by a lunatic who thinks he is God. "Yes sir, very well indeed."

He moved on and Tighe gave me a tight grin through clenched teeth.

After the captain had seen us all, he remarked to Corporal of Horse Tighe how well pressed the uniforms were, and Tighe told him that it was thanks to a Hoffman Press.

"Hoffman press?" he asked quizzically.

"Yes sir," Tighe replied, "Trooper Marx here was trained on them before he joined the army."

"Oh, I see, well done Marx." Then looking at Corporal of Horse Tighe, he said, "For a moment I thought Hoffman Press was the name of a recruit."

For a moment Corporal of Horse Tighe didn't know whether to laugh or cry and just said, "Very good, sir.

We felt fairly relaxed as they went into Room Two and then down the other end. Eventually, we got the call to muster at the top of the staircase. Captain Forbes-Hart gave us a quick debrief and told us he was pleased with what he has seen so far. "I know it has been hard work during the past three months, and there is a lot more to come. But it was a good inspection and I look forward to seeing you drill." Then he left.

A buzz was just beginning when Corporal of Horse Tighe shouted, "Shut up, it was good enough for the stage you are at. There is a long way to go and a lot to learn. Change into best uniform and then fall in on the square."

At precisely 1115hrs, by the clock on the square, Captain Forbes-Hart marched out. He came up and down the lines making little remarks about anything from, "Where is your home?" to "How is the training going so far?" or "Well turned out, good effort."

It took about fifteen minutes to get around us all by which time we were ready to drill, if only to get the blood circulating properly.

"This is where you get to show Captain Forbes-Hart how good you are. If you don't, I will keep you here all weekend if necessary."

That's better, this is what we are used to, so let's do it.

Corporal of Horse Tighe marched us around the square in ranks of four, putting us through our full repertoire. Lots of saluting on the march, eyes left or right, wheeling, and quick and slow marching and apart from a couple of small hiccups, which a quick check step fixed, it was a good and solid thirty minutes.

We were halted in front of Captain Forbes-Hart and Corporal of Horse Tighe smiled at him. "As you noticed sir, I gave a couple of orders on the wrong foot, to show you how quickly they would correct it."

"Thank you, Corporal of Horse, never doubted it for a moment."

It was close to lunchtime and Captain Forbes Hart said, "Dismiss the squad, Corporal of Horse, I will speak to them before they leave." He saluted and marched off.

Corporal of Horse Tighe told us to go and change into number-two uniforms, DMS boots, put on cloth belts, have lunch, and be back in the foyer at 1255hrs.

The noise in the block was over-powering; we all had something to say and we were all feeling good. There was a sense of achievement and a realisation that we were different from when we arrived: fitter and more confident. We were going home to show people how we had changed, that we could take it, and then come back for more.

Priorities first. There was a really good feed in the cookhouse to do justice to, and we all ate a huge meal to help us on our way. The atmosphere was totally relaxed. Two cooks were going on a long weekend, and the remainder had twenty-seven fewer mouths to feed, so it was a win-win for everybody.

At 1300hrs Captain Forbes-Hart entered the Lecture Room. There followed a ten-minute talk on what we had achieved, his impressions of today, and what to expect on our return. The news that had us wriggling about, was that on the Tuesday of our return we would begin sword drills, which had me thinking of Sir Lancelot again.

When the captain had gone, Tighe gave us his version of a reality check. "Your hard work hasn't even started yet. Be pleased with where you are at the moment, and we will be pleased to show you hard work on your return."

There was a knock on the door and two NCOs from the Orderly Room entered, and for the first time Tighe smiled. "Listen for your names; these are your travel tickets. Remember your return times and do not be late back."

We all eventually signed for them, and Tighe gave us his parting words. "Get your greatcoats from your rooms, lock your lockers, and we will lock the rooms when you are all out. For those leaving Windsor by train, there will be transport outside the Guard Room at 1430hrs. Enjoy your weekend and don't get too drunk."

We all burst out laughing at his completely impossible request.

A large group of us were travelling to London, then dispersing from there, so we made our way to the Guard Room. I already knew that Dave and Chris Pratley were going to Manchester, and Paul Smith was also on our train, going about two-thirds of the way.

There were a lot of us on the Bedford, including Timmy, Big Alex, Bob McCann, and Danny Williams plus at least seven or eight more. It must have sounded like a hundred men cheering as we drove out of the barracks for the first time in three months, without our shepherds.

THE WEEKEND OFF BEGINS

We arrived at the train station in Windsor and at 3:00 pm were in a carriage all talking at once about what we were going to do, amid much laughter and joking. Before we knew it, we had arrived in London. We walked off the platform and spread out with the speed of bird shit on a car windscreen as we all went our different ways.

When we got to our station, there was a one hour wait for the train, so Dave, Chris, Paul Smith, and I went and enjoyed the luxury of a beer while relaxing, then boarded our train for Manchester. We neatly folded our greatcoats on the overhead rack, placed our caps on them, went and got six cans of beer each, and returned to drink them around a carriage table.

The train journey set the theme for the weekend. The majority of people were very friendly, asked us about various aspects of the army, and constantly wished us well. We were the centre of attraction and were secretly totally enjoying it.

A youngish couple not much older than us were sitting across the aisle and the male asked us how we came to join up and where. Dave and I took them a beer and we sat having a good chat when the female said, "Don't you even think about joining the army."

They both burst out laughing as the female stood and opened her coat to reveal her bump. We hadn't realised until then that she was, as her husband put it, slightly pregnant, so we drank to the good news.

They left the train an hour later after a lot of good-natured banter, especially asking her to keep calm, as the only deliveries we knew about were in a mailbox.

A while later, Paul got off after we had checked our train times and we agreed to sit close to these seats on the way back.

I woke up to the train juddering, and opened my eyes to see we were only a mile or so from Manchester, so we smartened ourselves up.

We put greatcoats and caps on and virtually marched through the ticket box and outside of Piccadilly Station. We again confirmed our plans for meeting on Sunday, and Chris jumped in a cab. I walked with Dave past the bus station where he hopped on a bus, and I walked the last mile to Victoria Station to get the 10:00 pm train.

I found a phone and called Mum and then jumped on the train to the closest bus depot to home, in Whitefield. The train was nearly empty and the excitement built up in me during the twenty-minute ride.

This was the station I had got off at for five years to go to school, and it was smaller than I had remembered it. I had passed my eleven-plus, which gave me free entry to a grammar school, and my parents had scrimped and saved to keep me there. There always seemed to be a stigma around eleven-plus pupils, and I often got into scrapes as I rebelled against the system. This also led to friction between me and Dad.

I stood a short while, looking up the road towards a school that I had never felt a part of, which had made it clear I would never amount to much. I felt a great release in saying out loud, "Well fuck you all," and I proudly walked across the road to catch the bus.

When the bus arrived, I sat across from the driver, chatting, and he said just give me shout when you are near home. The bus conductress came back after a smoke, went upstairs collected the fares, did the same downstairs, and then sat with me. She said, "Put your money away son, my son is away in the Royal Navy," then she patted my hand and went to the driver. Less than five minutes later, I told them that my house was on the next junction, "the one with all the lights on." He dropped me off outside the house.

I waved to them both as the bus drove off and turned to see Mum standing at the front door. I walked the twelve or so strides up the path and couldn't believe how many emotions were present at the same time. I felt extremely proud, yet sad, at seeing the house again. I didn't know whether to laugh or cry, and my chest felt as if it was bursting.

I reached the door and Mum said, "John, is it really you?"

"It is from now on, love," and then I hugged her forever.

We went in and I saw my brother and sisters in the hallway, removed my cap and greatcoat, and gave them my best man-of-the-world look. We all hugged and I became aware of Dad at the living room door smiling. "Nice to see you, lad," he said, as we shook hands.

I hung my greatcoat and jacket in the stair cupboard, along with my cap, but only after they had all tried them on.

Upstairs I changed into some old baggy clothing, looked at baby-sister Helen in her cot, and then came down to a barrage of questions. We sat in the front room around Mum's huge plate of sandwiches and just talked.

After around a half hour, my younger brother Len and sister Barbara went to bed, ready for school in the morning. They had been too excited to sleep, and Mum had let them stay up. They were followed another half hour later by my eldest sister Celia, who was working at 8:00 am. I chatted with Mum and Dad and it turned out they had a loose itinerary for the weekend.

Tomorrow, with Mum and baby to see her friends, then a local pub for lunch. A family meal together later, and a night out with Dad for a beer or three.

Saturday, visit friends, then watch Bury play football, and an evening with Mum and Dad in the other local pub with some other friends.

Sunday, a big brunch with the family, as I would have to leave midday to return. It was a little like being in the army, except I had a say in it.

The three of us talked to around 1:30 am and went to bed. I got into my bunk bed and tried to get the rhythm of my brothers snoring.

I pondered on the day and how the house was just the same, yet at the same time totally different.

FRIDAY

I awoke to the strange sound of a gurgling baby, and saw Mum with baby in one arm, putting a cup of tea on the dresser and opening the curtains.

"It's 8:00 am love, and safe to get up now, all the others have left."

I hadn't heard a thing, but the tea and Mum saying there were bacon butties in the kitchen, made a nice start.

I washed up, and went and played with the baby; she had changed a lot while I was away and was normally very pleasant to have around.

Suddenly, Mum said that she had to go to her group meeting for 10:30 am, and had told them I would be with her. Much to Mum's amusement I got out the ironing board and then polished up my boots, changed, and put Helen in a pushchair. I pushed her to the nearby meeting room, while Mum talked twenty to the dozen.

"We are calling in to the Young Wives Group. I normally bring Helen here most days," then she started to laugh as she said, "I'm the president, only because no one else will do it."

We both found it funny as she was twelve years older than the next wife and at least fifteen years older than the majority of them. I felt a bit conspicuous as we went in and saw at least ten wives with very young children.

"Wow, you are looking good." I recognised Annie from before.

"You never said anything like that before."

"I know, but you were a bit of a tit before." This broke the ice.

I said to her, "Don't hold back Annie, just say it as it is."

We stayed about an hour then went to The Swan next door and had a drink and a sandwich. I knew the landlord from when I used to go in playing dominoes with Dad. He brought a beer round and we chatted for a short while. By the time we left over an hour later, we had talked to virtually everyone in the pub.

Everywhere we went, Mum would say, "This is my son John, he's on leave from the Guards," whether she knew them or not. I would nod, say hello and chat, still enjoying all the attention.

Later we walked to a shop and the lady asked me how old my baby was, and said it must be hard to leave her when I go back. As soon as we got outside, Mum looked a bit embarrassed and said, "It must look that way to anyone who doesn't know us."

I said to her, "Do you think she thought I was your toy boy?"

She blushed again and then laughed as she knew this story would improve over the family table and improve a lot more over time.

I had changed for a family meal at 5:00 pm where the conversation from the girls was mainly about weight loss and my clothes only fitting where they touched.

At 6:30, Dad said we would get the bus into Bury, have a few beers and then get back to The Swan for the last hour. I changed back into uniform and at 7:15 we were having our first beer.

An hour later, we went into the last pub as it was straight opposite the bus stop, and met the only bit of badness through the whole weekend.

I had put my cap on the corner of the bar, and we were talking on and off to the barman. There were about ten tables around the edge of the smallish-sized room, but only two were occupied. At the bar were stood five men who seemed to be together, though two talked mainly to each other. One of the men at the bar was getting louder, and it was becoming obvious I was the topic of his annoyance. He made a remark about, "Fucking smart-arsed Guardsmen," but not directly to me.

Dad looked at me and said, "Just ignore him, son."

Two minutes later the loud one suddenly turned sideways and said, "I was in the Lancashire Fusiliers and we got five VCs before breakfast." (Victoria Cross-the army's highest award for bravery.)

Dad said to him, "How many of them did you get then?"

The guy turned to face him saying, "I'll fix you, you smart arsed twa—"

He never finished the sentence, as a huge blow from Dad caught him flush in the face, knocking him backwards across one of the empty tables, where he landed on the fixed wall seating. The two guys nearest to him rushed across, and the other two seemed frozen.

Dad said, "Quick, get out of here," and was through the door like a greyhound with me right behind him.

We met up across the road and Dad said, "Looks like a good time to get on the bus." I told him we couldn't, as my cap was still on the bar.

We initiated emergency plan two, and went to another pub to let the dust settle before creeping in the back way for the cap. We finished our beer and went to the back entrance and looked in. The barman saw us and shouted us over. We began to apologise for earlier, and he stopped us short.

"He had it coming. They are long gone now, and he's barred from here for good,"

We went back into the front room. There was still a table full of people from before, and the two guys at the bar. It turned out they were friends of one of the others, not the one Dad punched. They got us a pint each, and by closing time we were all chatting happily together, and Dad and I missed the last bus. We drank up and decided to walk the two miles back.

"I thought you told me not to get into any trouble tonight."

He just smiled and said, "And you didn't."

He was a bit worried about Mum finding out as she might not go out tomorrow, so we agreed not to mention it.

When we got home, she said, "You're a bit late back."

"Yes love, I left my cap and had to go back and get it, which caused us to miss the bus."

Dad smiled and we settled down for a chat with the family over Mum's sandwiches, telling them about the night, missing one little bit, and exaggerating all the rest as only a few beers can do.

SATURDAY

This began just as if I had never been away. My brother had gone to his part-time week-end job. I lay on the top bunk looking out of the window, listening to Celia and Barbara trying to coax Dad out of the only toilet by shaking the door shouting, "Dad, stop reading the newspaper, we're in agony out here."

I realised I'd just swapped one bedlam for another.

As always, right at 8:00 am, he walked out, newspaper under his arm. "Morning girls." Then he went into the bathroom for a wash, while the girls decided who would be first to venture in and open the window.

Soon Dad had gone to work; he was in insurance and Saturday was his busy day, but he was finishing early as I was home. It was hard to make definite arrangements, as we had no car and relied on public transport or walking. By the time I got downstairs, Helen was fed and fast asleep again, and we were helping ourselves to the inevitable bacon butties.

Celia had arranged for me to go over to see Stuart and Arthur. She was in early courtship stages with Stuart and any excuse was a good one. I had worked with Arthur, who was a friend of Stuart's, who became my friend and I had introduced him to Celia.

We walked the half-mile round to Stuart's house and chatted with him and his parents. Then Arthur showed up and we arranged to meet at our house at 1:00 pm for our old Saturday ritual.

After Stuart and Arthur arrived and chatted to Mum for ten minutes, I told her to let Dad know we would be in The Swan until 2.30 and then we'd go up to Gigg Lane and watch Bury play football. It was only a five-minute walk to the pub and ten minutes from there to the ground, so it was already fairly busy. We had just got our second pint when Dad came in, and this was turning into a dream, as I couldn't buy a beer. First, two guys we used to play dominoes with, and then one of Mum's friends sent one through from the front.

We walked up to Gigg Lane with a group from the pub, and at the turnstile I asked for two tickets.

"Is this your father?"

"Yes."

"Then squeeze in together."

We stopped and talked to two sailors in uniform on the way across the car park, then ran and met Stuart and Arthur at the Manchester Road end goal, as Bury were kicking that way.

Bury were 1–0 down at half-time and we went around to the Cemetery Road end, stopping to get a meat and potato pie, and a Bovril to drink—all a part of the ritual. We then stood behind the goal becoming footballing experts, along with everyone else, while eating these great pies in the open air. A great day was getting better as Bury won 3–2 and it was back to The Swan for a quick one and a happy post-mortem, as we all waded in with our thoughts.

Stuart called into the house and we arranged that we would go to the other local, The Bridge, at 7:45 pm and Mum and Dad would come down at around 8:15 pm. Celia would babysit as she was still only seventeen.

Stuart left, I changed, and Len arrived in from his Saturday job, then we all sat around the table and enjoyed a good and lively meal.

Mum didn't go out very often and when she knew we were going to The Bridge she said to Dad, "If you get up and sing 'I'll take you home again Kathleen,' I'll leave."

This had us all in hysterical laughter. Mum was called Catherine, and I think this was the closest song to her name that Dad knew. She had many funny stories about Dad's attempts at this song, but had she planted a seed in his mind?

The front room of The Bridge was of the day: ladies were only allowed in the front room, not the "tap room" in the back. At weekends it was sing-along time, when various people would get up and sing with the resident pianist. It wasn't very often Dad would get up and sing (he needed a few beers to relax), but when he did, he had all the attributes of a great crooner except the voice, of which I inherited every tone-deaf note.

Rules were in place here, especially no swearing due to ladies being present. They were really good sing-along nights with everyone joining in, as Mum knew.

We had a terrific meal, and the girls even volunteered to do the washing up to let Mum enjoy her night out.

I went and changed again and by the time I got dressed, Stuart was there, so we strolled to The Bridge. I grabbed two tables near the bar and

Stuart came back with two beers and a big smile saying, "I see what you mean about buying beers, Harry (the landlord) got these."

I gave Harry a wave. Officially, Harry, his wife, and her mother ran the pub. His mother-in-law was an immaculately groomed lady about eighty years old, very prim and proper, and she never put up with any nonsense. She ruled the tap room with a rod of iron. She was renowned in the area for this, and for her great love of cats. We thought even Harry was a bit intimidated by her. She had apparently been quite upset during the week, telling Dad one of her cats was missing.

One of Dad's friends, Big Ronnie (ex-Royal Navy) and his wife, on hearing Mum was coming, came in with their son, also Ronnie.

I knew Ronnie well as he was my age and we had played darts together previously. By the time Mum and Dad arrived, the pub was in full swing. In a lull in the singing, Dad went to the bar and we heard Harry's mother-in-law shout, "Good evening, John."

Without any change in expression at all he replied, "Good evening, Mrs. C, how's your pussy?"

Mum's eyes opened wide, Harry froze, and we looked down laughing. The bar kind of looked on, fearing the worst, but she just said, "I don't know, John I don't think I'll see her again."

Dad looked very sympathetic as he came and sat down.

Mum said, "John, just behave yourself," but she was smiling.

He looked at her saying, "It must be in your mind, Cath. I was only enquiring about her missing cat, right Ron?"

Like the rest of us Ron couldn't see for laughing.

There were two spare chairs, but they were never empty as people kept coming over for a chat. It was apparent that I was now being talked to, compared to before I had joined up when I was just there.

I was enjoying this, no sense in being a shrinking violet—I stuck out like a sore thumb, so enjoy the moment.

It was good beer-wise also, as at one time I had so many in the pump that I had to get Stuart and Dad to help me out, but it was also good to go and thank the ones who had bought them.

Around 10:00 pm Dad said, "Watch the guy who has just come in," and we watched the man sidling his way round to the piano.

He would come in every Saturday night and the routine was always the same. He would take the mike and start to sing.

"PASSENGERS WILL PLEASE REFRAIN FROM URINATING WHILE THE TRAIN."

Harry would be running to get from behind the bar, to get to the piano, with everyone cheering.

"IS STANDING IN THE STATION AT THE STOP."

By now Harry would be shouting to let everyone know he was on his way.

"PLEASE RETAIN YOUR NATURAL FUCTION TILL WE GET TO CLAPHAM JUNCTION."

Harry always arrived at this point, taking the mike off him, and "barring" him from the pub.

This happened most weekends, and the room always cheered the singer and booed Harry. So good was their timing, we never knew the rest of the song. This put the room in a good mood, and Mum and Ronnie's wife were thoroughly enjoying the evening.

A lot of people knew Mum from the church and the "Young Wives" and there was a constant stream of mini-skirts coming for a chat. Young Ron kept looking at me and Stuart, amazed.

I said to him, "There's something wrong with this equation, all these attractive young women in mini-skirts coming over here to chat to Mum." But it was nice to see.

Mum was enjoying herself now; she'd had a couple of glasses of wine, plus she knew so many people. Not long after the singer was "barred" Dad went to the toilet.

Suddenly we heard the familiar refrain of, "I'll take you home again Kathleen" drifting over from the piano and Mum saying "Bloody hell" then looking round at her friends and rolling her eyes back. By now we were joining in with him singing—he was giving it his all. Secretly, Mum was really enjoying it, yet another saga of the song for the archives. We knew he only had one song, so we shouted "More, more," and Mum said, "Don't encourage him he doesn't need it. I'm going to kill him."

All too quickly it was 10:50 pm, last orders were called, and we drank our last drinks. We spent ten minutes on the long farewells, hugging and hand shaking, then wobbled up to the house. There were even more farewells and then into the house.

We had a brew, another beer or three and more sandwiches, then sat around exaggerating the evening to the girls and Len.

Mum fed Helen, while telling the girls about who was there.

Dad had become a mix of Joseph Locke, Slim Whitman, and Lassie.

It was around 1:30ish when Stuart went. I watched two of him leave, and we all went off to bed.

SUNDAY

We were all up around 8:00 am and had a good breakfast together. It was an altogether different feeling, as I knew I had to leave at lunch time, but we still had a laugh at Dad's antics and Mum's reactions.

I cleaned up and went for a walk with Mum and Helen, and enjoyed seeing her friends who were on their way to church, especially when one of them shouted across the road, "Did he take you home again, Cath," as we strolled back.

On a bus stop there was a timetable and I decided I'd go all the way to Piccadilly on the bus. It was direct, had few stops, and arriving at 1:00 pm would give me another fifteen minutes at home. I had arranged to meet Dave and Chris at 1:15 pm at the train station, so all in all it was a win, win situation.

I had a good chat with Dad until he left at 11:00 am to go to work and Mum suggested that it had better be John Senior and Junior, not Big John and Little John any more, as I had outgrown him.

All too soon it was time to leave. As we stood near the front door, Mum gave me an envelope, saying not to open it until I was on the bus.

I gave it straight back to her. "You'd better look under the teapot."

She said, "Oh John, you haven't."

"Yes, but I want to. I've spent very little this weekend, so get what you really need, or go to The Bridge again next week and pay Harry not to let Dad sing."

It was a little easier saying goodbye this time, as we knew I would be back soon, for longer. It was quiet, being a Sunday. I crossed the road and as the bus approached gave Mum a long wave and got on.

As soon as I got on and sat down, a wave of homesickness swept over me. It was only five minutes to Whitefield and during the quick stop there a guy in RAF uniform got on and we sat together all the way to Piccadilly. This was good for me and took my mind off leaving, as we bull-shitted the ride away.

We parted at Piccadilly Bus Station and I strolled down to the railway station. Dave was already there. It was chilly and we went inside to wait for Chris, who showed up at 1:35 pm. As the train was delayed twenty minutes, we went and got a beer.

It was good to travel back together, as we talked constantly about the weekend.

On arrival we got on a tube and went to Waterloo for the 8:00 pm train to Windsor. As we were early, we went to the bar for another beer. Obviously great minds think alike, as Timmy, Ginger, Alex, and a few more were there, and among much hand shaking, we managed a beer and then boarded the train.

The passengers must have thought it was an invasion, but the people from Windsor were used to the guards being around and were very friendly. The plan had worked out well and by 9:30 pm we were in The Raglan, a pub on the corner of the barracks, joining Pete, Jay, Don, and Bill Allen. The pumps ran flat out for the entire hour, all the food was devoured, and the whole deafening noise began again.

As closing time was 10:30 pm on a Sunday, we were walking back into the barracks by 10:50hrs and booking in. We went to the window, and wonder of wonders Corporal Fletcher was there and ticked us off one by one. "Good, everyone is back. Tomorrow we will hit the ground running, so go and cough and fart the beer out, or we will do it for you."

Pete who was a little tipsy said, "And a facking pleasure to see you again too, Corporal."

"Get upstairs, and tell me that again tomorrow, Hughes, when the glow has gone."

We made our beds and cleaned some gear, after a fashion. Don took my boots as we'd arranged over my getting him a beer in the pub.

Fifteen minutes later he returned them.

Bob said, "Look at those, mine look dull beside them, and I'm clean out of spit."

"It's that shite beer you drink, it's enough to dull anything down," Don told him.

"No such thing as shite beer," Bob slurred, "only types of good." He lay back in his wisdom and fell fast asleep.

We got on with our work and through constant talking it was soon apparent we had returned with a different outlook on life—more focussed. Another month and who knew what the future would bring.

It was 0100hrs as the lights were going out. I took a while to sleep as my mind was all over the place. Reflecting on the weekend, I felt sad at leaving the family but was laughing at Dad, and the "young wives" run by Mum. A very eventful weekend, I remembered lots of faces of the many people I'd met, but eventually sleep took over.

WEEK 13

MONDAY, DAY 82
"HANDS OFF COCKS...MOVE IT!"

My mind took a short while to process what was happening as the light flicking machine began and reality dawned slowly. I heard Alex say, "What the fuck was that?"

With all the speed of a frog with a brick tied to his leg, I hopped out of bed. I passed Bob, who was on the edge of his bed with his head in his hands, practicing some kind of medieval groan.

I was halfway through shaving when Bob came in looking rough, eyes on dipped beam, so we all made as much noise as we could.

He went into a toilet stall and we banged on the door wishing him a good morning. The best he offered was, "Fuck awf 'awa' ye's lousy basterts." (Go away, but emphasised) in his broad Scottish accent, so we did it a bit more. We swung straight into our regular routine and after breakfast stood by our beds at 0759hrs waiting for God.

"Stand by your beds."

And we definitely knew we were back. Not having seen him for three days was washed away in a split second, as he marched into the room. "Morton, what's on routine orders?"

Ginger stared at him blankly.

"You've not read them, have you?"

"I didn't see them when I came from breakfast, Corporal of Horse," Ginger stammered out.

"Are you suggesting that I have only just put them up?"

"Not for a minute, Corporal of Horse."

"All of you go and read them."

We rushed down, closely followed by the other three rooms. It was bedlam, as all twenty-seven of us had failed to see them on our way up from breakfast. It seemed the routine-orders fairy had waved a wand and made them magically appear. No great shocks: four more weeks of this then onwards and upwards.

Monday —Road Run—Gym—Drill
Tuesday —In Park—Swords Arrive
Wednesday —Gym—Sword Etiquette
Thursday —Sword Drills
Friday. —Gym—Drills
All Subject to Change.
No Phone Calls This Week.

Nothing much had changed, except the excitement over sword drills. The phone calls had been mentioned before we went home, so no shock there.

Drill was still on the cards today, but not first thing. As soon as we got back upstairs, we heard, "You look half asleep; we will run it off."

By 0830hrs we were in coveralls and web belts jogging through what was a damp and chilly morning around the barracks. There were only Corporals Miles and Fletcher, who must have been on a weekend throat massage course as they never stopped shouting.

"Green, look lively, you must have put on weight."

"No Corporal I don't think I've put—"

"You don't fucking think, I do, and that was not a question so shut up."

I did.

"Backhouse, that had better be a grimace not a silly grin."

"No Corporal, it's not a—"

"That's an observation not a question, shut up."

He did.

"Jackson, you look as if you are chewing a wasp."

"No Corporal, I was going to—"

That was not a question it was a remark but answer it."

"Are wasps still asleep, Corporal?"

"You are not a wasp, Jackson, you are a dozy prick."

"No Corporal, I was going to say—"

"That's an observation not a question, shut up."

And he did.

For the next hour we jogged gently around, as the mobile lesson in the English language carried on.

We went upstairs and changed for drill. Bob looked a bit ashen but insisted he was alright. We had a push and pull inspection from Tighe who had returned, tugging tunics and rearranging caps just to let us know who is boss, and then we went into a drill session.

It was a good hour and went really well until the last few minutes. We had been standing at attention for at least two minutes when Corporal of Horse Tighe shouted, "Right turn."

There was a wonderful, crisp, sharp crack as twenty-six pairs of boots hit the parade ground in unison, followed by a single one a split second later.

"What is that McCann, a fucking full stop?"

Bob stayed silent.

"Are you fucking deaf?" filled his left ear.

"Pardon Corporal of Horse," Bob said innocently, which caused a few of us to inwardly laugh, but completely went over Tighe's head, as he was busy giving Bob a full dictionary definition of a wanker. It turned into a bollocking for all.

"That was crap, any more of it and some of you will get another home visit permanently. Be back here at 1305hrs ready for the gym.

We went straight to lunch and Bob still looked a bit rough, but said he just needed a good meal and he would be fine. He told us he was thinking about the weekend and must have had a brain fart.

Ginger was laughing. "That's assuming you have a brain, which is a bit of a stretch."

We left him alone after this, as he was having a rough start to the day.

We ran across to the gym, feeling glad to be indoors, as the morning had been a windy and damp one. Such was our programming that even after a weekend off, we went immediately into our demented wind-milling.

We got into our three groups and received a quick welcome back from Corporal Kelly, who told us they would expect more effort for the last month, and then promptly set about proving it. There was one group on the wall bars, one on mats and the other jogging around doing backward running and leg stretching exercises. We started off at a fairly quick pace, which soon had us breathing for two.

There was a brief respite as we got out the complete circuit with the vaulting horse at full height. This was looking ominous.

Group one went off with five men, then a minute later the other four.

"Those of you not on the circuit yet, encourage the ones that are."

This was not for long as the first four of us in group two began and it did not take long to realise this was a tough workout.

As each minute passed, there was less encouragement, and more sounds of exertion and grunting, followed by cursing. It seemed at one point that there were bodies everywhere.

The whole gym was alive with writhing, grunting bodies urged on by shouts of "Gimme, gimme more, faster" coming from all areas of the gym. The air was full of the smell of sweat, with little puddles forming on mats. Then suddenly it was over. We began pulling air from another universe and sounding like an orchestra wind section warming up.

We were slowly recovering when Bob ran towards the door. I looked up to see him puking all over the floor, then sinking to his knees to get the last bits up. Al Hopkins and Corporal Kelly immediately ran to him.

Corporal Kelly said, "When you've finished McCann, clean this up, and then come and see me." Al went to help him and Corporal Kelly shouted, "No, his fucking mess, he cleans it."

Bob wobbled off to get a bucket and mop, plus loads of paper, then spent another five minutes cleaning the floor, while trying a few more dry heaves into the bucket. It was not long after this that we all went for a shower and then over to lunch, but Bob was kept back to see Corporal Kelly.

When Bob arrived, he had improved a lot to only looking bloody awful. He came and sat down with a bowl of soup and a slice of bread, plus a large, cold drink, and could hardly breathe as we gathered round to hear what he had to say.

He told us that he was standing in front of the table and Corporal Kelly sat facing him. Kelly looked him up and down for what seemed a lifetime, and Bob thought, *Here goes, I'm right in the shit now.*

Corporal Kelly pushed his chair back and eventually said, "Are you feeling better now McCann?"

"Yes, I need to apologise for—"

Corporal Kelly cut in. "A word of advice McCann, the next time you go on the piss, eat some solid food. It looked like baby puke." He pulled his chair back up said, "Now fuck off and eat something."

"Is there anything solid in that soup?" Don asked him.

"Nae laddie, bairn steps for now."

We had just got back in the block and Corporal of Horse Tighe shouted,

"Dress for drill number-two uniform, we will sort out this morning's fuck up."

And soon we had fallen in ready to go.

These lighter evenings were good mainly but lent themselves to a longer day outside. We did over an hour's drill with a ton of left and right turns, then a march around some of the barrack roads, and back to where we began.

"Back upstairs, NAAFI still 1930hrs. Then I expect cleaning to carry on, until it is completely finished."

Everyone went to the NAAFI full of stories about the weekend, and all came to the same conclusion. We had seen some of the big picture, and on the whole people were much more open, friendly, and chatty than before. Our confidence and bull-shitting levels were also much improved.

Once we had been served, Alice and Jenny came over to chat, and were soon laughing about Bob's bad day.

Alice said, "Ah, that's why he had two pies," and by the time we left it was three. It was apparent that Bob was back to his usual self.

Keith saw Jenny talking to Bob and shouted, "Jenny does a man have to be sick to get attention in here?"

"Obviously not," Jenny replied, "Or you would never be alone."

Completely unphased, Keith looked at her saying, "I feel rough, can you stroke my forehead?"

Alex who was walking past said, "My pleasure," and smeared Keith's forehead with his cream cake. We were all roaring laughing as Keith calmly leaned back swiped a finger through it and said, "This is at least four days old."

Alice said, "Your mental age then," and the place erupted.

We returned and got cracking on boots, belts, and brasses plus plenty of ironing and washing shirts and collars, then got into room and block cleaning.

It was around 0100hrs before we settled down. Having had little sleep last night, we followed Bob's example of being asleep before getting fully into bed. Most of us didn't even put a bedside light on.

TUESDAY, DAY 83– WEDNESDAY, DAY 84
"HANDS OFF COCKS!"

B*loody hell, not again, you noisy pillock.* The lights were flashing and the voice was at high pitch. *Enough, this is the day you pay.* I leapt out of bed and realised that for the first time in weeks I felt stiff and sore. It was not a lot, but enough to get him off the hook.

As usual at breakfast we were hungry and noisy. The cook corporal, who was back after his long weekend spoke to Danny. "How did your weekend go, Cassius?"

"Too quick," said Danny.

A short while later the corporal came for a chat and was asked where Trooper Casey, the junior in the cookhouse was, as we hadn't seen him since we got back.

"He has joined the regiment in Cyprus; he had two days off and flew out yesterday," he told us.

It went quiet for a minute as we realised this would be our future soon, and how quickly our lives could change.

"Lucky bastard," Timmy said, and we all agreed.

Today at exactly 0745hrs we were back upstairs and waiting for inspection, but five minutes later, nothing.

Alex stood with his back to the door and said to Timmy, "I'll bet the pricks have forgotten inspection times."

A voice at the door said, "What pricks, Stay?"

Alex ran to the side of his bed, came to attention, turned, and saw Billy at the door.

"I'll nail you yet, arsehole," he yelled, as Billy smiled and saluted him.

At this moment Billy froze as a voice from the other end of the corridor shouted, "Where is that idiot, Jackson?"

Alex was down the room in a flash and threw Billy out of the door.

"He's here, Corporal of Horse."

Tighe shouted, "Get down here Jackson, why are you not ready for inspection, you bloody dimwit?"

Alex smiled. "Run along now, dead man," he said, enjoying seeing the biter bit.

We heard every word of his bollocking from our end of the corridor. In fact, I think all of Windsor must have heard it. Tighe must have been saving it up all weekend.

"This weekend must have shrunk your already tiny brains. Ten minutes on the square, ready for a run in the park."

It soon became obvious it was pre-arranged as the Bedford was waiting there with sandwiches and drinks.

We disembarked and went for a run led by Alex and Billy, as in Tighe's words, "You are both fools." An interesting pairing as Billy was a runner, but Alex was built more for the shot put.

We spent a pleasant morning going through a fairly moderate set of exercises and team games. At lunch time we had to run back to the Bedford along the damp path, and Alex kept on varying the pace.

Tighe said, "Stay, keep your timing with Jackson."

Billy turned to Alex. "Come on big boy, spread those tree trunks and keep up with m—" never finishing the sentence, as he put his foot on the edge of the path, and fell down the slope ending up under the hedgerow. Even the instructors couldn't stop laughing as a bedraggled and damp Billy got to his feet.

We ate our sandwiches and mentioned swords, but this was quickly taboo.

"After this morning's debacle, I wouldn't trust you with a nail file."

I guess that's a no, then.

The afternoon was similar to the morning, and eventually we jogged off back. It was only a half hour jog, but as we were passing a group of girls, John McGrath, seeing the "Peacock effect," asked one of them the time. She said, "Half-past four," and gave a huge, beaming smile. John completely lost his step and we all piled into the back of each other, while admiring the view.

In the evening, Corporal of Horse Tighe and Corporal Fletcher called in and seemed genuinely interested in our weekend off. Tighe went down the other end and talked to Jay and Pete. When they were on their way out we heard them laughing all the way downstairs.

As soon as we got in the NAAFI, Ginger asked Jay what it was all about.

"How was the weekend, Bird?" Tighe had asked him.

"Terrific Corporal of Horse, we had a really good time and his family were great."

"Did you go anywhere?"

"Yes," said Jay, and in a real cockney accent said, "Seeing as Jay is here let's go down the facking pub, and have a facking good sing-song."

"Was his mother there?" asked Tighe.

"That *was* his mother," said Jay, as Pete just shrugged his shoulders and smiled.

The next day was buzzing as after a morning in the gym we had lunch, and then went to the Lecture Room. There was a knock on the door and two troopers entered with a long box.

Tighe made a point of saying, "Are all twenty-nine sets there?"

We helped them to bring in the other boxes, emptied them, and put them back in their vehicle.

This opened a worrying question, why only twenty-nine sets?"

It got worse as Corporal Fletcher asked if he should issue them to all of us, and Corporal of Horse Tighe said, "Yes, at least we'll know where they are, and we'll sort it out in the next day or so."

We all received a sword and scabbard, a sword knot, long and short slings, and a pair of white gloves.

Then began the learning curve before we could touch it.

A history lesson on Pooleys of Sussex, who'd made it since 1892. A thirty-seven-inch single-edged blade weighing two pounds and four ounces. Grip is wood bound in fish skin and then copper wire. Scabbard is nickel-plated with a protective shoe, all made to the highest specifications. Now primarily a ceremonial sword. Only one regiment, the 1st Life Guards, had carried it into battle.

By the time we were back in the block, we were aware of the bravery of our predecessors, who had endured terrible conditions and fierce personal combat. Failure was not an option and loyalty to monarch and country was prized above all else.

As enjoyable as this was, there was still the nagging doubt about the sword sets. It did not seem to worry the instructors, as they carried on with how to clean them.

They constantly re-enforced not to touch them with bare fingers, to clean them with newspaper or tissue paper, and occasionally a light oil or a little Brasso.

"Any questions?"

"Yes, Corporal of Horse, I'm left-handed," said Tony Mahoney.

"Set it up on the right-hand side and see me tomorrow. Is that everything?" he said, grinning. "There must be something you want to ask me."

Arnold lit the blue touch paper. "Yes, Corporal of Horse, you said only twenty-nine sets were needed."

"What day is it today, Moore?"

"Wednesday, Corporal of Horse."

"No, you lame prick, the date? Anyone."

"April 1st, Corporal of Horse."

Then it dawned on us. April Fool's Day. *What a sick fuck, all that worry since lunch time, was your idea of a joke?*

There was a brief delay and then Corporal Fletcher stood up and said, "I would like to thank you all for your co-operation and hard work, and I wish you all the best in the future."

Corporal of Horse Tighe then informed us Corporal Fletcher was being promoted and going on a gunnery instructor's course. "I'm sure you all wish him well."

We applauded him and gave three cheers, partly due to his leaving, and mainly because he wouldn't need a sword set.

The day was getting better, and a total dog's bollocks event happened next.

Tighe said, "I also wish to inform you that Corporal Wheeler is leaving at the weekend to join The Life Guards in Cyprus. He will try to say goodbye, but we wish him well also.

The noise level grew to a crescendo, when we realised he didn't need a sword set either.

As soon as they left, it was like a carnival atmosphere that carried on into the NAAFI.

Afterwards, we gave the swords a good clean, and only put them in and out of the scabbard about fifty times.

It reminded me of when I was ten years old and went to stay with my Mum's brother, who after the war became a career naval officer. While I was there, Uncle Fred attended a ceremony in a Fleet Air Arm hangar in full dress, including his sword. Because of this, I assumed for years he must be royalty.

The rest of the evening passed off quietly, and I fell asleep thinking of the first sword drill tomorrow.

THURSDAY, DAY 85
"HANDS OFF COCKS ON WITH SOCKS AND GOOD LUCK TO YOU ALL!"

When the awakening mist had cleared, we realised that this was the last time we never saw Corporal Wheeler, and by the time we had adjusted to being human beings, he was gone.

We were feeling positive that this would be an easing in of swords day, as they lay gleaming on our beds.

Corporal of Horse Tighe arrived and stood between Timmy's and Bob's beds. "All of you show me your swords," he said.

I was just about to grab it when I heard a manic shout. "Green, touch that with your bare fingers, and I'll chop the bastards off."

Everyone else did a quick digital detour and put on their white gloves.

As we were changing soon after, we heard from Room Two, "Smith, touch that sword with your bare fingers—"

We looked at each other and smiled and all gave him the finger, very quietly of course.

At 0815hrs we were lined up in the downstairs corridor and shown how to march with a sword in the scabbard. Eventually we lined up outside the block and marched down into the open doors of the empty riding school arena.

While this was going on, Corporal Miles spent a large part of the morning with Tony, teaching him how to use his right hand. By lunch, Tony said he was feeling comfortable and within two days it was perfectly natural.

This was the way it had to be for the future. One man in a squad being left-handed, would have ruined the overall effect and spoiled the uniformity, meaning the man would have stuck out like a sore thumb (these puns).

For the next two days we spent hours on just getting the sword in and out of the scabbard and marching with it in and out of the scabbard.

We had a demonstration from Corporal of Horse Tighe on the various drills we would be learning: standing at ease, drawing swords and saluting, then the next two hours were spent on withdrawing the sword and how to hold it. It soon became obvious that he had made it look easy.

At first it was done very slowly in four stages just to get the sword out and into the 'carry' position.

One —left hand holds scabbard so top is slightly forward and right hand on the sword hilt.

Two —pull sword up level with shoulder, arm at right angle, tip still in scabbard.

Three —draw sword out of scabbard, keeping it close to the body. Twist and bring it round, so the hilt is five inches from the mouth and the sword vertical (recovery position), while straightening the scabbard to attention.

Four —into the carry position, which is upper right arm vertical, elbow into body, and lower arm at ninety degrees.

Both instructors were used at each stage. They went to each of us pulling fingers and hands into the correct place, then practice, practice, and more practice for the whole morning.

It was obvious why they had us well spread apart, as the third stage was the hardest. At first it was difficult to keep the sword anywhere near the body, after it left the scabbard.

It did pass the morning quickly, and when we were back in the block getting changed for lunch, we marvelled at how difficult it was to make something look easy.

The cooks were having a field day. All good-natured stuff, about lopping ears off and cutting ourselves, and the bravery of the instructors. For about five minutes we couldn't get a word in.

As soon as they eased off, Timmy said, "Wait until next week when we do bayonet drills."

We all perked up, as this was news to us.

"That's bloody scary," said one of the cooks. "I hope you are a long way from us, those things are bloody sharp."

A big smile and Timmy said, "No, we are coming over here to try and cut these fucking steaks."

"Touché," said the cook, and Bob asked him if that was a sword-type term.

"No that's a cooking term, at the weekend we will have Steak Touché."

The rest of the lunch went on as normal, daft and noisy.

By 1315hrs we were back in the riding school. We carried on for another hour, until they felt a bit more confident with us.

"Draw swords."

We did it at their timing, then after twenty minutes, at the correct timing.

On the very first attempt, a forage cap rolled at the feet of the front rank.

"What happened Pratley?"

"Cap fell off, Corporal of Horse."

"Tell him why, Allen."

A squeaky, wavering voice said, "I caught it with the tip of my sword Corporal of Horse."

"Lucky you didn't take his head off, you dozy prick. Tell him what he is Pratley."

Chris turned to Bill and shouted, "You're a dozy prick."

"Out here, both of you!" Their swords were handed to Corporal Wheeler.

"Right Pratley, punch him in the arm."

Chris seemed a bit unsure, but punched Bill hard in his arm.

"Fall back in, I do not want to see this happen again."

Agreed, I don't think we are too keen either.

It went well for the rest of the afternoon until we had about ten minutes left before evening meal. As we were doing probably the last return swords, the dreaded forage cap bug struck again.

Why is your cap on the floor, Jones?"

"Knocked it off with my sword, Corporal of Horse."

"Your own sword. In all your life, Corporal Miles have you ever known any fucking idiot chop his own ear off?"

"Only Van Gogh."

"Van who?" Tighe replied. "What kind of an idiot hits himself? Why did it happen Jones?"

"I think my arm was aching, Corporal of Horse."

"Jones, tell everyone why it happened."

There was a whisper.

"Louder."

"I'm a wanker."

"Correct, fall in."

We were marched back to the block, put our swords and bits on the beds, and went over for evening meal.

Later, halfway through NAAFI, we weren't sure whether Jenny was kidding when she said, "I thought I knew everyone, who's Van Gogh?"

I said, "Ask Pete. It's complicated, but he will explain it."

She looked at Pete saying, "No, it's ok, I don't really need to know."

We got into a good clean up and as the evening went on, the conversation got back to having free punches at each other, so we decided to practice rolling with the blows, and soon the whole block was enjoying the game.

It was going well until we heard Bill Allen shout at Arnold, "You fucking twat," and he went at him like something demented. He dived at him and they hit the floor with a mighty crash, and immediately everyone was all over them, getting them apart. There was blood coming from Bill's nose.

He was still straining to get at Arnold who said, "It was your fault, you were supposed to move your head back."

This infuriated Bill even more and he tried to lash out again. It was a full minute of restraining him until he was taken to the washroom, where he was calmed down, and his nose plugged up.

We kept him there until he seemed calmer.

Arnold came in and apologised saying, "I'm sorry Bill, it was a pure accident, I thought you would move."

Bill shook Arnold's hand telling him, "You are still a prick," but the moment was over. Bill mumbled something else, but the cotton wool stuffed up his nose was affecting his speech.

I gave Don his gear back somewhere after midnight. We had a chat about how the tempo was building up a bit, which may have helped towards the earlier incident.

When I eventually got back to the room, everyone was either in bed or getting in bed, and only bedside lights were on. I heard Ginger say, "I don't want to appear ignorant, but would you call this Van Gogh a really famous painter?"

"Call him whatever you like, he probably wouldn't hear you," Bob told him.

FRIDAY, DAY 86
"RISE AND SHINE—MOVE IT"

This was Corporal Miles at his civilised best, no light switch fandango, and by the time we got in the washrooms the conversation was centred on the fact that both the "hands off cocks" guys had gone, so it would be less of a noisy awakening from today.

That being said, not much more would change, as the mornings were speeding up.

"Stand by your beds." Tighe hit the room like a tornado. His riding whip was set on super twitch, and within five minutes it had flicked over clothing, shaving brushes, and soap containers, all with little moans of disgust and pulling back as if he would catch something. The whole outlook of the room was transformed.

It soon became apparent that Bob was today's 'educational recipient' as Tighe picked up his sword knot. "There's a crack line here, McCann." He pointed in the general area of Bob's sword knot.

Bob raised his eyebrows and said, "I think it must be a hair, Corporal of Horse," but he had opened the door to instructor apoplexy.

"This is a crack line here." Tighe bent the knot backwards and forwards. "Now can you see it?"

Bob got the message, staying silent.

The gym was not as fearsome now as we knew it had improved us no end, and we expected to push ourselves a bit more.

Once we were good and warmed up out came the circuit. We went off in threes. The circuits were hectic and physically hard.

By the end of one, we often felt that dying was a reasonable option, but after a minute or two of cursing and gasping we would slowly recover.

It was around 1015hrs when we got back in the block to change for drill.

We practised quick march/slow march. This was made more difficult by being stopped and started and made to stand on one foot while they moved around, making sure knees were at ninety degrees, or toes were pointing downwards correctly.

It looked more like a field sobriety test than a drill movement.

The morning was a good one as we had no cockups. Most of the problems were instructor induced to see how we would react. As our eardrums were still intact, things must have gone well.

To stop us getting too cocky we were told, "Be back out at 1315hrs in number-two uniforms and sword fittings. I will be inspecting all swords and attachments." Tighe stared directly at Bob.

When we got upstairs, Bob was a bit down and said he would have to miss lunch. I told him not to worry as I had a plan. I lightly removed crack junction, and we all went over to lunch.

When we returned, I gave Bob mine and I took his, as I never had a problem with my belt and attachments, so probably wouldn't get the close-up treatment.

"No, I can't take yours, Jimmy," Bob said, as he fitted it to his sword, "I owe you for this." He went from looking like he needed a sick bag, to smiling in one second.

We fell in and then marched over to the riding school.

Corporal of Horse Tighe began his inspection and as Bob was behind me, I didn't know what was happening until I heard Tighe say, "Did you do this during lunch time, McCann?"

"Yes, Corporal of Horse."

There was a long loud, "Mmmmmm," from Tighe. "Improved, needs more work."

The next hour was spent practising draw and return swords, from attention to the carry position and return to scabbard. This was all about timing and hand and finger positions, and a lot of confidence in keeping the sword close to the body.

Mid-afternoon and we went outside for a break. Bob walked past, all smiles, and said quietly, "Your knot looks a bit ropey, needs more work."

I was talking to Timmy at the time, and we both burst out laughing.

"Something you would like to share, Green?"

I said the first thing that came into my head. "I was wondering how you mount a horse with haemorrhoids, Corporal of Horse."

He looked at us almost despairingly saying, "Our horses do not have haemorrhoids, they are thoroughbreds."

I was going to say I meant us, but he was enjoying his reply, and I was pleased to have got the moment over with.

We viewed the afternoon as a success and so must have they, as it was decided we would march back.

"I think I can expose you to any unseen eyes by now."

At "Quick march" we hitched the scabbard forward and marched up the road, round the back of a block and onto the square. We did a bit of wheeling around the square and were doing return swords prior to being dismissed, when suddenly a cap rolled along the floor, and the intake of breath was deafening.

"Stand still, McGrath, you fucking half-wit!" By now Tighe's head was on John's shoulder. "You do not have to prove you are a total prick, the whole world can see it. Get out front and tell us all how it happened."

John faced us, looking as if the floor opening up would be a blessing. "It seemed to fly off when I turned my head, Corporal of Horse."

"Give your sword to Corporal Miles. After thirteen weeks here you still can't put a fucking cap on your head. You want to do things by yourself, punch yourself in your stupid head."

With no further prompting John swung his right arm in a big semi-circle. Then last night's training came in and he staggered sideways for about four paces and shook his head, like a very under-rehearsed music hall act.

We had gone in a second from total fear for John's safety, to having great difficulty holding in laughter.

Tighe looked up to the sky and said, "Whatever it was, I will never do it again." He looked at us and shouted, "For fuck's sake, dismiss."

We rushed into the block laughing, as we became aware of the instructors walking off, pretending to stagger.

In the NAAFI the chat was mainly based around John's terrific bollocking, and he joined in quite happily as he had come out of the last session unscathed. He showed the ladies how it worked, and we found it was almost impossible to hit yourself hard in the head.

On our way in we stopped and read Routine Orders, which had appeared while we were in the NAAFI.

It could have been quickly written as guard duties and more of the same, but would probably change a lot as the week went on. The guard duties were taken in our stride now, as we had completed two, so no great worry there.

At the first chance I got, I spoke with Timmy, and we agreed that the "Hound" theme should be resurrected.

As the evening wore on, a competition was breaking out to see who could do the most elaborate and realistic stagger and head clearing shake. It was a noisy period between the applause and piss taking.

It took a while to settle down, as we chatted about the increase in physical work, and sword drills.

SATURDAY, DAY 87–SUNDAY, DAY 88
"GET YOUR BODIES OUT OF YOUR PITS —LIE-IN IS OVER"

This was a strange voice with a strange accent—must be a guard NCO, letting the instructors have a lie-in. As usual, we were up and moving at the speed of three-legged tortoises. Everyone seemed to be in good humour, though, having had a lie-in.

We were chatting at the sinks, when Dave came in and tried all the toilet doors, but there was someone in them. He began to get desperate. "Hurry up, I'm in agony here."

There was total silence from the toilets, although we were laughing at Dave's cork screwing attempt at rock n' roll.

Suddenly Big Hippo's head appeared over the top of the door totally deadpan saying, "I'll be out in five minutes." Then Paul Smith did the same in the next one. Tom Peter's head appeared and Tom said, "Sorry Dave, a bit constipated this morning."

Dave was red faced and holding his stomach as two doors opened simultaneously and they came out. Dave moved to the nearest as if he had an apple between his knees, and as he got there Timmy ran in and locked the door.

This was now or never. Dave dropped his towel as Tom came out and he leapt into the toilet. Before he could close the toilet door, he exploded into the toilet with a huge sigh of relief that must have been heard all over the barracks. He slammed the door saying, "Don't any of you bastards throw any water over."

What he couldn't see was they had hidden the toilet rolls behind their backs.

"You bastards, where's the bog paper?" Six toilet rolls were lobbed over the top.

The laughter got louder as we heard Dave cursing, and Ginger shouting, "It's ok, you've plenty of time to clean up; breakfast isn't until 0730hrs. If you've filled that one the others are empty now."

There was no inspection today, so beds and lockers were soon in the middle of rooms and the Bumper wheeled out. At 0945hrs, Corporal Miles came in, and after pointing out a pile of "necessary" work he left, but nothing was upended or air mailed, so we saw it as a success.

The weekend was more of a drill period than block cleaning, plus a run in the park.

The run was memorable, not for the run itself, but our return to barracks.

"Everyone, shower now."

We ran to the showers with towels round our waists.

"Oh, by the way, the hot water is off."

It was like being hit with a wet fish; it wasn't just cold, it was freezing. It started a fuck fest of cursing and swearing, between gasping for air and big body shudders. We were definitely wide awake now.

The squad was drilling all morning to allow us to go in pairs for a hair trim, so there was a constant movement back and forth. I was first to go with Keith, and on our return Tighe was drilling the squad on the far side of the square, and shouted, "Squad halt."

Keith and I did a smart halt and Tighe came marching across saying, "What are you two clowns doing here, do I have body odour?"

Seeing as you ask, yes you do. And your breath smells, and you are a prick.

"I was halting the squad so that you pair of idiots could join them."

Try telling us first then, for crying out loud.

This came across as "Sorry, Corporal of Horse, I misunderstood." It calmed down after this, as everyone else had been told after we left.

In the afternoon we reverted to sword drill. We practiced "draw swords," with just a nod of the head from the right marker. Initially, because of their pulling and pushing us around, our view was getting obscured. Instead of a crisp, sharp crack it was more like "drawing a pair of bloody curtains together."

"Walters, why are you two days behind the rest?"

"Corporal Miles was—" Then he stopped as he was going to say, "In the way."

"Finish it," said Tighe.

"Was helping someone perfect his movements, Corporal of Horse."

We were totally impressed with Joe's quick reply, as was Corporal of Horse Tighe, who could only say, "I wish you could think that fast normally."

The block was gleaming after lunch on Sunday. The block had been cleaned so often it could be designated a place of outstanding blood, sweat and tears with no bit of dust bigger than a flea's left ball. There was a smell of polish everywhere, and it was a happy bunch of recruits who went to lunch.

I sat on a separate table to Timmy and said to him, "I don't care what they say, I'm not going near that rear gate."

"Nor me," said Timmy, "Going near it at any time gives me the willies."

"And me," chimed in Bob, and feigned a shiver.

After Bob's toilet antics this morning, the cooks had got him a table near the toilet door with a newspaper and a toilet roll on it, but he wouldn't sit there. He probably wished he had, as the guys who sat there kept calling out to him, "Hey Bob have you seen this newspaper? It says recruit changes his name to Dai o'Reah."

We fell in on our guard duty with two new NCOs. I was the spare man and Timmy was first stag on patrol. The corporal asked me what I did after I'd helped the duty driver, and I told him that I would go with the patrol man on the midnight stag.

At midnight we went off to build on the "Hound." As we approached the area, I said to Timmy, "Are we checking the back gate?"

"What do you think?"

"I think we've done such a fucking good job of this rumour, we've screwed ourselves up."

As we got near, I picked up a stone about the size of a half house brick. I threw it into the bushes causing a rustling sound followed by a loud thud as it hit a tree trunk.

I looked around and Timmy was ten feet back up the road saying, "What the fuck was that?"

"Half a house brick."

When we calmed down Timmy said, "It sounds locked to me," and we walked off laughing.

We settled on it being not much bigger than three weeks ago, but when I threw the stone there was an awful, ungodly smell.

This would improve in the cookhouse tomorrow.

WEEK 14

MONDAY, DAY 89
BLOODY WELL EXECUTED

I had only been back about five minutes when I heard a commotion down the other end. Alex had apparently asked if he could give the guys their wake-up call, and as soon as he switched on the lights, he ran to Billy's bed again, and tipped him onto the floor.

All I heard was Billy shouting, "You stupid arsehole," as the guard NCO left to look up the definition of insanity.

I was in the washroom by the time they all came in, and you could tell which room was which, just by who was talking. People who are awake make so more noise than those trying to wake up. This especially applied to Dave, who went straight into the toilet where he brought a whole new meaning to 'regular soldier.'

"Stand by your beds." Tighe came in the room, went straight to Keith, and said, "Did you clean those boots ready for inspection this morning?"

"We were on guard last night Corporal of Horse."

"I couldn't give a shit about last night, it's a yes or no."

Miserable shite house, you know he couldn't possibly have done it.

Keith said, "No Corporal of Horse, sir," almost resigned to his fate.

"The whole room will parade in the foyer tonight at 1915hrs with two pairs of boots for inspection." Then proceeded to upend bed packs individually, saying, "Change your sheets," and we couldn't get out fast enough.

"Square, five minutes, sword drills."

Six minutes later, the body pushing and pulling was underway, and others were told to show up gear at 1915hrs as well. Only a handful remained unscathed.

No time to worry now, as we marched across to the riding school for another session of sword drills. They still didn't trust us enough to risk a public display, and not much farther down the line we began to see why.

For now, we felt it was going ok. A quick break, then we had to watch four marching past us. One of us would have to give constructive criticism, which never bodes well, and it didn't this time. We had been doing it for about ten minutes.

"Green, observations."

Oh shit, that bit of straw blowing past had caught my eye and my name bought me back with a jolt. All I could think of was, "A well-executed drill, Corporal of Horse."

The flood gates opened. "Well executed, fucking well executed, you should be executed, you blind pillock. Look at his thumb position."

Look at his thumb position? He's so far away I can barely see, him let alone his thumb.

"Yes, Corporal of Horse I can see it now."

"You are not relaxing at this stage, re-focus, or I will do it for you."

"Atten-shun, carry swords, quick march."

Off we went on a fifteen-minute march around the barracks ending outside the block.

"Upstairs, remove swords, back here in three minutes."

We fell in on the square and realised that he had missed a little word off and had meant to say, 'I will re-focus you *now*, as we set off at a quick pace. Lots of mark time, then marching around the square as they stood in the middle, turning in a small circle. Sometimes they appeared to be miles away, then as if by magic, were on our shoulders.

"I'm fucking watching you."

I hope so, you pair of wankers, I would hate to think this was just a private show. At 1215hrs I don't know who was more screwed up, us or them. I do really, and it wasn't them.

"Back here with swords at 1305hrs."

There must have been a smell of burning rubber as we raced off the square.

At lunch Timmy and me were on the next table to Paul Smith and Tony Mahoney, who were on guard tonight. Behind them sat Keith and Ginger. I said loudly to Timmy, "I'm glad we're not on guard again tonight," but only half looking at Tony.

Tony asked, "Why, what happened?"

Timmy butted in. "Jimmy threw a brick into the bushes as we got near the gate. There was a huge rustling sound, then a bloody awful smell like a skunk filled the air."

Keith, the great disbeliever said "Bollocks."

I looked at him directly and said, "You went and checked the gate last night?"

"Not quite, you said it sounded locked, and I believed you."

"Oh, so you didn't," Timmy said.

Keith shrugged and carried on eating.

Timmy looked at me. "I don't blame him, Jimmy, there's no way I'd go near there on my own."

Knowing Room Two only had six men, I shook my head in disbelief that anyone alone would even consider it.

Soon we were out on the square and spent two hours on non-stop drilling from draw swords to quick and slow marching, slope arms and saluting. By the time we stopped at 1520hrs, we were all drilled out, and stone deaf.

"Fall in here at 1530hrs, combat trousers and pullovers."

As soon as we fell in, we were marched across to the Lecture Room and saw the young NCO from last night's guard. We were seated, and Corporal Miles introduced him as Corporal Nicholson, fresh back from Cyprus, at which point he took over.

He was a tall, fairly rugged-looking character, with very dark hair cut short, and piercing blue eyes, that always seemed to be smiling.

As time passed, he showed an unlimited amount of patience. His turnout was immaculate, and he was very interesting to listen to, as he explained his career. He started with being a recruit and outlined his ambitions and achievements, all in a very unassuming way. He talked about the United Nations Peace Keeping force in Cyprus.

He discussed the troop set ups, and how the vehicles were ready for the role, and that they could electrify them, if in heavy crowd situations. By question time he had sold us on our chosen careers.

After lots of questions Corporal Miles said, "One last question. Backhouse?"

This caught Jack by surprise, and he blurted out, "Is it very dangerous in Cyprus?"

The corporal started laughing as he looked at Alex and said, "Not as dangerous as letting you lot wake each other up in a morning." This was a great finish to a good afternoon, and we all stood up and applauded him.

As soon as we got back, Room Two started to get ready. We gave them a collar strangulation and brush down, and they went to the foyer.

The guys got stuck into their gear, and of course there was no inspection.

I went over to the phone for 1800hrs. It was a terrific fifteen minutes and Mum and I talked about the weekend at home, sword drills, and today's lecture. She couldn't wait to proudly tell me that the girls at the young wives had talked to her about me being a smart and confident young man, which made us both feel good.

In the NAAFI, Keith was sniffing around, and as Jenny was clearing some bits from a table he asked if she'd missed him last night.

"Yes," she said. "Like missing smallpox when it has cleared up."

Keith looked forlorn. "Jenny you are breaking my heart."

He looked amazed as she said, "Up a bit, it's between your shoulder and chin I'll break, if you go on."

Alice shouted across, "Atta girl," and Keith went quiet for the rest of the night.

TUESDAY, DAY 90
"COME ON, YOU LAZY TARTS. GET YOUR SWEATY BODIES OUT OF THOSE PITS"

Shite, Room Two has caught it now. Even the normally quiet Joe Walters is at it, sounding as if he has something rammed up his arse, and he may well have soon.

We were in the washroom when Dave and Bob shuffled in doing the new version of the tortoise and the hare, namely the tortoise and the tortoise, heading for the only free sink. Bob won by a hare's breath.

On the way to breakfast we heard Paul Smith had been on the midnight stag, so over breakfast we asked him if he had checked the back gate.

"Yes, no problems," he said and carried on eating, which shut us up for now and soon we were back in the block.

"Stand by your beds."

Now here's a new approach. He entered the room slowly, looked around, went next door and did the same, then came back into the corridor and yelled, "Get in the washrooms now."

We sprinted in with a distinct feeling of *WTF*. My mind was racing as I thought, has the roof collapsed? A flood, toilet bunged up? No, according to Tighe much worse.

"Look at *this*," he said pointing to a sliding door catch. Most of us had difficulty seeing the door catch let alone, *this*. We were made to look at it in turn.

"More, why?"

Timmy looked completely baffled. "Why what, Corporal of Horse sir?

Kaboom. "You want to take the piss? I'll show you how. Downstairs for drill in three minutes."

It was a hell of a rush and trying to get the collar on was sheer hell, and I swear my Adam's apple ended up under my left ear.

"Too slow. Swords, back in three minutes."

We raced upstairs put on swords and ran back.

"Three minutes and five seconds, back upstairs, remove swords and back here in three minutes."

We sprinted upstairs pushing and falling over each other, but this time were back very fast and fell in.

"You like to take the piss, that was three minutes and four seconds. Get upstairs, swords on, back here in three minutes."

I heard a gasp of, "You twat," and Tighe said, "Do you have a problem, Bell?"

"No Corporal of Horse, I was just asking what was that."

It didn't matter, as Tighe was already chasing up someone else. Twice more up and down then he said, "Change into gym kit."

We had realised a long time ago that if one of us was singled out, it could be any one of us. We had long since stopped the blame game, knowing the best outcome was to suck it up, and get on with it.

Soon we were in the house of correction doing our wild warm ups, not that we needed to warm up.

The session was like most of the others in the gym, starting off slowly and building up as the morning went on; it would peak in the middle and then a long warm down.

For the first hour it was a good easy pace in our three teams doing the usual wall bars, mats, medicine balls, and jogging around the gym with an occasional sprint thrown in. Nothing too exhausting, followed by a ten-minute break.

Then, as if a switch had been thrown, they were all tiptoes and tongues, as they set us off again.

We watched Team One set off led by Al, who was going to do his mat work at the end to allow the PTIs full freedom to get amongst us.

"Team Two, first three."

Off we went and right from square one it was tough going—everything was faster or there was more of it. The PTIs were living up to their names, it was all "Gimme another," echoing all over the gym; Ticker complaining, "That's not correct do it again, another," and Jeeves, "Hurry up I can't wait all day."

I was hanging on the wall bars doing knee bends and straining for "Gimme another," and I thought my stomach muscles were going to burst.

The first vault was good, followed by forward rolls, then straight round to the beam for pull-ups. "Gimme another." I thought my arm muscles were on fire. A sprint the length of the gym and then the ropes. Lots of agony at the top, we had to shout "ceiling" and wait until called down, but after three shouts I thought fuck it, and came down.

I reached the floor.

"Green, go back up until we hear you."

Shit, this is painful, but I eventually reached the ceiling. At the fourth shout Jones looked up, smiled, and said, "No need to shout we're not deaf."

My answer was absolutely unprintable.

By the time I was on the floor doing more mat work, it was a relief to do sit-ups. Another run back to the vaulting horse and harder this time as I only just cleared it, then forward rolls on my aching legs and back to a mat to do press-ups.

Just as I thought I was finished with them, there was Corporal Thomas alongside doing press-ups and staring at me. "Another."

I creaked and strained, sweat running off my face.

"Another."

Shit, you bastard, why don't you fuck off.

"Good, well done, move on."

I reached the last mat, and my body was doing its best to disown me. As I was doing a medicine ball lift, I saw Ding Dong let go of a rope from about six or seven feet and hit the mat with a thud. Corporal Thomas ran across as Corporal Kelly's sympathetic voice shouted out what by now could be our slogan. "If he's ok, start him running again, if not, tread him into the floor."

While this was going on, I ran and flopped down on the finishing area mats, and for around a minute hovered between life and death. As soon as we were feeling fit enough, we put all the circuit away and cleared the gym floor.

A mat with a medicine ball on it was placed in the middle of the gym, and we formed two teams. One team had to surround the ball, the other had to get it to the top or bottom end of the gym. The main rule being that there were no rules. The whole thing was designed to give us a higher class of bruising. It was a brawl really.

It was around 1150hrs when we had a kind of debrief, which was mainly to tell us there would be a final assessment next week, and it was not too late to fail.

When we sat down to eat, Ding Dong got touchy about the ribbing he was getting about his fall from the ropes. It had left him with a sore arse, and an even sorer disposition, almost like the old proverb in reverse "Pride comes after a fall."

Timmy and I decided to move on to setting Billy and Arnold up for tonight. They were on a table between us and Paul Smith. Billy said Paul had been to check the gate last night, no problems, so it was a load of bullshit.

Timmy shouted to Paul, "What stag were you on last night?"

"The first one."

"Oh, so you went down after midnight," Timmy replied.

"Well, no, I did it about 1900hrs."

"During daylight hours," said Timmy, giving Billy and Arnold a knowing nod of the head.

It was a hard afternoon with only two short breaks and constant movement, and by the time evening meal arrived, we were more than ready for a longer break. As we had overrun, it was a rush to get back and get Room Three ready to go on guard.

There was more often than not someone in front of the mirror making sure that positioning was correct and trying to make some of the moves more instinctive, but the spectacle of sword drill in plimsolls and underwear kind of took away the effect.

By 1930hrs most of us were in the NAAFI laughing about Ding Dong's, "fall from grace." About 2000hrs Ding Dong appeared and sat giving us the finger with each bite of his pie, as we joked with him. Eventually we stopped as he just sat quietly, seemingly in his own world.

I was marching back with Timmy when we saw Jim Jones, who was on the middle stag, and I asked him if he had checked the rear gate.

"No, but Billy did it earlier."

"Right, so you are doing it early morning."

We knew from the laugh he gave as he walked off, it wasn't going to happen.

It was back to carrying on with various work, and most of us did the floors and got them out of the way. Around 2230hrs we were back sitting in a group in the cleaning room. Someone mentioned jokingly about Ding Dong having a heavy fall onto his "most attractive feature."

This led to a whole raft of jokes.

"Would he need to see a brain surgeon for anal disfunction, as that's where his brains are?"

"He'll need an X-ray to see if his head's up his arse."

Thankfully Ding Dong was at the other end of the floor.

We fooled about for a while, so I made an impromptu story up. "You may remember in the gym I got a wallop in the nuts and there was a lot of swelling, and enough pain to have killed a normal man. I was thinking about going to the doc tomorrow to see if I could get rid of the pain, but keep the swelling." This effectively killed off any further conversation.

WEDNESDAY, DAY 91
THE FINAL BELL

This was probably the strangest and most unusual day to date, but it began just like any other.

We were out on the square with Corporal of Horse Tighe and Corporal Miles doing sword drills, when after an hour Corporal of Horse Tighe left us with Corporal Miles, who drilled us until about 1040hrs and then told us to be ready for Pay Parade at 1055hrs.

As we ran into the block, Captain Forbes-Hart was already in the foyer with Corporal of Horse Tighe, and they were deep in conversation. We lined up in the corridor at 1055hrs. I was standing next to Jay and he whispered that Corporal of Horse Tighe had gone off with Ding Dong.

"Why?"

"Fuck knows," replied Jay, "All very hush-hush."

By the time the pay officers were behind the tables, Corporal of Horse Tighe was back with Ding Dong, and the Pay Parade went off without a hitch. We must be improving as Tiber was no longer in a corner twitching at every move.

We did notice that Ding Dong went off with Tighe again, but had no time to think about it, as we changed into combat trousers and pullovers and went for a run around the barracks.

At lunch, Ding Dong was a hot topic for missing a complete session. No one in his room had much of an idea what was happening, but suspected the fall on his backside was behind it. (No pun intended).

As soon as we got into the block, Captain Forbes-Hart was in the foyer, and then we heard Corporal Miles's voice telling us to fall in upstairs. We knew now that something big was in the air—Captain Forbes-Hart and a corridor line-up were for special occasions.

There is nothing like getting to the point immediately. Captain Forbes-Hart said, "As from now, Trooper Bell has exercised his right to leave the army."

The silence said it all, as none of us had seen this coming. After a short halt for it to sink in, the captain carried on. "We fully respect his wishes, and his resolve in the way he has handled this. He would like to say goodbye to you all."

As he said this, Corporal of Horse Tighe appeared with Ding Dong dressed in civvies, and he looked very different than we were used to seeing him. He was looking very emotional and seemed to be going to speak, but it was too much, and he came and shook hands with every one of us. We were all still in shock, and most of us could only wish him good luck, as we shook his hand.

Forbes-Hart handed over to Corporal of Horse Tighe and left.

Corporal Miles went with Ding Dong, and the guys from his room put his army gear back into stores and took his empty bed and locker downstairs. Corporal Miles went off with him to the Orderly Room, and Corporal of Horse Tighe took us to the Lecture Room for an update on what had happened.

It was very different from the others who had gone, and he wanted to clear the air. He explained that Trooper Bell had spoken to him on the Monday we returned saying he felt this might not be the life for him. They'd had a lengthy chat and eventually he agreed to give it another week. If he still felt the same then they would discuss it further, but he was asked not to discuss it with anyone.

He had been approached by Bell yesterday and had arranged for him to speak to Captain Forbes-Hart this morning, before Pay Parade.

Bell had spoken to his father on the phone last night, and he told Forbes-Hart his decision to leave was final. During this morning's discussion with Captain Forbes-Hart, his father was also involved again.

After this discussion, due to a unique set of circumstances, it was deemed in the best interests of all concerned to allow him to leave.

The silence was broken by Corporal Miles entering the room and whispering in Tighe's ear. Tighe said, "Recruit Bell has left with our best wishes—anyone else will not. Corporal Miles, take them back to the block, and out on the square in fifteen minutes, dressed for sword drill."

We marched back, changed, and then out onto the square. Tighe was already there.

We were not even remotely understanding the logic as we began a non-stop two-hour drill session. Once more it was almost manic, giving us no time to dwell on anything. For them it was probably therapeutic, being able to unload their frustrations.

We took pride in ourselves for not showing any signs that they had got through to us. Just listen and when ordered, do it. This was all part of the greater scheme of obeying orders, though for us at this time it was also survival.

By the time the session was over we felt physically and mentally drained.

The cooks, like all of us, were surprised by Ding Dong leaving. He had done a tremendous job of keeping it quiet, and we had thought he was in it for the long haul.

We went back and Room Three helped Room Four to get ready to go on guard, mopped out their room, and closed the door. As Don put it, "It was a bit like closing the door on Ding Dong."

At 1930hrs we were running down to the NAAFI through the drizzle. It always amazed me how Alice and Jenny seemed to know when anything big had gone on. When the rush had died down, they came around and asked about Ding Dong.

"Yes, it's true," Jay told them, "He left just after lunch today, and surprised all of us."

Alice asked if we knew why.

No, was the reply, but we were told it was a unique situation.

Alice said, "What does that mean, unique?"

"It means kind of one off," Tom Peters told her.

Alice said, "I know that." If looks could kill Tom was already underground. "I mean in his case."

To diffuse the situation Jenny asked what his name was.

"Bell," laughed Don, and already Jenny was dragged in.

"I know that. Jesus it's like pulling teeth, I mean his Christian name," she said as she glared at Don.

There was a brief silence as we looked at each other blankly, and then Bull said, "Ding." Alice and Jenny walked away, shaking their heads.

We were reasonably early in bed and strangely subdued, listening to the wind outside and thankful that Room Four was out there and not us. It had been quiet for some minutes when Keith suddenly said, "I wonder if Ding is donging someone tonight?"

A voice replied, "Goodnight o' cess-pit brain," and we turned out the lights.

THURSDAY, DAY 92
OBSTACLES

We had just finished in the washrooms when Corporal of Horse Tighe showed up.

"Early breakfast 0645hrs, foyer 0730hrs, combat kit, pullovers, and boots ready for a day in the field."

At least no inspection today, bed packs and straight over for breakfast. We knew it was going to be different as Corporals Thomas and Jones also appeared dressed for a day in the field.

Corporal of Horse Tighe took Corporal Jones and four recruits in his Land Rover and the rest of us piled in the back of the Bedford with Corporal Miles.

Miles was enjoying every minute of our not knowing where we were going, and whenever he was asked, just tapped his nose and smiled. We knew it would be a physical day but not where, but about twenty minutes after leaving Windsor, we heard Pete shout, "Facking Hell, we are going to facking Pirbright again. It's got to be that facking obstacle course."

There was a moment's silence as we all thought, *Holy shit,* broken by Miles's huge grin.

We drove through the barracks and followed a rough road out of the back before the Bedford stopped. We all jumped out and lined up in front of Corporal of Horse Tighe and Sergeant (Honorary Corporal of Horse) McMoody, plus our junior NCOs and a couple of theirs.

We received official confirmation that we were the lucky recipients of a thoroughly enjoyable visit, centred around the obstacle course.

"Thank you, Sergeant McMoody, we will certainly make the most of it," said Corporal of Horse Tighe.

Speak for yourself you conniving bastard, I will bet it's the royal "we" again.

"You will leave in your teams at three-minute intervals and we will guide you round. The objective is to get everyone to finish, help each other, and where possible we will make decisions for you. Team One will go in five minutes." Sergeant McMoody then gave us a full water bottle to put on our web belts. At least it wasn't raining here, but the weather was chilly, and the ground was very slippery and damp.

We watched as Corporal Miles and a Scots Guard corporal set off with Team One, running about fifty yards to two fixed logs, one at two feet high and the next three feet high, set one stride apart in a sandy pit.

The first three or four did it, but then we laughed as the next guy slipped off into the damp sandy pit. The ones behind him tried to slow down and two more lost their balance and joined him but had to get up and keep going.

The laughing soon stopped, though, as Corporal Jones and another Scots Guards lance corporal got us underway, and we did the same at the logs. It was now more slippery and getting muddy as the ground was cutting up. It was also noticeably the royal "we" as encouragement was constant but from the drier areas.

We came out the other side, down a short path and onto more logs about six feet high and pulled ourselves along them. Next, we ran towards a ten-foot-high wall, where two men stood at the bottom and cupped their hands, getting two men up on the top and they would then help the rest over. Except Ginger had a brain fart and jumped off the other side. The resulting bollocking must have been heard back in Pirbright barracks.

"What are you doing, you fucking balloon? Go back and do it over again."

Ginger was now last and ran at the wall, and the two on it missed his hands. He slid down again, getting a bit of skin rash. This quickly focussed him and the next attempt was good.

Another run through more trees and down into a ditch area where we had to get up an embankment. After Team One had gone up, it was a slippery, muddy mess, and we grabbed and tugged at anything we could. I was behind Jack Backhouse, who slipped backwards, as I was holding on to a bit of a shrub. He slid into me and got going again, which dislodged me, and I slid back and had to do it over again.

"Move it, come on, we don't have all day."

I remember thinking thank fuck for that.

Once at the top it was around the trees to a low net stretched along the floor, by now a sandy wet mess, and we grovelled under it on our bellies. This was an annoying exercise as the water bottle kept getting caught in the netting. I got a boot in the side of the head, as the guy in front of me got caught up. I cursed the shit out of him, but he was too busy thrashing about under the net to even care. There was shouting coming from all sides. Despite the running we were never too far apart, and we could hear the other teams getting an earful.

Eventually, we emerged onto a flatter piece of ground and ran to a seven-foot wall. Earlier, we would have gone over no trouble but due to things being slippery and bodies aching, it became more difficult.

Some did it ok and others needed a couple of attempts, but we pulled and shoved and tugged at each other until we were all on the other side.

This was getting to be bloody hard work and tempers would flare up, aimed mainly at the instructors, but as long as we kept going it was as if they were deaf. Our bodies were feeling heavy, and it was all about mind over matter and keeping going.

Through the next clearing I saw this fifty-thousand-foot-high, heavy netting meshed together in squares, going up one side over some huge poles, and down the other side. It was probably only around twenty-five feet high, but in our present frame of mind it looked like Mount Everest.

There was almost an audible gasp as we saw Team One was still only clamouring over the top, but it did give us a quick break. An encouraging instructor said, "This is the last obstacle, so give it all you've got."

And off we went. We ran to the net and began scrambling up it, and soon knew what the difficulty was. From about a third of the way up, the whole net would shake and bounce each time someone put their weight on it or took their weight off it. It was hard to get a foothold; more often than not our boot would go through the netting and we had to heave ourselves back up. This was happening to all of us as we pulled ourselves a little higher, each time struggling mainly to get our feet on the netting. It seemed to take a lifetime to get to the top.

We could hear the shouting from below. "Hold on tight as you swing over the top."

It was a given, as aching arm muscles hung on for dear life. We soon found going down was as hard as climbing up. Arms were hurting more each minute and we had great difficulty in finding the bouncing footholds as we slithered and slid the last few feet. Two of the guys were having a real rough time of it, and one instructor stayed with them. The other instructor took the rest of us back through a wooded area to where we'd begun.

Tighe was there, and before we could collapse, we heard, "Don't relax, we will go back round again."

My mind went numb, as it was programmed for a rest, but we fell in ready to go.

"Just testing, well done," a smiling Tighe said. "Not too difficult then. Get a drink all of you."

The other two from our group arrived, and we just lay and stared at the sky for a while, until we felt good enough to stand.

We were getting a drink when we heard loud voices from the other side of the wood, in a barrage of encouragement. "Keep going, hang on, don't give up now. Keep a good grip at the top, swing over, good, good."

A minute or two later, "Don't lie there, get up and join the rest."

That didn't sound too good, but suddenly a Guards lance corporal came running into sight with six men. They were doing a complicated-looking stagger as they arrived back and commenced sucking moisture out of the ground.

A minute or two later and Sergeant McMoody was heard in the distance. "Keep going, keep going you are almost there, heads up, show some spunk, come on, come on."

We all saw Bull (who had his hands on his thighs) and Arnold (who looked like a beetroot on legs) shuffling into sight, with Sergeant McMoody on one side, and Corporal Thomas on the other.

Someone shouted, "Twenty yards!" and we all joined in with "Nineteen–eighteen–seventeen," until they were in front of us and McMoody said, "Well done lads, good recovery, fall out."

Alex sank to his knees looking as if he was either going to get a knighthood, or the guillotine.

It was lightly raining again, and nobody complained as we cooled off. Sergeant McMoody collected the water bottles and drove off with his men, followed by Corporal of Horse Tighe and Corporal Miles in the Land Rover.

Corporals Thomas and Jones lined us up in twos, and we leisurely jogged for a mile into an area of older-looking buildings. We jogged in single file over to Corporal Miles, who hosed most of the mud off us, and then we went into one end of a building.

It was a big room with benches against the walls and some decrepit tables and chairs lying around. To us it was heaven, warm and dry with the only good table full of sandwiches, fruit, urns, and mugs.

"Hang your jackets over there and grab some food."

The sandwiches were a king's feast and the tea like nectar, and we all began to chat about the obstacle course. It turned out that Team Three had a pig's arse of a problem with the embankment, as it was a muddy mess when they got to it. The slipping and sliding back had sapped a lot of their energy.

By now we could hear Arnold telling some guys that by the time he reached Mount Everest his legs were ok, but his arms were like lead. "Especially as that netting tied me in knots because of that fucking water bottle." We saw Sergeant McMoody, with a big smile on his face, wink at him.

A debrief from Sergeant McMoody took place, and it was very easy to listen to, finishing with, "For the Household Cavalry, you are almost as good as the Foot Guards."

We were ready for this dig and shouted out, "Thank you Corporal of Horse," as he pointed his finger at us and smiled.

We grabbed our jackets, got into the Bedford, drove back close to the Foot Guards drill square, and came to a halt.

Twenty seconds later there was a collective gasp of "Fucking hell!" and everybody, including Corporal Miles, slid away from the tailboard. The biggest head and paws, of the biggest dog I had ever seen, appeared over the tailboard. He was huge, and just rested his head and paws over the tailboard, and leisurely ran his eyes over us. There was total silence in case he was weighing up his meal options. We heard a voice call him, and he loped back to a group of soldiers, who were enjoying every minute of it.

Corporal Miles told us he was an Irish wolfhound and the mascot of the Irish Guards. If he had a saddle on, he could have been the mascot for the Household Cavalry. Of course, by the time we were on the road, he hadn't worried us at all.

By around 1800hrs we were told to go change and then begin cleaning.

At 1930hrs everyone headed for the NAAFI, where the pies, cakes, and drinks became an endangered species. As the NAAFI break went on, it was clear that it had been a very physical day. Most of us were feeling a bit sore, but everyone was tired.

"Looks like you've had a rough day today, boys," Alice remarked, and there was a general murmur of agreement.

Keith looked very sincere. "It's been hard Jenny, as hard as it's been since we began."

"Any more of that and I will snap it off," Alice told him.

At this point most of us cringed and realised that there were worse things in life than a physical day. Even Keith pretended to feel the pain.

Then, more room cleaning and lots of talk about the days getting more physical, with everyone having a story of pain on the obstacle course. Ginger, waxing lyrical, said, "At least we are still here." There was also total agreement that Ding Dong had picked the right time to leave.

There was no banter at all tonight, as we were just happy to get into bed and grab some welcome sleep.

FRIDAY DAY, 93–SATURDAY, DAY 94
"ARE YOU GOING TO STAY IN THERE ALL DAY? WAKEY-WAKEY!"

A little voice in the mist said; *Yes, I'd love to stay in here all day*, but as the mist receded, I joined the rest of the room shuffling into another new day.

We compared cuts and bruises and all felt a bit sore, but a good breakfast hit the spot. By the time we were ready for inspection all aches and pains were receding.

"Stand by your beds." Tighe came into the room like a tornado and it was as if he had turned the clock back.

Bed packs demolished (and not even Monday). "That's a half-inch too small, Green," as he wrecked it.

Fuck you, you lame-brained arsehole. I used a template, but it was condensed to silence. By the time he got around the room not a one of us escaped unscathed. It had been a long time since we'd had total chaos visited upon us.

"Absolute shite, do you think you are beyond cleaning properly?"

"Parade ground 0830hrs, number-two dress uniform with swords."

We were in two lines and an inspection took place and again we were absolute shite. Caps not brushed correctly, brasses neglected, belts and swords not fit to be associated with the Senior Regiment in the British Army and boots crap—hell, this was the old days.

He singled out guys at regular intervals, and as he stood in front of Jay he shouted, "These boots look a fucking mess, obviously you don't care about your personal turn-out."

Jay stared ahead without flinching.

"Well, are you going to look at them?"

"No, Corporal of Horse."

Corporal of Horse Tighe went three shades of purple, but before he could speak Jay carried on, "You said they are a fucking mess and as I respect your judgement, I have no need to look at them, sir."

For a moment Tighe appeared tongue tied, as he stared at Jay, then through a series of grunts he said, "Correct, remember that," and moved on.

Tighe must have seen the look of amazement on some faces. We thought Jay would be dismembered by now. Looking sideways, Tighe said, "Bird, do two laps of the square, while I decide if you are taking the piss."

As Jay passed the squad he gave a little smile—some things are just worth the pain.

The remainder of the morning and part of the afternoon was strange. Corporal of Horse Tighe kept on vanishing into the block and then he'd come out and move someone around, then go back into the block again. The WO, also spent an hour watching us drill, then he spoke to Corporal of Horse Tighe and left.

We were marched into the Lecture Room and Corporal of Horse Tighe said, "I must be insane, but after much soul searching, I have decided to begin continuity drills tomorrow."

We stared at him blankly, as we hadn't a clue what he was on about. Was he having some sort of episode?

"For the next two weeks, we will practice a six-minute drill session that you will be able to complete without any orders from me."

This almost confirmed our worst suspicions: *You? Quiet for six minutes?* Then we realised he was deadly serious.

"You have been placed in the most aesthetic positions for height and stride patterns. These are now permanent positions. During the next week we will work on distances, pacing, and drill timings, during the second week we will put it all together."

He then left a very quiet room of *what the fuck just happened* recruits.

Corporal Miles explained the day's events, including the WO's presence. It seemed the WO had given permission after he was satisfied that we were capable of doing it. Miles finished by saying, "On a positive note, Corporal of Horse Tighe would not have put his neck in a noose, if he did not believe in your ability to carry this off. Don't let him down."

We went back in a great mood, knowing that Tighe had this confidence in us. This still did not stop Billy from doing his best piss-take impression of Tighe though. "Right, you dead legs, fall in at the top of the stairs. Bird, march this riff-raff out of here."

Jay was already laughing, and Billy turned to me and said, "Green, do *you* think I'm insane?"

"Not insane, Comical of Horse, but if you think you are, I fully respect your judgement."

At this point Jay probably wet himself.

I was sometimes having difficulty seeing myself, so much had happened in a short period of time. Depending on the next path I took, I could be training for the Sovereign's Escort in London or doing UN peacekeeping duties in Cyprus.

It seems a million years ago that I was a nervous, wet-behind-the-ears boy. My world was opening up and I was opening up with it.

Later, I was with Don, listening to Jay and Pete talking about their weekend, and they were already laughing a lot before Jay told us the story.

They got into the pub with Pete's parents and Jay ordered a pint and turned around to see what everyone else wanted. The barmaid shouted, "Hurry up for fack's sake, I haven't got all night."

Jay thought, *Holy hell, I haven't even had a pint yet.*

Pete leaned over and said, "Meet my sister, Desiree."

She was smiling and said, "It's Maude really, but who the fack wants to be called Maude?"

"Well, not me, for sure," Jay replied, and they were all off laughing again."

The next morning there was no inspection, just a shout to be in the Lecture Room by 0830hrs, and this time there were three large drawings on the blackboards.

They showed the three phases of the continuity drill and again it was death by Indian raiding party arrows. There was a large number of crosses above the middle one, denoting seating, and a large rectangle showing where we would start and finish. The phases were marked with directional arrows, number of paces, and approximate timings.

He was into his spiel now, and for a while we may as well not have been there. It was infectious and he had it all clear in his mind—all he had to do now was get it into ours.

Our enthusiasm was rising, as we knew by now that he was totally positive that we would succeed.

We went on the square and for ninety minutes we practised the first half of phase one. "Right turn, thirty paces, about turn sixty paces, about turn thirty paces." We began to feel more confident as we practised this over and over again until lunch.

"Is he teaching you how to drill or count?" asked a cook.

"Both," said Danny. "We are going to drill on our passing out parade, with no words of command."

"Well, I'll be fucked," the cook replied, sounding surprised.

Danny laughed, "Yes, but get in line, I think we may be first."

Another hour and we were expanding the phase. A right turn twenty paces, about turn forty paces and about turn twenty paces. By evening we had progressed from the instructors counting out the paces, to the squad counting the paces out loud.

At the end of the day, Tighe seemed really pleased, and you could have knocked us down with a feather, when he said, "I have decided to give you the morning off tomorrow to relax. Clean the block in the afternoon, and we'll pick this up again on Monday."

Alice looked startled when we walked in. "You are all in a loud mood, have they fired you, or something?"

"Nearly, we've got all tomorrow morning off."

Keith's voice piped up, "Jenny, would you like me to give you a—" And Alice leapt in saying, "If you finish that, I'll finish you off. You and your one-track mind."

Keith was completely unabashed. "I was going to say, would you like me to give you a chorus of my favourite song?"

Don't bother," Jenny said, "It would have to be in the three-to-five age group."

The laugh was deafening.

Probably the remark of the evening came from Billy at the counter, as everything calmed down, "Can a man get any food in here?"

"Jenny, can you keep some baby food hot for Billy?" Alice remarked.

"Ok. What would you like Billy?"

Jenny blushed as Billy said, "Breast feeding."

We had a long chat and fooled around enjoying the thought of our longest sleep since the course began.

SUNDAY, DAY 95
"RISE AND SHINE! IT'S 0730HRS, BREAKFAST AT 0800HRS!"

The lights came on, although we didn't really need them this morning. We stretched and yawned, slowly looking around at each other. Then a slow meander off to the washroom, waking Bob and Dave again on the way and wondering how the two best sleepers in the world had ended up side by side.

It was a great feeling to enjoy a normal type breakfast sitting around, feet up, drinking extra tea, totally relaxed.

It was 0845hrs before we got back to the block and another shock as we saw four Sunday newspapers outside each room: two *Sunday People* and two *News of the World*. (It had lots of risqué stories in it and was more commonly called the *News of the Screws*.)

I grabbed one and lay on my bed reading it. This was living: a lazy Sunday, good breakfast, newspaper, what more could we ask for? In Bob and Dave's case, more sleep, as they had already dozed off.

It was hard work doing nothing. At NAAFI time, most of us went down there more for the walk than to eat and then back to the block and more of the same.

The print was nearly worn off the papers with all the usage.

I strolled down to see Don, who was already bulling his boots. He laughed, "I ran out of being lazy, so thought I would do something to pass the time." We agreed it was hard doing not much, after being organised twenty-four hours a day. By the time we were going for lunch, we were not upset about getting back into routine, though the novelty had made a great change.

As I stood in line talking to Timmy, a cook walked down and placed a container of sizzling hot steaks onto the hotplate and said to Timmy, "As promised 'steak touché.'

"They look fucking delicious," Timmy said to him. "Do you cook them just like any other steak?"

"Yes," the cook replied with a broad grin, "Except when we tenderise the steak, instead of a mallet we use the dick bone of a dead donkey."

"Thank fuck it's dead," said Timmy, "It would be bloody upset if it wasn't."

The picture in my mind made me decide on fish but the guys farther back, who hadn't heard the chat, had steak, agreeing afterwards how tender it was. When they had mostly finished, the cook came over and told us he was only joking about tenderising the steak. After he had everyone's attention he said, "It was a mule's dick bone," and we were all laughing at Alex's quizzical expression.

We had only been back in the block for twenty minutes when Corporal of Horse Tighe came in. Fortunately, we'd begun to pull out beds and lockers and prepared the Bumper for its afternoon assault. Even more fortunately, we had finished rolling the oranges at a banana, to see who would operate it.

Tighe arrived dressed in civvies. It turned out later he had been to a christening, and looked as immaculate in civvies as he did in uniform. He spent a long time talking to us and was still excited about his continuity drill and our ability to carry it out. He also made the point that next week would be very physical as there would be assessments, drills, field work, and a ten-mile bash. Having planted this in our minds, he left.

We got stuck into the cleaning amid much fooling about, which was highlighted mid-afternoon. About ten of us were in the cleaning room when John McGrath appeared at the door. He was dressed in forage cap,

PT kit, white belt with scabbard and the sword in his right hand, with the left one holding a long-handled brush between his legs.

He started shouting, "Whoa boy, easy, easy," while jerking the brush wildly between his legs and leaning back while spinning around. "Easy boy, easy, relax, whoa, whoa."

We were all fully into this now, roaring laughing when John said to his "horse," "Easy boy, relax, the cooks only remove it when you are dead," and the "horse" immediately calmed down. John replaced his sword in the scabbard, stroked the brush head, "Good boy, well done," and looked at us saying, "Carry on," then he "rode" off down the corridor.

By the time we went for evening meal all of us were in a good mood and strangely hungry, but mostly opted for something that didn't need tenderising.

Later we trooped off to the NAAFI. When we'd all been served Alice came around and said she had heard a rumour about a strange kind of steak, so we referred her to Timmy to explain. He told her the story from the beginning, and how the steak was specially tenderised.

She looked straight at him. "Yes, but how is it specially tenderised?"

Timmy was floundering a bit here, and we were all staring at him smiling.

"Instead of a mallet they use an...umm...an, you know."

Sensing his struggle, she egged him on. "No, what?"

Timmy said, "Ok, there's only one way to say this...a donkey's donger."

"Oh, the bell round its neck."

"No, his big thingy," said Timmy, going red.

"Ah, his main bone," she said, and Timmy looked relieved to be off the hook.

"It's ok Timmy, Jimmy told me while he was getting his pie." She walked off laughing, as we enjoyed Timmy's discomfort at being tongue tied.

We got back, showered and shaved, then cleaned up the washrooms ready for tomorrow, and after a personal gear clean-up were in bed by midnight, knowing that the next week would be a major challenge.

WEEK 15

MONDAY, DAY 96– WEDNESDAY, DAY 98
DIAGRAMS AND DRILL MOVES

The pace was beginning to pick up even more as we were coming into the final stages of the course.

We had a full morning in the gym preparing for our final assessment on Thursday. A long morning but not over physical, just back to doing the exercises correctly. The circuits were done without time restraints, followed by the last hour of personal goals.

I did one forward roll unaided and felt confident to go it alone. It was a good spin in the air but I had to run and then do the forward roll. I was pretty sure that it would be there, or thereabouts, on Thursday. The morning was enjoyable without pushing our limits.

After lunch, the priority of continuity drill took over, and we incorporated it with sword drill. We carried on from Saturday, did phase one a few times out loud, and then on to phase two.

Four right turns, three at twenty paces, then one at forty paces. Left turn for twenty paces, left turn ten paces, eyes right for twenty paces, eyes front ten paces, and left turn for forty paces.

We practised for over an hour up to the eyes right, then added it to phase one, still counting out loud. It was almost lunch time when we heard, "You stupid, dim-witted arsehole," at which point we lost count.

Tighe ran into the middle of the squad and leaned into Joe's ear. "How many times do I have to tell you? If you lose step, do a smart, precise check step, don't bounce around like a fart in a colander. Corporal Miles, take over before I lose my bloody patience. Back here 1700hrs."

Wow, nice to see it was under control—hate to see you really lose it.

A cook asked Alan Ladd what all the shouting was about, and Alan explained it to him. Halfway through the meal the cook walked between the tables waving a colander saying, "A colander for Joe, colander for Joe," and amid the laughter everything was back into perspective.

Back on the square we carried on up to eyes right, still beginning all over any time there was even a slight hiccup, and slowly but surely it was falling into place.

As soon as we were off the square I was on the phone. Mum said, "I must tell you quickly, Dad has taken a week off work and Dad, me, and Helen are going to stay with Fred. We are going by train, then he will pick us up at Godalming in the car, so next Monday call this number."

"Oh, that's great love, you deserve a break."

I could hear her laughing saying, "As you know it's only about an hour to Windsor from there," and the penny dropped.

"Are you coming to the passing out parade?"

"Yes, we got a call last Friday. They said we can confirm vehicle details and numbers through you next Monday."

I suddenly felt very emotional knowing they would travel halfway across England to see my passing out parade.

"You've gone quiet, maybe I should have left it until next week?"

"No, no, this is great news, I'm just so pleased you can make it." My time was up, and I wandered back to the block in a dream.

It made me realise a number of things. How the time was closing in on the end of the course. How I felt more capable of dealing with things now, but most of all what it meant to my family, to Mum, Dad, Fred, and Betty.

As more of us came back from the phone it became the major topic of the evening. We had seen the crosses on Corporal of Horse Tighe's diagram and knew they were for our families, as well as army personnel. I could hardly sleep thinking about it.

Last week they had promised us one more big run and today was it. We drove to an area of Windsor Great Park that we knew quite well and disembarked.

"We will jog to the Long Walk, head towards Windsor Castle, loop around and end up back here. After a break we will do a few exercises to check fitness levels."

This was a better jog, no rucksacks or bricks, just water bottles. The pace was nice and consistent, and we got into a good rhythm. All went well until we looped back to the start, which was still about three miles away. The path was shaded from the sun and became slippery. This led to our feet sliding around a bit and it all got annoying. The water bottles were bouncing up and down and sweat under the arms and crotch was more noticeable. My arms ached and shoulders felt sore.

We became two groups, a main one and a slower one of six or seven. The PTIs dealt with our main group, and Tighe and Miles dropped back with the others. It put a lot of extra strain on the last two or three miles and we were relieved to see the Bedford. All pain vanished as we jogged down to it, flopped down, and began to get our breathing back under control.

Not long after, the other group came in and they were absolutely shagged. We watched while they made strange gurgling sounds as they lay flat out.

I had a full mug of Gatorade and drank it in one go—it was delicious. Within seconds it hit me in the middle of my tender stomach which went into spasm as it decided whether to throw up or not. Luckily, the god of puke was having a day off.

We had a relax, ate sandwiches, and enjoyed a good chat between everyone, and then it was time for some 'little' exercises.

"Crawl to those trees and back."

If we slowed down, our boot soles were given a kick. We did a few field exercises and then heard, "Last one, carry a man to the tree, change over and return."

I looked round and saw Bull behind me, got an energy burst, ran round him, and picked up Tom Peters. Tom carried me back, slipped twice and left me with sore nuts.

Corporal Kelly said, "Are they still in the right place, Green?"

I replied in my best high-pitched voice, "Is under the armpits the right place?"

"Depends whose," he said and walked off.

We returned to barracks, showered, and were out on the drill square by mid-afternoon carrying on up to eyes right until evening meal when Tighe looked at Corporal Miles and smiled.

The conversation in the cookhouse told us that our drilling was also being discussed by other soldiers in the barracks, who were reacting quite positively to it.

It made us feel we were achieving something that the others hadn't done before, and we were determined to do it well. We were also seeing how our fitness levels had improved a lot, after our jog and exercising. There were no big mishaps—if we had done this three months ago there would have been guys littering the countryside in various stages of distress.

The drills carried on all day Wednesday, and we soon learned why we were stopping at "eyes right." It was a bit trickier. If anyone twitched just before it, someone else would do it early and it was like scattershot. This could also happen with "eyes front" as well.

After an hour Corporal of Horse Tighe said, "We need to see the big picture again," and marched us into the Lecture Room.

It did help, as even the arrows began to make sense. It was easier to follow now, as we had got into phase two. He showed us the seating again, and how the captain's chair had to be in the very centre, hence the ten paces.

We returned our swords to the block as it was difficult enough doing eyes right without adding them to the mix.

More and more practice, until we were getting to the end of phase two, while counting out loud.

After lunch, a warrant officer joined us on the square and Tighe stood him where Captain Forbes-Hart's chair would be. He explained how the salute was central to the parade, and how we would start and finish in the same place. He then gave us the order and we did the full phase-one without any further orders.

Later, in the Lecture Room, Corporal of Horse Tighe introduced us to Warrant Officer Class 1 Wheater, BEM (British Empire Medal). We had seen him on Pay Parade previously. None of us knew he had the BEM, as the medal ribbons meant nothing to us, but we knew it was rare if it resulted in initials after his name.

He was a tall man, around six-foot three inches, with a tanned, craggy face. He had a slightly thickening waistline, but a strength of character that made him stand out. He stood there in his full uniform, and we were totally impressed.

"I have a confession to make. When Corporal of Horse Tighe approached me a week ago, with a crazy idea of doing drills without commands, I did not believe it could work." He paused and smiled, "Especially as I remembered my table being upended and money spread over the foyer. Corporal of Horse Tighe assured me that was then—this is not now. After your display today, I am in full agreement with him. Keep up the good work, and I look forward to your big day." He thanked Corporal of Horse Tighe and left.

"His words, not mine."

This further enforced to us that Corporal of Horse Tighe was missing the day they covered praise on his instructor's course, but then he smiled. "Corporal Miles, take them back to the block." Then as an afterthought he said, "Have a good evening."

All the talk was about the warrant officer's talk—we knew we were good, and he had just confirmed it.

The NAAFI was bouncing and Alice and Jenny were interested in who we had coming. Alice asked Keith if he had anyone coming.

Making sure Jenny could hear he said, "What, besides my wife?"

Jenny looked amazed. "Good grief, are you married? That proves there is someone for everyone. Is she coming?"

"It depends on our babysitter she can't really bring both the kids."

Jenny was surprised, "How old are th—" Then she saw Keith laughing. She turned to Alice. "He isn't going to make it. I'll strangle him before then."

As we turned in, Alex couldn't resist, mentioning Keith having kids with his tiny todger. "How old are they, did you say?"

"The youngest is twenty-four," Keith replied…which would have put him in the *Guinness Book of Records*, as the first man to have two kids before he was born.

THURSDAY, DAY 99
"IT'S 0600HRS. EVERYBODY UP AND OUT OF BED!"

Not very novel, we are more used to something more dramatic, but I guess the end result is always the same. A grunt followed by thirty seconds of brain re-focussing, then a stagger off to the washroom with the speed of stagger directly related to the call of nature.

Bob went into a stall and within two or three seconds farted so loud and so long, we thought his health was in danger. We never really knew how Bob constantly did it, going into the bog with the bearing of a limp rag and five minutes later emerging like a newly minted wallaby.

At breakfast it was decided to eat sparingly. I was all for that, so instead of going for seconds, I had a healthy bowl of cereals. Then it was back in the block ready for 0745hrs.

"Stand by your beds."

We looked as smart as you can be in ironed PT shirts, ironed baggy shorts, and plimsolls and we lined up and got a lengthy preamble from Corporal Kelly. "Everything you do today will be based on previous assessments, we have it all documented." (Outside the office was a long table groaning under the weight of clipboards and paper, not the only thing groaning soon, I thought).

"Your results will be based on today's performance, no more chances. Questions? None, good. You will go in threes, two minutes apart and a whole team will finish before we begin with the next. Remember, if you bleed, break, or bruise, carry on—no finish-no result." He gave us a wry smile. "Get your mindset in order and good luck."

The usual warm up took place with us feeling a bit apprehensive as this was the day that all the hours in the gym and in the field had been leading up to.

Team One began while the rest of us did a bit of jogging and exercising to keep warm, all the time watching what was going on and constantly urging them on. Soon we were engrossed in watching. This was our "fit" group and after fifteen minutes it looked as if they had been through a washing machine. They were still under a constant barrage.

"Gimme more, gimme another," and Ticker in his style of; *Is that the best you can do?* "Not good enough, another."

I was feeling knackered just watching them, but eventually they completed their circuit and collapsed in a sweaty, twitching mess on the mats in the corner.

Corporal Kelly came to our team and gave us another pep talk. (I think he could see the *What the fuck was all that?* setting in). "You are all at different levels; we are judging you personally. It is how you perform individually that we are interested in."

He turned to Al Hopkins saying, "Keep the rest occupied until we are all done." (Done being the operative word.)

Al was already standing, but no one else was, as our "elite" were still trying to get up off the mat, and even Al only answered with a nod.

"Begin."

The first three were off with the instructors hot on their heels, and two minutes later two others and I joined the fray under guidance from Corporal Jones. We did a sprint to the top of the gym, then mat work, just press-ups and toe touching, but already "Gimme more." Onto the ropes and a climb to the ceiling and of course they were too busy to look up, so we hung around until, "Carry on, arms only." It felt as if my arm muscles were popping, and I dropped the last six feet and ran to the beam where it was more of the same. I tried to keep doing pull-ups. "Two more, more effort, heave yourself up," as neck muscles also started to ache.

We were spreading out a bit now, yet the instructors were all over us. A welcome sprint up the gym, then run and vault the horse, followed by forward rolls down the mat to the medicine balls. Lift them overhead and back to the floor, reach your target number, sweat running into my eyes.

I could taste the salt on my lips, but it was over to the wall-bars with toes underneath and sit-ups.

"Too slow, another," and "Gimme, gimme."

Major grunts as the effort set in. Cursing the *bastards*, and *fuck you*, but nothing mattered except for getting it done. Grit your teeth and concentrate on mind over matter.

Hang off the wall bars and lift knees, stomach muscles and back muscles straining and then feeling the relief as we dropped off. Then onto another mat to do star jumps. The final agony as leg muscles, backs and arms ached.

"Legs wider, arms fully over your head, another, good, now two more."

Just as the world was closing in, a tap on the shoulder. "You've finished, back to the corner mat."

Although it was only about five yards away, as I reached it my body and mind separated. My mind went completely blank. As I fell onto the mat, my body tried to regain some kind of normality. Soon I was breathing in every bit of spare air in the vicinity, sweat now pouring freely off me, and steam rising from my slowly recovering body. I rolled off my back with someone shouting at me.

I realised it was someone shouting at Team Three on their circuit, and they were well into it. I slowly got to my feet still breathing in big, deep breaths and made my way to Team One, who were shouting encouragement at them.

I watched as a tiring Bull Durham vaulted the horse and his legs buckled as they hit the floor. He pitched forward rolling into the medicine balls, then began grinding out the exercise. On the final test, Bull, who was really strong in the arms, was doing a weird-looking star jump, with his arms waving above his head and his legs barely able to get off the floor.

As Team Three were thrashing about in their death throes, Corporal Kelly shouted, "Take a fifteen-minute break."

It was done before the words were out of his mouth.

The instructors started marking their paperwork while we drank the Gatorade provided. As we felt better, we began to bull-shit about it not being as bad as we thought it would be, making sure the instructors didn't overhear.

"Fall in your three teams."

Looking quite serious, Corporal Kelly said, "Did anyone find that too difficult?"

Not a word as we stood to attention, giving the impression it had been a piece of cake and smiling just to prove the point.

"Good," he said solemnly, "We have a big problem with discrepancies in the marks for Teams One and Two, who will have to go again."

It was as if the roof had fallen in. Smiles vanished and shoulders dropped—even Team Three looked totally deflated and they were not involved. There was a horrible silence that filled the gym as we stared and glared at them.

They looked a little crestfallen. If looks could kill, there were three stone-cold dead instructors.

It seemed forever and then, completely deadpan, Corporal Kelly said, "Just kidding," and they all burst into smiles.

They must have felt the *you sick fuckers* stares we gave them, but it was soon over. The relief we felt when we knew it was a sense-of-humour test, soon had us feeling upbeat again. It's not as if this type of thing hadn't happened before.

When we had put the circuit away, Corporal Kelly said, "After lunch back in here for personal achievements. Go and shower and we'll see you at 1315hrs."

There was no shortage of noisy chatter at lunch mixed with relief at a major obstacle being reached and overcome. We were sure that we had all done enough to get through it all. It would not be totally confirmed until Monday, but we were positive that they would have let us know if there was a problem.

Anyway, we had all finished, so we were looking forward to this afternoon and a lighter-hearted, more relaxing session while we strutted the fun part of our training.

We all lined up and one at a time did our personal achievement, cheered on by everyone else. All of us had something to do; some were extending a skill and some of us were mastering a completely new one. We were called out one at a time, there was a quick explanation by a PTI, and then the ones who didn't need equipment went first.

We made a big space for them and as they began the gym was a riot of noise as we all yelled encouragement at each other. In front of our peers, failure was not on the cards.

Timmy walked half the length of the gym on his hands with us all around him. Danny did an exhibition of skipping at speed. Jim Jones faced the wall bars and travelled the length of them by swinging from side to side. All met with loud applause.

Al Hopkins climbed up and down the rope using just his arms and made it look easy. One other went up and down just using his arms and did not make it look as easy. Two more did it using arms to go up and feet and arms to come down, one of who was Tony Mahoney, who got a ton of cheering, as he had never climbed a rope in his life until he began training.

Eventually we got to those using the vaulting horse and got out the mats and a number of them did a forward roll along the top of it and landed upright. Two guys did handsprings off the end of the box. Chris landed like a bag of shit on the mats and asked if he could do it again, where he proceeded to show it was not a one-off error. The other was Pete Hughes, who did a good handspring then hit the mat fast. He did a kind of foxtrot and three steps down threw his arms in the air and we heard, "Facking brilliant! Abso-facking-lutely great!" as Pete couldn't contain himself. They put the vaulting horse away and left the mats for the last three of us.

"Green, forward spring through the air." And the noise kicked in again.

I was really confident I could do it, and as soon as I began didn't hear much until I landed a bit hard, momentum still going forward, did two weird forward rolls down the mat and jumped up, arms aloft. I remember Pete grabbing me shouting, "Facking good, Jimmy, nice facking recovery!" It was all over as I took a bow, along with lots of back slapping and hand shaking.

I was so elated I don't even remember the next one to go. The final one was Alan Ladd, who did a backspring. Due to his tall, gangly build he resembled a spider spinning in the air and even he was laughing, obviously pleased to get it over with.

When we'd finished a good evening meal, we were greeted in the foyer by Corporal Miles. "Drill with swords, ten minutes on the square."

We did the first phase counting out loud, then twice more quietly, which went very well. It was extended to the start of the eyes right and after an hour it was all falling into place. A quick break, then two more run throughs to the eyes right. There were a couple of minor mishaps, quickly rectified, that went almost unnoticed, and it was fast becoming second nature. A number of run-throughs doing just eyes right, and soon to the end of phase two counting out loud.

"If you get to the end of phase two quietly, we will finish. If not, we will be out here all night."

It was a good drill. Corporal Miles seemed quite content as he dismissed us, or maybe he was saving us for Corporal of Horse Tighe tomorrow.

Before we were dismissed, he told us to pay special attention to swords, number-one uniforms, and best boots for tomorrow's photos.

In the NAAFI it was like the cork had popped out of a bottle and released a torrent of noise. We were full of the day in the gym and the hard assessment, but by now everything was open to exaggeration to suit a story, and we all had one to tell. Pete's handspring carried him at least twenty feet from the horse, I leapt at least fifteen feet into the air, and Timmy walked the full length of the gym on one hand.

It carried on back in the block as we cleaned and cleaned and cleaned. It was a riot of laughter and pure bullshitting, but all the time we were working really hard on getting our gear gleaming for tomorrow's photos. It was well into Friday before the last of us got to bed and went straight to sleep.

FRIDAY, DAY 100
PICTURE PERFECT

Not another strange voice—at least he is different. Who cares, let's get up and begin another day.

We carefully laid out all our hard work from last night, touched up the floors, and went off to breakfast, all excited about the morning, especially the photo session.

"Stand by your beds." In seconds, Tighe was in the room inspecting all uniforms, swords, white belts and boots, but this was different. Whatever he pointed out was fixed immediately, but although we thought we were immaculate, he was in flea's left ball syndrome. By the time he left we were all cleaning something, even if we might not be able to see it.

"Outside, ten minutes, road run."

Soon we were enjoying a pleasant jog around the barracks on a nice April morning, with no after-effects from yesterday. On entering the final week, it felt as if it was all coming together.

We had a good drill session with us putting our all into it, as we knew this was the last sword drill of this course.

It seemed no time at all that Corporal Miles was heading to the Guard Room to see if they were ready for us. Five minutes later we were marched to the Guard Room by Corporal of Horse Tighe.

Outside the wall of the Guard Room there was a row of chairs laid out for a photo shoot. There were dusters to touch up boots, and clothes brushes for uniforms and forage caps. The first half of the guys were seated with the centre chair left vacant, while the rest stood behind.

We were enjoying this, especially as cameras were few and far between, so getting a picture taken was a novelty. The back row moved around until the photographer was satisfied with the uniformity (of course), then Tighe sat in the middle and the pictures were taken. The chairs were removed, and we came out of the Guard Room in pairs, and had another picture taken in front of The Life Guards cypher on the wall.

This was taking longer than expected, so half of us were taken to the Lecture Room to place the swords and slings into the boxes provided. I had just laid my sword in the box and was staring at it as the remainder came in. Corporal of Horse Tighe asked, "What are you staring at, Green?"

"Just feeling a bit melancholy, Corporal of Horse."

"Don't be something you can't fucking spell, get a move on."

I looked up with a faint smile, and saw Timmy and Alex turn away laughing.

The first bunch of us went for lunch slightly late, which one of the cooks remarked upon. We told him we'd had our pictures taken.

"Bloody hell, they must have really tough glass in those cameras, if your ugly mugs didn't break them."

Don said, "They have, but not as tough as your steaks."

"Oh, touché," the cook said.

Timmy rolled his eyes back saying, "Oh shit not again."

It was a bit later when we got back to the block where we were told to change into number-two dress and be on the square for 1330hrs for continuity drill.

We could almost feel the impatience in Corporal of Horse Tighe to get started. "We will begin with phases one and two out loud."

He must have felt our own impatience as this was already firmly imprinted in our minds, and we didn't want to count out loud—that was for learners.

By the end of the afternoon, we were doing it quietly, and initially the only hiccup was at the eyes right. Corporal of Horse Tighe came up with a solution. The right marker would say "Hup," so that only we could hear. As this worked to begin with, he was happy with his tweak, and if he was happy so were we.

Evening meal wouldn't be until 1700hrs to give us extra time. After over three hours we were feeling very pleased with ourselves, as we were getting to the end of phase two, with no instruction. Even Tighe seemed pleased as he remarked that it was "Coming along," which from him was a major compliment. "Go and change into pullovers and combat trousers and be in the Lecture Room at 1735hrs."

As the meal was a little later, there were more regular soldiers in the cookhouse. Although we weren't supposed to get involved with them, the rules had relaxed due to doing guard duties, and seeing them around more often. In the near future we would be joining them anyway. Some of them came across for a chat, mainly about the continuity drill.

"Do you really count all that in your heads?"

"Yes, and that's only two-thirds of it."

They walked off impressed, and this really bolstered up our confidence.

We lined up at the Lecture Room door and Corporal of Horse Tighe appeared. "Shut up, sit down, and shut up again."

He ran through phase three, then we all had to count it out loud a couple of times, as he and Corporal Miles took the timings of each phase again. He showed us where we would finish up and where he would take over to give us the order, "Right turn, salute to the front, stand at ease," and it would be over with.

He looked at the drawings. "Any questions? None, good." He then proceeded to give us a quick lowdown on parts of next week, mainly the five minutes on the phone and Tuesday morning being the cut-off for visitors.

Pointing at his masterpiece he said, "This will be perfected by Tuesday evening. If not, we will drill all night until it is." He had a half-smile on his lips. "See Routine Orders on your way back: they will give you an outline for your last week of training."

This was music to our ears: "Last week of training."

Minutes later we were looking at our final Routine Orders.

Saturday —Drill—Cleaning—Press Uniforms
Sunday —Relaxed Morning—Clean—Finish Uniforms
Monday —Drill—Gym—PT Awards—Last Phone Calls
Tuesday —All Day Drill—Hair Cut—Final Marks
Wednesday—Pay Parade—Drill—Collect Photos—Travel Passes
Thursday —Final Rehearsal—Officers Block Inspection
Friday —1100hrs Parade—Awards—Meal
All Subject to Alteration.

It was 1900hrs by the time we got upstairs and we were all talking at once after having read orders, and the reality that this time next week we would have finished recruit training.

Even though we had a late meal, everyone trooped off to the NAAFI for our hour away from the mayhem in the block.

Alice and Jenny were in the same frame of mind as us. "Does it feel strange, your last Friday evening as a recruit?"

"Whatever will you do with yourselves when we finish?" Keith asked Alice.

"Pardon?" Alice said.

"I said, what will you do when do when we finish?"

Alice cupped her ear and said loudly, "Pardon?"

Keith, almost shouting by now, said, "What will you do when we have finished?"

Alice put her fingers up to her ears and said to Keith, "In your case I will remove these earplugs." She took them out to a huge bout of cheering and Keith's face showing he had come second again.

We returned to the block still on a high and looking forward to drilling tomorrow, realising this was the show piece of the parade. As it was going well, we wanted to show ourselves and others how well it could be done. We were even beginning with a bit of a swagger.

Eventually, we did a perfunctory clean up, knowing that there was one hell of a follow up to come in the next few days, but it was still well after midnight before we began to turn in.

As we settled down there was a squeaky sound coming from Keith's bed.

"Hey, are you pretending to clean your sword tonight?" Ginger said to him. "Can you just polish it quietly?"

Keith's bed started squeaking at a hundred miles an hour for a few seconds then his voice said shakily, "I've polished it off now."

"Ok, show it up for inspection in the morning," Alex called out to him.

There was a ton of laughter as Keith said, "Will you lend me a hand, Alex?"

SATURDAY, DAY 101
"EVERYBODY UP—NOT IN THE BIBLICAL SENSE!"

Where are they finding these voices recently? Is there a nearby school for failed one-line instructors? In truth it was probably a guy coming off guard who would rather be lost in the jungle than coming into a recruit's block. A meander into the washrooms while the warm bed mist receded, and soon the banter began.

"What did that guy say this morning about the biblical sense?"

"I didn't get it," shouted Bob from inside his royal box.

"You would in biblical times," laughed Paul Smith.

Tony grimaced. "With a smell that bad you probably never will."

Bob was oblivious as he relaxed and enjoyed his best five minutes of the day.

At 0801hrs we were on the square getting our first drill inspection of the day, another push and pull along with the usual remarks. "Stand up straight. Are you a weird shape, Green? When you were born, they must have delivered you with a corkscrew."

Ah I get it, that's a good one, just had to get it in, you donkey.

From the kick off of the drill it was phase one and two counted quietly, and it was beginning to feel good. The tiniest hitch, a knee not at ninety degrees, a thumb not on the seam, or in their words the eyeballs didn't click on eyes right, and it was back to doing it from the start.

We went into phase three, which in essence was the simplest: a lot of marching but an easy pattern to learn, and it consisted of the last twenty paces on phase two left turn, then forty paces about turn, forty paces about turn, forty paces left turn, twenty paces to a left wheel, and then Corporal of Horse Tighe would give us, "Halt, right turn, salute, stand at ease."

It was a lot of marching to look impressive, but easy to learn. By midday we had progressed to phase one and two quietly and were counting phase three out loud.

Tighe, looking at Corporal Miles, nodded and said, "Improving, keep it up. After lunch, room cleaning, we will be around. The tailors will be open from 1315hrs–1630hrs today and from 0900hrs tomorrow until all number-one uniforms are done. If there is time, we will press number-two uniforms.

We had only just got back upstairs when we heard the instructors coming into the block and we all pretended to be working.

"Marx, start with McCann," and off they went.

"Green, you go in ten minutes and when one returns the next one goes."

We know that arsehole, do you think we are stupid? On second thought, don't answer that.

"You can stop pissing about, pretending to look busy. Starting now you will wash down all the walls throughout the floor, including corridors, landing, skirting boards, doors, and hinges. All corners, everything above floor levels, paint if required, oil window catches and hinges, get to work."

We all ran into each other trying to get away.

They wandered around the floor, finding more stuff and making sure everyone had got the message, and then they vanished only to return an hour later.

By now we had transformed a clean, neat floor into a scene of total chaos. Anything within a foot of the wall was pulled out to the centre. Buckets of soapy water and clean water were everywhere to clean off suds, plus mops to get it off the floors.

As we progressed, it was into the washrooms with old toothbrushes to get behind pipes and cisterns, polish up toilet and sink chains, and get under sinks. Whenever we saw perfection, a voice would boom out, "Get over here, there's a fucking huge dust ball," always in a difficult-to-reach space.

We looked like a bunch of hobos, all a bit wet from the sponges with bits of polish smeared on coveralls, and as usual we were hungry. I thought I'd try something different and pointed to an interesting mix of finely shredded meat, onions, peas, carrots in gravy and well-roasted sliced potatoes over the top. "That looks good."

"Of course, we don't serve crap in here. It's an alternative corned beef hash."

"Alternative?"

"Yes, there's no corned beef in it."

I looked at him quizzically and he carried on.

"It's a medley of fresh vegetables grown lovingly in our own back garden. Exquisite, freshly imported Spanish onions, glorious white-fleshed Jersey potatoes cooked to perfection in a five-herb sauce and all layered on top of a newly crushed-up goat's ball patty." He walked away smiling.

When we got back it looked as if a bomb had hit.

Corporal Miles was there and shouted, "Marx, the tailor's shop is open until 1930hrs, do some more."

It was all about putting things back together for the next stage, and it was done with Corporal Miles's non-stop pointing at things. We thought we'd finished but at 1830 hrs he gave half a dozen guys the job of cleaning the windows, which was a daunting job as there were so many of them.

A little later Tighe came in unnoticed. "Who is cleaning the windows? Get in here now. We are not the bloody navy cleaning port holes, get into the corners."

At 1930hrs the windows were only a third of the way done, and Tighe lined us up in pairs in the corridor. "All windows will be finished tonight. Tomorrow morning will be the same as last week. Breakfast 0800hrs. We will be in after lunch. Marx, carry on from 0900hrs." He threw Dave a bunch of keys, which Dave wasn't expecting so he ducked. The keys hit Jack Backhouse, who was day-dreaming behind him, on the side of his head.

"You twat," Jack said, startled. He instinctively kicked out at the keys, and they slid nearly back to Tighe.

"Did you say something to me then, Backhouse?"

"Absolutely not Corporal of Horse, I meant him for ducking."

"Pick them up and give them to Marx."

Just as Jack was going to pick them up, Tighe kicked them to Corporal Miles. "Make a note Corporal Miles, Backhouse moves at the speed of a penis in an ice-pack."

We all began to laugh, even Tighe, who didn't seem to have heard it before either.

"Marx, check the keys for damage, they have hit the densest thing in the block. Dismiss."

My corkscrew story got twisted (excuse the pun) out of shape by Ginger producing the best laugh of the night. He got silence to tell them all that he believed I'd been born the normal way, then they took one look at me and used a corkscrew to try and put me back.

Alice and Jenny came over in a lull, to tell us that they would be coming to the passing out parade and were looking forward to it.

Jenny obviously remembered Keith winding her up and said, "I'm bringing my children, and sitting next to your wife."

"How many have you got?" he said.

Jenny looked really serious and said, "Four by five different fathers."

I don't think Keith took this in, as Jenny winked at Alice and we kept laughing. The laughter was made more prolonged by the blank look on Keith's face.

We were all pleased to hear they were coming, especially as Alice had been like a second mother to us and was always ready with a sympathetic ear if we were a bit out of sorts or wanted a little chat. We had all grown very fond of her and Jenny during the past weeks, especially of their ability to have quick, funny remarks for all occasions, as we had just witnessed.

Back in the block we had a raucous hour tidying up, then spent a relaxed couple of hours in each other's rooms chatting, and the time passed quickly.

We were in no hurry to go to bed, discussing where we would be next Saturday. Although we knew it had to end sometime, there were times in the past when it seemed it never would. Now that the end was in sight, we were struggling to come to terms with it.

It was around 0100hrs when I wandered back to our room with Keith. Alex, Timmy, and Ginger had switched the main lights off. We were lying in bed chatting and in a good mood when we heard Bob and Dave saying goodnight from down the corridor.

Ginger said, "Quick, turn your lights off."

Dave and Bob came in and quietly put on their bedside lights. As Bob climbed into bed he shouted, "You basterts." He was cursing everyone, including Dave, and I could hear the others laughing.

They had folded Bob's sheets in half and tucked them in tightly, so he couldn't get into bed. Bob switched on the main lights, still cursing us all, except Dave, when he saw they had done the same to him, and they had to remake their beds.

It took ages to settle down and I was just about asleep when I faintly heard Bob saying "Basterts, fuckin' basterts."

SUNDAY, DAY 102
"UP YOU GET—BREAKFAST AT 0800HRS!"

As I strolled into the washroom, someone said that it was 0715hrs and we had forty-five minutes before breakfast.

Bob was still muttering some deep Scottish threats about a plague being visited on anyone committing such a sacrilegious act on another man's bed. But Bob being Bob, he went into his well-organised bowel routine, and when he emerged was a much quieter and calmer person.

It was great to go over for breakfast and enjoy the luxury of time. Around 0900 hrs Dave gathered up two more guys from Room Three and took them on a more pressing engagement. The rest of us picked up the newspapers and lay idly reading about the world outside and dozing off here and there.

It was around 1000hrs when Big Hippo decided on the spur of the moment to play a new game, He stood up stark naked, placed a pair of sunglasses in his pubic hairs, and walked up and down the room saying, "Who does this remind you of?"

We all did our pretend throwing up and showing apparent distress. As soon as the noise died down, he pointed to his masterpiece saying, "King Farouk."

This had us rolling around laughing at the likeness, to us anyway. He lay down, removed the sunglasses, and with only the paper to cover his modesty fell fast asleep.

A few minutes later, Billy appeared at the door and then vanished for a minute, returning with his finger on his lips for us to be quiet. He crept down to Alex's bed, lit the paper, and raced on tiptoe back down the room. He had just reached the door when the paper flared up and Alex leapt off his bed slapping Farouk and shouting, "Fucking hell! I'm on fire."

This rendered the room incapable of doing anything for laughing, as Alex stomped on the paper.

He looked around, saw Billy laughing at the door, and set off down the room after him. Billy's face went straight to panic mode as he turned and broke the world sprint record, running down the corridor and outside the block.

Everyone came rushing out into the corridor in time to see Alex at the top of the staircase, stark naked, rubbing his singed pubic hairs shouting, "I'll fucking strangle you when I get my hands on you, you little twat."

Not knowing what had happened, the rest apparently thought Alex had cracked up and was shouting at his penis, but by the time he got back to the room everyone knew what had happened.

We helped Alex clean up, but every time he started to speak, we just burst out laughing. Eventually, when all the singe had gone and "Farouk" was uninjured, he was reluctantly seeing the funny side of it himself.

At 1030hrs we set off for the NAAFI and Billy was still outside, so Alex called over to him saying, "It's ok, we're going to the NAAFI."

Billy, not believing Alex, waited until we were well on our way. It was a hilarious half hour with nobody being able to speak to Alex without bursting out laughing. This was made funnier by Billy getting a drink, sitting on the table nearest the door and never taking his eyes off Alex. Suddenly Alex got up to brush some crumbs off his lap, and before they had hit the floor Billy was halfway back to the block.

When we got back to the block it was more reading and chatting and discussing King Farouk. After a while, Alex went down to the other rooms and even checked the cleaning rooms and toilets, but there was no sign of Billy.

A few of the guys had gone over early for lunch, and by the time Alex got there they were having a field day. Two of them tried a rough version of, "Goodness gracious great balls of fire."

We sat down to eat and through the window saw Dave, Jay, and Billy come out of the tailor's shop. On entering the cookhouse, Billy was trying to appear invisible as he hid behind them in the queue. When the meal was partway through, Billy must have thought *screw it,* and he went to the opposite side of Alex's table.

"I didn't think that would happen like that, I'm sorry mate."

While still eating Alex slowly looked up and smiled, "Oh you will be," and carried on eating.

On the way back I said to Alex, "That was very calm with Billy, I think he was expecting you to go for him."

"I know," Alex grinned, "and now for the rest of the time he won't be sure whether I will or not."

The noise quickly stopped when we saw Corporal of Horse Tighe at the top of the stairs, and he immediately began organising the afternoon. All the time he was pointing out our "flaws," but also having more friendly chats about families or sport, though we had to keep our wits about us in case the "other" Corporal of Horse showed up.

A minute later, Keith popped his head in the room and said, "Jimmy, number-two uniform to Dave," and I couldn't get out quickly enough. When I got back, the cleaning was still in full swing. By the time we went for evening meal it was looking much better, and we were feeling pleased with our afternoon's work.

We were all in good spirits and relaxed, except for Billy, who had developed a major twitch every time Alex moved.

On the way back Alex said, "See Jimmy, he's a nervous wreck and doesn't know what to think." He was enjoying his revenge.

Dave had only a handful of uniforms to do and on our return Corporal of Horse Tighe decided it would be a good idea to get some exercise, so at 1715hrs we were out on the square being inspected.

We went through phases one and two, "Once out loud," then did them quietly. We had done this so often by now, especially phase one, that I'm sure if we took our boots off and said quick-march they could have done it without us. We did this for an hour, and for the second hour added on phase three counting out loud.

By 1915hrs Tighe seemed pleased with the session and not one eardrum was assaulted in the last half hour.

We all remarked how fresh and clean the block was looking as we had a shower, then went off to the NAAFI. Alice and Jenny remarked on how it was supposed to be a quiet drill, but it hadn't sounded like that earlier.

A cheer went up as Alice said, "That's a lot of learning just to stop Pete from swearing for a few minutes." Pete went to speak, but Jay put his hand over his mouth, so we never knew what pearls of wisdom were stifled.

We carried on cleaning personal gear, but with both uniforms freshly pressed we did our shirts and starched collars, and a bit of posing in the full-length mirrors. It would be a brave bit of dust that dared to settle in here tonight.

WEEK 16

MONDAY, DAY 103
"RISE AND SHINE—IT'S THE LAST WEEK BEFORE THE REST OF YOUR LIFE!"

Holy shit, philosophical at 0600hrs—they must be fed a special diet known only to the Army Instructors Philosophical Corps.

"Stand by your beds."

They did a good equipment check, but it was more positive than previously. They pointed out little things that needed to be rectified, which in earlier days would have been air mailed. "Foyer 0815hrs, dressed for the gym," and then they went next door.

As usual we waited until they had gone down the other end, looking at each other in surprise, at the different type of inspection we just had.

We were ushered into the gym to see the smiling faces of the PTIs. Corporal Kelly said, "Into your teams and then warm up." When we had been all wind-milled out there was another spiel. "Today will be your last in the gym. You will all receive verbal assessments, then the best recruit and most improved recruit will be announced."

Al went into the office first then came out and one by one we followed. It was a great morning as we played six-a-side football, then a form of rugby with medicine balls, then bean bagging—in fact, all the team games we'd played over the course of training.

My name was called out and I was marched into the office. Corporal Kelly was sitting behind his desk and he smiled. "Trooper Green, what can I say, relax and feel free to answer at any time."

We had been here often in the last few weeks, the atmosphere was not intimidating, and he was always open to quips or suggestions.

"Corporal Thomas, background."

For a couple of minutes Corporal Thomas read out facts and figures that showed my improvement had been consistently regular, and that initial observations had been pretty accurate.

"He will not always win the race, but he will always finish it."

Corporal Kelly was looking at me so I said, "I'd still like to think I'm not a camel."

"He laughed. "Ok, a gorilla then."

"No, I can't be a gorilla."

"Why not."

"I don't like bananas, Corporal."

This he found funny remembering our past conversations.

I had relaxed by now as Corporal Thomas went on. "He really persevered with his forward springs, I thought he would remain the king of splat, but he got there in the end."

Corporal Kelly took the chart off him and looking at it said, "You have worked very hard since commencing this course and quite rightly you feel proud of your achievements. Do you realise that you have lost the equivalent of 7 x 2lb bags of sugar? I have finished your final report."

The first part stated that I had great perseverance and stamina to enable me to finish the tasks, giving me the ability to help others along. The second was that I had the ability to interact with others, often through a sense of humour. These assets would serve me well in the future.

I handed it back to him feeling two feet taller.

"You have earned this Green, and I do not say this lightly," said Corporal Kelly. "Well done, very well done."

I ran back to the squad about a foot off the floor.

A while later we had another break with Corporal Thomas in charge. All of us who had been in the office were in a talkative mood, as the nerves were all gone, and we were still here.

Corporal Thomas said, "Green is now a gorilla. As he does not like bananas, he is in charge of the total NAAFI supply of coconuts."

As none of us had seen a coconut this was an easy task.

Big Hippo said to Corporal Thomas, "What will they give a hippopotamus then?"

The gym was in an uproar as Thomas said, "In your case a wide berth, and nothing that makes you fart."

At around 1145hrs the last one had been assessed, and we were told to relax as the three PTIs went into the office, followed soon by Corporal of Horse Tighe and Corporal Miles. Five minutes later and we were lined up in the gym with Corporal of Horse Tighe and Corporal Miles on one side. Corporal Kelly faced us, flanked by Lance Corporals Thomas and Jones.

"Before we announce the best and most improved recruits, we want you to know that there are no losers in here today. The sheer fact that you are here makes you all winners. It has been a deliberately long and hard physical journey. We were just discussing that collectively you have lost the weight of one corporal of horse and one corporal."

We all laughed at this and then Corporal of Horse Tighe, looking deadpan said, "That is purely theoretical, we are going nowhere."

Corporal Kelly took over again. "Now to the awards, and it will probably come as no surprise to anyone that the best physical recruit is Trooper Hopkins."

There was a burst of clapping and cheering as Al stepped forward. From day one he had been streets ahead of the rest of us, his only challenger having gone over the wall early on. He shook hands with the PTIs then returned to his place.

"Now to the most improved recruit. This was a considerably more difficult decision to make as any number of you were deserving of it. We eventually gave it to this recruit for two reasons: the first his great weight loss, and secondly his resolve to carry on when at times we were thinking he would not make it." He paused then said, "Trooper Moore."

Arnold was genuinely in shock. Corporal Kelly said, "Well done Moore, from one of The Three Stooges to anything but."

Arnold recovered enough to shake hands.

From here Corporal of Horse Tighe took over and began by congratulating them in his own inimitable way. "Well done you two, but the weight of this Corporal of Horse is still here, and there are still four days to survive. Do not relax." He was smiling as he said, "Back to the block, lunch, on the square at 1315hrs, ready to impress me. Dismiss."

The lunch was a hubbub of noise as we ate, especially at Arnold's attempt to look as if he had been shot, and the knowledge that a major obstacle had been overcome.

By the time we were lined up on the square at 1315hrs we were standing taller and more erect, looking like soldiers and wanting to strut our stuff.

We did an entire run-through with him counting out loud. Then one with us counting out loud. We were feeling the part. Backs were straighter, turns crisper. Uniform creases we could cut butter with and brasses gleaming so much that the sun bouncing off them could damage eyesight.

"Good, now phase one and two silently, and phase three out loud."

In a way it was enjoyable, as a bunch of individuals were expressing themselves as a team, quite often trying to outdo each other on personal performance, but coming together as an effective unit.

After three or four times we took a break and during this time a different warrant officer came over to Tighe and had a quick chat. Then Tighe told us to fall in.

We were at the top end of the square facing the cookhouse and the warrant officer stood on the grass facing us. He would move left or right and we would centre ourselves on him, but eventually the dance ended when they both agreed on a position. A soldier nearby put a chair on the spot and the warrant officer sat on it.

"This will be the position of the centre of the visitor's chairs on Friday. You will start and finish continuity drill exactly where you are now." The chair was secured to the ground.

We did a number of run-throughs involving the start and finish, all under the commands from Corporal of Horse Tighe. The first part where we marched from the block would also be under his words of command, which took a lot of pressure off us.

We marched from the block to the starting position, had a couple of run-throughs on where to start and finish and eventually the positions were sorted out. The rain was beginning just as predicted, and it was getting quite dark. If they were correct, it would be windy tomorrow and clear up for the rest of the week. Tighe marched us back to the block to change into coveralls and berets.

Corporal Miles ran us across to the Lecture Room with the rain getting harder. We went straight in to see Corporal of Horse Tighe, who sat there with the warrant officer. We were told to shut up, sit down, and remove our now-damp berets.

"I would like to introduce Warrant Officer Two Cannon," said Corporal of Horse Tighe. "Tomorrow he will help at the start of continuity drill at the chair, and the finish, including the officer's salute."

He went through the diagram again from start to finish. It was like a military exercise, precisely planned and well-rehearsed. "There is one minor change. The last left turn will now be a left wheel. I will still give the commands: squad halt, right turn, salute, stand at ease, and then there will be an address by Captain Forbes-Hart, after which I will dismiss you. Questions? None, good."

The warrant officer got up to leave, then stopped and asked Corporal of Horse Tighe if he could speak to us. Tighe looked a bit puzzled as obviously it was off script.

It was on the same theme as Warrant Officer Wheater. "At a general meeting to discuss this, I was a no vote. I am now pleased to say I was wrong. I did not think you would be able to carry it off. I was going to wish you good luck, but I see you don't need it."

Corporal of Horse Tighe thanked him and as the warrant officer went through the door Tighe raised his eyebrows and smiled at Corporal Miles. Corporal of Horse Tighe happy equals us happy, and we were feeling pretty chuffed after Cannon's speech.

Once again Tighe remained Corporal of Horse Tighe. "We still have a lot of work to do. Drill and haircuts tomorrow, and we will drill all night if I am not satisfied, so no fuck-ups."

Fifteen minutes later we were in the cookhouse, all chattering away at the same time. Arnold was completely changed from this morning—now we couldn't shut him up. He was walking around shaking everyone's hand, telling us of his hard work, and all in all, being a bit condescending. No time to dwell on that now, as the rain was only light, and we were concentrating on getting to the phone.

I heard the pennies drop as I pressed the button and Uncle Fred's voice saying, "I know you haven't much time, I just wanted to say how proud we all are of you."

"Thanks Uncle Fred, look forward to seeing you on Friday.

He replied, "There is someone hopping from foot to foot here."

I heard Mum say, "Oh John, I can't believe it's nearly over with. We are really looking forward to it. This is Fred's car make and number, and there will be the four of us and Helen. How are you?"

"Better by the hour, Mum, but there's still a fair bit to do, so we are keeping occupied."

She asked if their being there would make it harder, and I told her, "Not as hard as you not being there."

"I'll put Dad on, he wants a quick word."

There was a silence and then I heard him say, "Are you still there, son?"

"Yes, you don't get rid of me that easy."

"You will never know how—" And there was a clunk and the phone went dead.

I handed the phone to Danny and wandered back to the block in a strange mix of melancholy, excitement, and pride as my thoughts were all over the place.

I took my boots down to Don and we chatted about Friday and he told me his parents, one sister, and a brother were coming. I said, "Between you, me and Keith, we have a football team coming and that's only three of us."

We suddenly took in how big an event it was going to be. There were about fifteen guys in the cleaning room and I could hear Arnold still holding court, and some of the others were looking a bit pissed off with him.

As I walked in Arnold said, "Hey Jimmy, do you want to shake the hand of super Arnold?"

I looked at him and it went quiet, as I said quite loudly, "Arnold, do you remember Corporal Kelly saying it was a really close decision as to who got the award?"

Arnold just stared at me.

"When I was in the office, Corporal Kelly told me it was between me and you."

The room went very quiet.

"I asked him to give it to you, as you are such an ugly little twat, and he agreed, so you should thank me."

Everyone roared laughing at the look on Arnold's face.

Later I was at a table with Danny and Bob cleaning when Arnold came across and said, "Did that really happen?"

I told him, "No, it didn't, but fuck, you just kept banging on and on."

He sat down and told us he had been so overwhelmed that he hadn't thought about anyone else.

We chatted about Friday, plus some of our past exploits, including Arnold being helped on his road runs with guys carrying his equipment to make sure he got over the line, and guys in the gym slowing things down, to help him along in there. Suddenly Arnold stood up and said, "Thanks guys, I get it."

We found later that he had gone around most of the squad and thanked them for helping him out.

We were really cleaning on top of cleaning by now. The mood was getting lighter— everyone knew who was attending.

The NAAFI, as always, was a hive of noise with people trying to outdo other people on the day's events. What with Warrant Officer Cannon's speech and the positive reviews from Corporal Kelly, it had been a good day for us.

We found out here that Jay had shared Pete's call for the leave period and had been asked to stay with them again. He even spoke to the "delectable Desiree" for a minute. Jay was very happy, as Pete's parents and Desiree would be coming to the passing out, and we were all looking forward to seeing them.

At this point Alex's booming voice said, "Do you think some people's destiny is decided at birth?"

There was a puzzled silence.

"What other job could a cannon go into?" Alex said as he carried on. "Can you imagine him organising a dance in the mess?"

We looked even more baffled.

"You'd get an invite for Warrant Officer Cannon's ball."

We burst out laughing and then it went quiet.

"What would you reply, Jimmy?"

I said, "It all depends on whether it's a dance or a raffle."

It was early morning before we turned in still talking about the day, Jay was a main part of the conversation as we all felt so good for him. Most of us were looking forward to meeting Pete's parents, who were obviously a big-hearted couple, and the "delectable Desiree," AKA Maude.

TUESDAY, DAY 104
"MOVE IT—MOVE IT OR TODAY WILL BECOME TOMORROW'S YESTERDAY"

Too early for this, you half-baked knob head. Get a life instead of a master's degree in talking out of your arse. Through the mist I heard Dave's dulcet tones shouting, "Come here, you noisy prick, and I'll ram tomorrow right up your stupid arse." But today's chosen one from the guard was off at speed.

We wandered into the washroom still growling but having enjoyed Dave's outburst.

We were partway into breakfast when two cooks who were sitting with Danny and Keith got up laughing really loudly and went back behind the hotplate. Next minute the others also burst out laughing.

About five minutes later I went and asked if there was any more bacon.

"No," one of them said. "That ugly little twat over there ate it all." And they were off laughing again. Thankfully Arnold never did find out what it was all about.

We had just finished the floors and raced back to our beds as we heard Corporal of Horse Tighe's voice: "Stand by your beds."

A quick glance. "It will need a lot more work before Thursday, and I will assist you in achieving that. Drill on the square at 0830hrs."

The next hour was spent getting from the block to the start of the continuity drill, as we kept going back to make the turns, where they would get us in exactly the right place. This was ok by us though, as it was bread and butter stuff with no need to think. We just had to listen to him. After an hour he seemed satisfied as we took a break, and then fell in facing the block.

As we marched up the square, we saw that Warrant Officer Cannon was sitting on the chair looking like an artist's model sitting for a portrait. We halted and got a right turn. As he stood up, we saluted him. As Warrant Officer Cannon had the only perfect salute the instructors were amongst us like sharks tasting fresh meat in a feeding frenzy.

"Longest way up, shortest way down. I should only see a blur, not a bunch of fucked up fingers." Our hands were pulled and pushed around.

Warrant Officer Cannon must have wondered why he was there for the next few minutes, as he reverted to artist's model, and we underwent a re-focussing.

From there we did a number of run-throughs, perfecting the timing of saluting and the positioning of the squad again. We were into this now, as the swagger was back, and we were all trying to outdo each other. By lunchtime it had improved no end and although all we heard was, "Better, needs more work," we knew that score by now.

"Stand by your beds at 1310hrs in number-one dress and best boots."

He came in the room at 1310hrs and started to take family and vehicle details for Friday, making sure the ones he had were still the same and updating those that weren't.

"Green." I gave him the vehicle make and number.

"How many?"

"Four and a third, Corporal of Horse."

"A third?"

"Yes, she's only one."

Quick as a flash he said, "She must mentally be the eldest then," and he began to laugh. He wouldn't have if he could have read my mind along the lines of *Coming from a practicing mental tit that must be true.*

This came out as a grimace-type of smile, but he was on a roll now as he said to Ginger, "Morton how many?"

"Two Corporal of Horse."

"Are they both of your probation officers?" He was off laughing again, as were all of us, but mainly as most of us, except Corporal of Horse Tighe, saw two of Ginger's fingers twitch up in the victory sign.

It was around 1345hrs when we were formed up on the square for the inevitable inspection, flicking off imaginary mountains of dust and adjusting caps and bodies.

"Haircuts will be done tomorrow. We will drill from now until I am happy, any screw ups you will not need a haircut."

It's inbred, can't help yourself, can you? Three days to go and still lobbing grenades.

"We will march from here to the starting position."

No Warrant Officer Cannon now, he was replaced by Corporal Miles, who was seated bolt upright on the chair looking for all the world, as if he was trying to pass excess wind.

"Stand at ease, we will commence with a full run-through as it will be on the day. I will give you squad shun, right turn, by the right, quick march, then away you go until you finish back here. I will say squad halt, right turn, salute. Captain Forbes-Hart (aka Corporal Miles) will salute, then present awards, after which he will address you and your families, return to the chair, and salute. We will return the salute and I will dismiss you. Questions? None, good."

A quick pause and we were off.

We immediately got in the stride and timing, with the sound of best boot studs on the tarmac giving us confidence, and it began to show. Backs were straighter, ninety degrees now the norm, arms pulled down sharply making turns crisper. We carried on until after what only seemed a couple of minutes,

"Squad halt, right turn, salute, stand at ease."

We relaxed into a happy place having done it all in one go. Our happy place lasted about two seconds.

"What the fuck was that? Eyes right looked like a bloody tennis match. Lazy, pure bloody laziness, I want to hear your neck bones crack as one. Squad shun, we will do it again. Right turn, by the right, quick march."

Off we went until we got to the eyes right, and halfway through he shouted, "Halt! It's crap, I want head and eyes over the right shoulder this quick." He snapped his fingers, went along every one of us, and turned our heads to where he wanted them. "Again."

He was still not happy. "Ladd are you saying "hup?"

"Yes, Corporal of Horse."

"Why have you begun to fuck it up this afternoon?"

Danny, who was near the back, said, "The noise from the boot studs is drowning it out, Corporal of Horse."

Tighe called over Corporal Miles, who said all he could hear were the boot studs. Tighe said to John McGrath, who was in the middle of the squad, "McGrath, you will say "hup." And the problem was solved.

We then began a prolonged session of continuity drill and with each run-through we could feel the smaller things improving.

By the time evening meal arrived we felt pretty good and well-rehearsed. There had been no lost counts, eyes right and eyes front were working, and it was looking and feeling like one smooth drill.

"At 1715hrs, back outside the block in drill kit."

After an enjoyable meal we were lined up outside the block in our starting formation.

"We will do a complete run-through, stopping for nothing whatsoever. Questions? None, good. Left turn, quick march," and he marched us up the square.

There can be a monotony about doing the same things over and over again, and occasionally drill had entered that category. At this stage, knowing that each one bought more awareness and cohesion, the improvement far outweighed any other consideration.

The squad at this moment knew it was good. Gone were the monumental cockups of the early days. The hard work was paying off. The work over the last four months had produced a squad that looked the part, could think for itself, and work as individuals and a team. We knew it and so did they. We saluted Corporal Miles in the chair, who came out, walked along the ranks as if inspecting, and then returned to his chair.

Corporal of Horse Tighe did an imaginary speech and we heard, "Squad shun, right turn, quick march."

As soon as we began, we were more relaxed, arms swinging straight and free, legs all at same height, turning together, confident. Like anything in life that is done well, we were enjoying it. By the time we heard, "Squad halt, right turn, salute, stand at ease," there was a feeling of achievement.

"Do you think that was acceptable for this stage of training?"

Not a murmur, just a déjà vu feeling of, *Oh fuck, not again.*

"Did you think that was acceptable?"

We all tried to shrink back and look invisible.

"Well, you should. A bit of fine tuning over the next two days and you might..." After a pause he carried on, "Just might, be at the top of that ladder."

We all stared ahead in a state of disbelief and shock. Did he say what we thought he said? Is he well? Has he mismanaged his medication? But we found an extra inch in height, as he marched us to the block.

We were all feeling very positive now, and even allowed ourselves the luxury of looking ahead to Friday night. It suddenly dawned on me that I had not even thought about it, almost in the mindset that the world would end on Friday. Now I knew we would be going to Uncle Fred's and a celebration would be involved.

I heard Corporal Miles come into the block and into the cleaning room. We stopped what we were doing as we asked him the same question different ways.

"Did we hear Corporal of Horse Tighe correctly earlier?"

"In the past week you have heard two senior warrant officers admit they were wrong, but you have finally proved him correct in his belief. Those who doubted his judgement, and your abilities, now fully support his decision. Because of you, his position throughout the course has been fully vindicated." Corporal Miles took a long pause then said, "Let me ask you the question, did you hear him correctly?"

There was a stunned silence with everyone in the room outwardly looking in shock, but inwardly bursting at the seams with pride.

There wasn't a murmur as he reached the door and looked around, "I think you have answered your own question," and he walked off into the night.

The silence lasted another ten seconds, then as it began to sink in, the noise level rose to an all-time high and was the only topic of conversation when we reached the NAAFI.

We'd had a confidence-boosting injection and if other nights had been noisy, this one topped them all; it was almost total bedlam.

"Goodness me, boys," Alice said. "Jenny and me are going to need earplugs, or we're going to be deaf."

"What's that you are saying Alice?" Bull shouted.

"Ok point taken." Alice walked off laughing.

Alice and Jenny were talking to everyone about Friday, their families, and how quiet it would be when we had gone.

Somebody mentioned our eyes right being like a tennis match and one minute later Billy was facing about twelve of us. He looked at his right hand and went "Clunk," then at his left hand and went "Clunk." After two goes we cottoned on, and at every "clunk" watched a ball fly over a pretend net and nearly everyone was joining in.

Suddenly Billy stopped and said to Danny, "You are not following the ball."

We were laughing as Danny said, "No, I was looking at the royal box."

Billy pointed the opposite way. "It's over there, we'll have to start the bleeding game all over again, and it will be played until I hear your neck bones crack," which led to a crescendo of foot stomping and table slapping.

As the noise subsided, Jenny's voice said, "Thanks Billy, that really calmed the place down," and the noise rose up again.

It was no quieter in the block. It was as if a noisy happiness tap had been turned on, and everyone was in a practical-joke mood. It was a strange night, as if we wanted it to last forever. I was feeling part of something so big I couldn't begin to explain it. I couldn't wait to show my family what I'd achieved.

On the other hand, I was part of another family, one that was showing us that in times of conflict we could rely on each other without reservation, different brothers than those at home, but brothers none the less. As with any family we had our differences, but when push came to shove, we were together, and one day our lives might depend on it.

There was time for one more wind up as we noticed that Bob was still down the other end of the block. We slightly roughed up Bob's pillows and sheets, then put his bedside light on so that it looked like a little film set. We turned everything else off, then lay there waiting for Bob to appear.

After ten minutes we heard Bob come in, gently close the room door, and creep to his bed. Then he shouted, "You basterts." He grabbed his sheets and blankets and pulled them off his bed, only to realise that he had just wrecked a perfectly good bed.

Most of the bedside lights came on at the same time and a voice said, "Been out on the beer Bob? That's a strange behaviour pattern, or is it some little-known Scottish ritual?"

"Basterts, aw' on ye,' fuckin' basterts, (all of you lack parents)." Bob's voice rang out as we were by now all helpless, laughing at his abuse of the English language. As Dave helped him make his bed, he slowly calmed down and was asleep in no time, the rest of us now wide awake.

WEDNESDAY, DAY 105
"RISE AND SHINE—GOD'S IN HIS HEAVEN AND ALL'S WELL WITH THE WORLD!"

After the frivolities of the night before, we were slightly more subdued on awakening and needed a bit more stretching and yawning time to get us mobile. This completely threw Bob a curve ball, as he was one of the first in the washroom, and a loud shout told us that even the most regular soldier could get a shock off a cold toilet seat.

We launched into a good breakfast and lots of conversation about the speech Corporal Miles gave us last night. We realised how Corporal of Horse Tighe had gone out on a limb, believing in us, when many did not agree with him. We were determined to prove him right.

"Line-up in the corridor in two ranks." Amid a clattering of running bodies and low mutterings we raced out there.

"Shut up, who told you to speak? Get in straight lines and listen, I will not repeat myself."

Aha, what did your job description say—Wanted, a complete arsehole with a permanent scowl, eyes up his arse, never satisfied and a voice that carries over a jet engine. You must have pissed it through the selection board.

Underneath though, there was emerging an appreciation for what he had achieved with us, and the pressure he must have been under from all levels.

"At 0830hrs you will be on the square ready to do a complete run-through of our drill on Friday. Later is Pay Parade, haircuts, and a last huge block clean ready for officer's inspection tomorrow. Fall out."

As we were getting ready, Corporal of Horse Tighe and Corporal Miles came into the room chatting in a relaxed mood. Of course, it being Corporal of Horse Tighe, he informed us that if it did not go well, we would be the only squad in regimental history to pass out with only one testicle each.

We marched to the chair occupied by Corporal Miles, who again did the honours, followed by Corporal of Horse Tighe's preamble to the imaginary crowd. Then we heard "Squad right turn, by the right, quick march," and off we marched.

All we had to do was what we had rehearsed so often and give it our all. We immediately developed plenty of attitude and body position, turns crisp and sharp—this was our show and we were going to make the most of it. At times when marching towards the block it looked like a cuckoo clock. People were going in and out of the doors and faces appeared at different windows then vanished, but there was not much time to dwell on it.

Keep counting and concentrate on the marching but soon, "Squad halt, right turn, salute, stand at ease."

Tighe marched to Corporal Miles, saluted and Corporal Miles pretended to present awards, deliver a speech and another salute and then "Dismiss."

We immediately fell in again.

He looked us over eventually saying, "I'm speechless," which we knew could only be a temporary state.

As we faced the block the cuckoo clock came to life and four men came out, two with stop watches. After much arm waving and nodding, Corporal of Horse Tighe came back to us. "It will take approximately forty-five minutes from start to finish and I am informed you look on the ball." He broke into a smile and said, "Their words, not mine."

Still smiling he said, "There will be one more run-through, and by the end you will know why."

I think at this stage we could have parachuted in without missing a step.

We did the full drill again and heard, "Squad halt, right turn, salute."

Corporal of Horse Tighe said, "At this point there is the presentation of awards, but there is one missing, the best overall recruit." This was followed by one of his long, dramatic silences. "We have based this on the results of the total course, the gym, the drills, the marches and runs, and saw that this man was consistently in the top bracket." Another pregnant pause. "He has also shown his ability to lead when it is necessary." Another very long pause. "Showing a strong inner self, it is my pleasure to give the award to Trooper Williams."

He called Danny out front, shook his hand and we had three cheers for a visibly surprised Danny Williams.

Tighe marched us back to the block ready for Pay Parade. "The storeman will be in attendance. When paid put the money in the envelope he gives you, sign it and he will keep it in his safe until Friday. When half of you are ready, Corporal Miles will march you to the barbers, the other half will go to the Orderly Room to sort out travel passes. Then change around. Questions? None, good. Again, well done Williams, all of you fall in down the corridor."

The tables were set up and Captain Forbes-Hart plus the pay officer and corporal, Warrant Officer Wheater BEM and the storeman were in place, with Tiber playing it safe at the back wall, in case the dyslexia bug struck again. We were in a much better place now than in earlier days and it went off without a hitch. It was also apparent that Danny's decision had been discussed on high. When he approached the pay table, both Captain Forbes-Hart and Warrant Officer Wheater BEM congratulated him, and he saluted and thanked them both.

By the time we went to lunch everyone had been to the Orderly Room, and about ten of us had to go to the barbers' shop afterwards.

There was a lot of congratulating Danny during lunch and in turn he thanked anyone who spoke to him, quite rightly enjoying it. The cook corporal even came across and congratulated him, "Well done Cassius, bet you are as pleased as punch."

We all groaned out loud at the awful pun.

At 1330hrs we were getting instructions from Corporal of Horse Tighe. "We will make this floor immaculate today ready for tomorrow's inspection. You only get one chance so we will be around the rest of the day to make sure you use it."

The work got under way, except for the lucky ones who got a bit of time off to get a haircut. This was no great shock as it was the way we had been doing it all along, the only difference was Tighe and Miles being there. We started to clean an area that under any other circumstances would be classed as 99.9% germ free.

As ever, we had to make a mess in order to put it back together, with a constant stream of "do this or do that" from the instructors.

There was no doubt that the bar had been raised again. We had gone through a flea's left ball, to a pimple on a flea's left ball, and were now elevated to a nipple on a pimple on a flea's left ball.

The Bumper was on its best behaviour as we polished up the floors, even though Corporal Miles and Tony still didn't get too close after past experiences.

By evening meal, lockers and beds were back in place on highly polished floors, and toothbrush-sized areas done and dusted. The mountainous piles of dust, invisible to the human eye, but capable of causing unknown diseases and plagues, were hopefully vanquished.

By 1900hrs it was looking terrific.

At 1930hrs Corporal of Horse Tighe told us to go and relax and enjoy a NAAFI break, ready to carry on when we got back, and the block cleared faster than a flushing toilet.

We got our pies and sat down with everyone still congratulating Danny on his award. Alice had told him to go and sit down, and in a quiet moment she and Jenny came over to him carrying a tray containing a steak and kidney pie, a large tea, and an elaborate-looking sticky bun.

"Well done, Danny."

The cheering and shouting began again, although looking at his tray I had a moment of jealousy.

"Speech! Speech!" and eventually a slightly embarrassed Danny got to his feet.

"I'd like to say you are the best bunch of people I have ever met." Pause for more shouting. "But I can't as I have never met another bunch."

Cue booing and catcalls.

"But if I had to pick a bunch again, it would be you lot."

More cheering and shouting.

"Well, most of you anyway."

More booing and catcalls.

"I would like to thank Alice and Jenny for not only this two-course meal," more cheering, "but being strong enough to look at some of these ugly mugs every night."

The catcalls and booing grew until he said, "Seriously, I have to thank Alice and Jenny for looking after us these past few weeks. We all appreciate everything you have done for us."

The NAAFI erupted into cheering and foot stamping as Danny went and hugged them both. For the next few minutes every one of us hugged them both and said thank you, which for once had them both lost for words.

Alice was tearing up and soon vanished in the back to compose herself, while Jenny tried to carry on, but soon joined Alice. When they were composed, they came back and the hugging began again.

On returning we tidied up and were just putting the cleaning equipment away when we heard, "Room one to your room."

We raced into our gleaming room and stood by our beds as Tighe came in.

"Do you think this is good enough?" he barked as he produced the eighth wonder of the world. "Look at the dust in here," and he unscrewed Bob's bedside light bulb. and pointed to the bulb holder. The fact that he must have seen it while coming up the stairs impressed us all.

"Why is this dusty in here, McCann?"

"Sorry Corporal of Horse, I must have missed it in the dark."

"Well switch the fucking light on then," he said, having completely missed the irony that he was holding the light in his hand. "All of you clean them now."

There was a pitter patter of plimsolls running back to the other end of the block to do theirs, but he never went to them. Having made his point, he then left the block. We had been here many times before and we knew that if that was all he found he was happy, so we carried on with touching up our personal gear. The relaxed atmosphere was back and by around 0100hrs the block was settling down under the very dust-free bedside lights.

Bob made a remark about switching the light on while Tighe was holding the bulb to see if it would light up as, "This would prove he was possessed."

There was a brief silence as we wondered if Bob was of this world when Alex said, "I think he was just trying to throw a light onto the day's events."

Cue groans.

Ginger said, "I thought he was in his element," which doubled the groans.

I remarked that I thought, "He was just showing us his dark side."

Everyone showed me their dark side as the lights were all switched off.

THURSDAY, DAY 106
"WAKEY-WAKEY! RISE AND SHINE WITH A SMILE ON YOUR FACE AS THERE IS ON MINE!"

Only our favourite alarm clock could get away with it, but he always had a pleasant start-of-the-day manner. We were up and ready to go, except Dave, who was nearest the door and nodding off again until Alex, on passing, squeezed his big toe. Dave leapt up ready to fight, saw it was Alex and decided better of it. This got Dave off to a bad start and the rest of us into a good one.

This mood quickly left Dave as he threw a bucket of water under the bog door that Alex was sitting on and soaked his plimsolls and shorts.

We heard Alex shout, "Right, arsehole, you're dead."

Dave in his best Scottish Bob accent said, "Awae an' fuck yussel (yourself) ye big tart."

The washroom was reduced to peals of laughter, except for Bob who kept repeating "It was nae me, it was nae me."

Even Alex joined in as he came out of the stall and saw everyone rolling about laughing, with Bob stuttering away thirteen to the dozen. Alex didn't know for sure who did do it.

It set the day off on a good note. The other rooms had heard the commotion, and after being told the story over breakfast kept walking past

Bob saying, "It was nae me, it was nae me," which was the key phrase throughout breakfast.

Bob's delicate response of, "Ah, fuck off awa ye stupid Sassenach basterts" set up a whole new round of laughing.

At 0745hrs we were standing by our beds as Corporal of Horse Tighe strode in. We leapt to attention as he said, "Good morning," causing a brain freeze.

Corporal of Horse Tighe saying, "Good morning." What the hell is going on?

"I said good morning."

We chorused together, "Good morning, Corporal of Horse," still a bit shaken.

"Right, gentlemen, 0815hrs on the square number one dress, best boots." Then he went next door. We kind of heard this in a haze, as if we'd been head butted by an angry bull.

By 0815hrs "twenty-six gentlemen" were lined up ready for inspection. Even this was a culture shock, a more relaxed one, more of a confidence booster.

"Keep your back straight, soldier."

"Thumbs in line with seams of your trousers, young man."

"Good turnout, keep it up."

By the time they had finished we were raring to go.

Corporal Miles marched off to the chair.

We were marched to the chair then waited, while they went through their pantomime routine, "To re-check the timing" and then it was our turn.

We were wanting to show how good we were, and it was a relief to get going. Corporal of Horse Tighe was totally relaxed as we went seamlessly through the drill. Six minutes later and we were coming into land. "Squad halt, right turn, stand at ease." They checked timing of speeches again, and seemed satisfied, as Corporal of Horse Tighe came to the front.

"We will have one more run through. If all goes well it will be your last until tomorrow, so plenty of pride and attitude to show everyone what you have achieved."

By the time we began our continuity drill, we wanted to impress and we did. It felt good because it was good, and once it had begun everything else was forgotten. We concentrated on doing it well, and by the time we were facing the chair we knew it had gone well.

A smiling Corporal of Horse said, "Well done, gentlemen. Once more tomorrow. With that depth of confidence what could possibly go wrong?" Smiling, he marched us over to the block, and we saw a lot of familiar faces leaving, including Captain Forbes-Hart, Warrant Officers Wheater and Cannon, and a number of people we hadn't seen before.

"Upstairs, change, finish off the cleaning, and after lunch a full locker and kit layout for the officer's inspection at 1430hrs."

On our return from lunch the instructors came in and the block was looking spotless. The next half hour was spent making sure everything was precisely in its place, creases smoothed out, locker gear in exactly the same place in all lockers, beds and bed packs immaculate.

By 1415hrs the block looked and smelled excellent. Our rooms were like an advert in a glossy magazine for a new, upscale boutique, and each room was identical to the others.

"Keep it up, stay by your beds, be quiet and don't be nervous. Answer Captain Forbes-Hart if he speaks to you."

After what seemed forever, we heard the sound of people coming upstairs. There was a hum of discussion and then the sound of officers' brogues, the pitter patter of a dog, and the noise of boot studs heading our way. We prepared ourselves, but they headed into the washroom.

We heard some laughter and lots of talking and eventually they came back into the corridor. We braced ourselves again but nope they went into the cleaning room. More muted discussion and laughter over a remark about a big mirror.

Oh, come on for fuck's sake, we'll twitch ourselves to death if this carries on.

Suddenly "Room-ATTENNN-SHUN" and Corporal of Horse Tighe marched in with Captain Forbes-Hart, Corporal Miles and an already bored looking Tiber, who just plonked himself down against the wall.

Corporal of Horse Tighe accompanied Captain Forbes-Hart while Corporal Miles wandered on ahead making sure that everything was fit for an officer's eyes. As in most big inspections, the build-up was more rigorous than the actual event.

Captain Forbes-Hart was going to have a chat with each of us, as Tighe did the introductions. He began with Dave, and then had a quicker one with Bob as he probably couldn't tell a word he was saying, then a longer chat with Timmy, and then I heard Tighe say, "Trooper Green, sir."

Captain Forbes-Hart did a glancing look over the bed and the locker. "Well done Trooper Green, good turn-out. Have you enjoyed your course?"

I looked at Tighe over his left shoulder giving me his best *I can kill you with a single glance* look. "Yes sir."

"Could we improve it?"

"No sir, it was well organised, and very beneficial."

Both I and Corporal of Horse Tighe relaxed as they moved on. I didn't hear any more after this, as the nerves I didn't have settled down.

"Room atten-shun," said Corporal of Horse Tighe.

Captain Forbes-Hart said, "Well done, thank you all, very impressive" and went next door.

We wanted to leap around now it was over but had to wait another fifteen minutes until we heard, "Thank you all, well done, very impressive," from next door, and they trooped off to the other end of the block. We had four months of hard work and cleaning coming to an end, and in twenty-four hours recruit training would be over with.

The whole inspection took about ninety minutes, and then we heard the voice shout "Foyer!"

We all legged it downstairs and were marched over to the Lecture Room.

There were three tables: two full of paperwork and one empty. Two Orderly Room corporals were behind the full ones. As soon as we were in the room, Captain Forbes-Hart walked in with Tiber. All protocols were different now, and Captain Forbes-Hart got up and came to the front of the table to speak. This caught out Tiber, who got up to leave and then realising they weren't leaving, spread himself back across the floor again.

"Good afternoon, gentlemen," the captain began in his beautifully cultured accent which seemed to drift calmingly around the room. "First,

I would like to thank you all for this afternoon. The block was excellent and reflects the hard work you have put in over the past weeks. Sixteen weeks ago, in this very room, I addressed a group of bewildered, dis-organised, and nervous young boys. I recall that it was mentioned that some would not be here at the end. As this is the case, it should make those of you who are here very proud of your achievements. Today I do not see bewildered, dis-organised and nervous boys, but in their place a fit, disciplined group of young men, to whom I am pleased to welcome into our army family. Although you are at the beginning of your careers, you have adapted enthusiastically, and proved you are fully capable of reacting to the many ongoing pressures that the army will put you under."

He waited for all this to sink in, as we felt a surge of pride and achievement in his words.

"Well done again to you all and I look forward to what I know will be an exceptionally good passing out parade tomorrow. Thank you, Corporal of Horse." He looked at us, smiled, said "Tiber out" and left.

Corporal of Horse Tighe soon filled the vacuum, "His words, not mine." He looked at Corporal Miles with a big smile and we all relaxed.

Tighe informed us that on table one there were two photographs per person: one of us all and one with just two of us on it. Then we were to go to table two and collect rail passes. "Check your passes carefully, there are two different return dates. When you have checked them, march to the store, and he will lock up the passes and photos with your pay.

At 1745hrs we were back in the block, changed and ready to put the last delicate tweaks and touches to our personal gear for the very last time as recruits.

We had only just begun when Corporal of Horse Tighe and Corporal Miles came in looking very cool in number-two trousers and pullovers. They wore cloth stable belts in the red/blue Life Guard colours, fastened with two leather straps through chrome buckles. They placed their forage caps and whips on a table in a cleaning room and got everyone in there.

For the first time it was totally informal, as we sat wherever we could, leant on walls, or just stood there as they sat on the table. "First a quick outline of tomorrow, the eight Royal Horse Guards raise your hands."

Don, Pete, Jay, Bull, Keith, Dave Marx, Joe, and Arnold Moore raised their hands.

"You will all return a week on Wednesday by 1500hrs, and fly out to Germany on the Saturday, to join your regiment."

By now most of us would have gladly given up the extra four days as we felt envious—this was one of the reasons we'd joined up, and soon they would be in another country.

"The remainder, back here two weeks on Sunday. The Household Cavalry will go to the equitation wing, and the remainder of The Life Guards will be out on courses soon after returning. Tonight, keep the block clean as you may want to show your guests around tomorrow. Breakfast at 0700hrs and you will all go, after which we will inform you when to hand in bedding, collect pay, passes, and civilian clothing to take with you, even if it won't fit. Lockers and rooms will be locked while you are away, so leave what you don't require in them. At 1050hrs we will parade outside the block ready to march over and begin at 1100hrs sharp. You will leave barracks in number-two dress and cloth belts, and leave best boots here."

The atmosphere was relaxed by now and we were laughing in the right places, as all of us and the instructors were unwinding. Soon the stories over the last four months were beginning to flow. We were surprised at how much they knew regarding what had gone on.

They would laugh and bring up their memories, and it began with Billy's remark about the idiot on the end of the whip. Tighe had told the mess members about it, and they were still laughing about it. They enjoyed it as much as our musical group moving the grand piano in the mess. They would ask someone to finish a story as in Billy/Alex and Farouk and were rolling with laughter as the two of them gave it to them blow by blow. At times we would add our own slant on things, and their remarks showed how much they had remembered. Bill Allen throwing his pay around and Bull's "mincing march." We all curled up laughing as they got onto Don's run to oblivion, and the "peacock effect," which they had come to expect when outside.

There didn't seem to be much they had missed as Corporal of Horse Tighe said, "Green, before you leave tomorrow, go and catch that fucking hound, and take it with you— even some of the regular Guard aren't going down there anymore."

I looked at Timmy and we were laughing along with everyone else when Corporal Miles said, "Yes More, and keep your boot polish to yourself, correct Trooper Stay?"

This had barely died down when Corporal of Horse Tighe looked at me and said, "Green, I believe you referred to me as a tit."

He was smiling, and laughed as I said, "That's a relief, I thought you'd heard the other words I'd used."

He looked at Corporal Miles and said, "Apparently I'm seen as a Tongue in Torment."

It carried on in this vein for over an hour with everyone at some stage being involved. "I don't think we missed anything do you Corporal Miles?"

Just as he was going to speak again, Ginger stood up and said, "One minute, Corporal of Horse," and ran out of the room, appearing thirty seconds later holding a piece of cardboard. We all clapped and cheered as Corporal of Horse Tighe and Corporal Miles looked at each other blankly. The noise subsided and Ginger said, "It's our template for bed packs."

"How long have you had that?"

"Most of the course," Ginger told him, and related the story of the day he was almost caught out. He'd had to leave it in his bed pack, and was going to throw himself through the window to cut out the middleman, if it had been discovered. The room erupted again as the instructors acknowledged the fact that they had no idea it was there.

"We wondered at times how you managed to keep them correct but—" and then they laughed saying, "You devious bastards."

They got up still shaking their heads and smiling as Tighe said, "Tomorrow, up at 0630hrs and breakfast at 0700hrs; we will be in your rooms just after 0800hrs. Until then, enjoy the rest of the evening."

We applauded and cheered them on their way out.

Alice and Jenny told us that the NAAFI would be open tomorrow, if anyone wanted to look around, but no food would be available. It became another evening of saying thank you to Alice and Jenny, impromptu war song renderings, and then back to the block late, as for the first time the NAAFI had stayed open longer.

It was a more sombre atmosphere on our return to the block, as we were realising not only was it the last night, but it was highly likely that some of us would not see each other again.

We had spent what was probably the most difficult period of our lives so far, as close to each other as we were with our own families. We'd laughed, fought, argued, sweated, tested our limits, helped each other, and been helped by each other. We had relied on each other in very difficult situations, shared intimate stories that would usually be kept inside our own families, and formed a bond of mutual trust. Tomorrow, having gone through all this together, some of us would go our separate ways, and would probably never meet again.

We drifted around with lots of hand shaking and little stories, but just after midnight we were moving back to our rooms to get a reasonable night's sleep. I made a point of shaking hands with Pete and Jay.

After a period of funny stories Pete said, "I'll be facking pleased when its mid-facking-day tomorrow, Jimmy," and I knew there wouldn't be another Pete.

I also went down and spent a while with Don, as we had got on so well during the course, and there wouldn't be time for this tomorrow. We had a general conversation and hoped we would meet again in the future. Knowing it was unlikely, we said our goodbyes and I went back to my room.

All the bedside lights were on and we chatted amongst ourselves, more subdued than normal, all aware that tomorrow was a big day. After that, Bob, Dave, and Keith would be off to pastures new, and our lives were going to change so much again.

There was only the small matter of a big Passing Out Parade to deal with. I think long after lights out we lay there in that hard-to-get-to sleep mode, as our brains were still working out what was to come.

FRIDAY, DAY 107
THE FINAL DAY

I slowly opened my eyes and thought that for the first time I had woken solely to the sound of the bugle playing Reveille, and looking through the window watched the bugler march back to the musician's block. I sat on the edge of the bed for a few minutes, then decided to go to the washroom. It was obviously infectious as by 0620hrs all but two of us were in the washrooms.

At 0630hrs Corporal Miles looked into the washroom, saw it full, then pretended to grab his heart and stagger sideways. "Good morning gentlemen, who wet the bed this morning?" and shaking his head he went to the other end of the block.

It was a very chatty and noisy meal, as we had all been herded into one small area of the cookhouse, with a large area cordoned off for the midday buffet.

"This looks good Chef, you are doing us proud," I said to one of the cooks.

"It's not for you riff-raff, so don't bugger it all up, it's for your guests," he told us.

The newest cook in the kitchen, nicknamed "Omelette," came out, full of bravado, in front of his peers. "Anybody here got a good-looking sister coming along today?"

Timmy said, "Yes, Jimmy has."

"Will you introduce me to her?"

"Of course." I smiled at him. "She likes anything that looks like a cartoon cut-out, so you'll be ok."

It was a great start to the day: a relaxing breakfast, and plenty of good-natured banter. By the time we got back in the block, the majority of us were in a good mood, ready for the rest of the day. Almost exactly at 0800hrs, Corporal of Horse Tighe and Corporal Miles entered the room and Tighe said, "Enjoy your breakfasts?"

"Yes, Corporal of Horse."

"Good, Corporal Miles bring Room Two in here."

Thirty seconds later we were stood by our beds, and Room Two had lined up at one end, like a choir ready to sing to us.

"As soon as I have finished, take all your bedding down to the stores and bring back a clean eiderdown and mattress cover and put them on your beds in case your guests come up here."

This didn't take long and fifteen minutes later they told us to go down in the same order and collect pay, passes, and civilian clothing. We collected our clothing, and it was a strange feeling seeing it again after four months. I was trying to remember the raw, apprehensive youth who had handed it in against the more confident young man collecting it, and it seemed a whole lifetime ago.

We came back into our rooms, and as the instructors weren't here, we tried on our civilian jackets to much amusement, as they were nearly all too big. I borrowed Big Hippo's and put it on. I was down to my underwear and socks and his huge jacket was more like an overcoat with the shoulders halfway down my upper arms. I strutted up the room with everyone laughing and then went into Room Two, and they began whistling. I did a very slow walk down the room for them, in a kind of catwalk style, stopping at each bed and posing.

"Green, have you lost something?"

I spun round and saw Corporal of Horse Tighe and Corporal Miles standing inside the doorway, attracted by the sound of laughing, and the first thing in my head was, "Seven two-pound bags of sugar Corporal of Horse."

Laughing he said, "I was thinking more like your marbles."

I saw that he and Corporal Miles had changed and were looking extremely smart, and we were more than ready to look the same.

It was around 1000hrs, and the instructors were down the other end, when Tom Peters popped his head in. "Hey, come and look at this."

We all went into Room Two and looked out of their windows, which looked over the square. In the last hour a hundred or more chairs had been placed either side of the officer's chair and already people were arriving. At this moment it went very quiet, as it brought it home that the time was very close.

We got back into our room and completed getting ready. We got into our best boots, jackets, and then white belts, which completely changed the whole scene into a smart and confident squad of men, getting ready to show what they had achieved. We moved around brushing each other off and flicking out imaginary creases, then took a minute or two brushing off forage caps and by 1035hrs we were ready to go.

A couple of us went back into Room Two and looked through the window to see that the chair area was absolutely full of people.

I suddenly saw a push chair at the end of the middle row and Mum holding Helen, talking to Aunt Betty. Dad and Uncle Fred had their backs to the square talking to someone behind them. For a moment my chest needed a couple of deep, deep breaths and a hard swallow and then thankfully, before I had time to dwell on it, I heard Corporal of Horse Tighe shout, "Come away from the windows, or you'll scare the shit out of the women and children."

It was back to putting the finishing touches to our uniforms. We carefully put on our caps, had a quick look in the mirrors, and by 1045 we were all in the foyer, where the sound of excited voices, and boot studs filled the air.

"Quiet!"

You could have heard a pin drop.

"The sun has co-operated, so let's get out there and shine."

At exactly 1050hrs we had fallen in, dressed off, and were standing at ease.

Corporal of Horse Tighe walked amongst us, putting any nerves we had at rest telling us to enjoy it. This was the last parade and drill session, then we were home and dry. Quietly, he said to us, "Get ready for it," and then at the top of his considerable voice shouted, "SQUAAAAD, SQUAAAAD - ATTENNNSHUN!"

There was one sharp crack of boots.

"SQUAAAAD, left turn."

The legs came up to ninety degrees with the right foot slammed in alongside it.

"By the right-quick march."

And we were off, eff-ight, eff-ight, eff-ight then a left turn and the long relaxing march up the side of the square. We realised then that anyone left in the barracks was watching. Many of the cooks were lined up along the front of the cookhouse, and groups of regular soldiers were along the edge of the square. No time to dwell on it though.

"Squaaaad, left turn, eff-ight, eff-ight!" And right on cue, "Squaaaad-Halt...right turn-salute."

Captain Forbes-Hart stood and returned the salute.

"Squad present and ready for your inspection, sir."

Thank you, Corporal of Horse." As Corporal of Horse Tighe introduced us one by one Captain Forbes-Hart had a quick word. "Excellent turn out. Family here?"

"Yes, sir."

"Good, well done, very smart." All in all, it took about ten minutes, and although I could see my family, it was eyes front and stay focussed.

Eventually it was finished. There were more salutes and Captain Forbes-Hart returned to his seat.

Corporal of Horse Tighe then addressed the audience and briefly explained Continuity Drill. He explained that this could only be achieved when a high level of drill had already been attained. To lighten the mood, he told them that the hardest part was to convince us that he could be quiet for six minutes. "The outcome, see for yourselves why you and I are proud of every single one of them."

He half turned to us and held the moment briefly. "SQUAAAAD, RIGHT TURN, BY THE RIGHT, QUICK MARCH."

We were finally able to stride out and have our moment.

Thirty paces and about turn, then the wisdom of sixty paces straight back past the audience. It gave us an easy long distance to get into the swing of it, then about turn thirty paces, and right turn twenty paces going away from the audience, a left turn for twenty paces to a halt.

About turn forty paces and halt, about turn for twenty paces and we knew we had it nailed. The adrenalin was going, and we were enjoying it. The timing of the studs on the tarmac was making it sound as one, and the hours of training were bearing fruit, as we were automatically into it.

Three right turns of twenty paces then forty paces, left turn for twenty paces and the ten paces, eyes right then the right marker salutes Captain Forbes-Hart who was on his feet. Eyes front ten paces and a left turn. Corporal of Horse Tighe must have been pleased with that, all necks at ninety degrees and no need to say "hup" all we needed was an audience, forty paces and left turn.

We were nearing the end now with forty paces and about turn. Another forty then about turn again and it felt terrific as we did a left turn marching up towards the audience and a perfect left wheel took us into the right position, and as we got back into our stride pattern we heard,

"SQUAAAD HALT (and Tighe was beaming). RIGHT TURN, SALUTE." A smiling Captain Forbes-Hart was already on his feet to return the salute. For a second or two we could feel the audience was restless, not knowing whether to stick or twist, clap or stand up, but a lot were ex-forces, and knew there would be no long pauses.

"Captain Forbes-Hart will now present the awards for the best over-all recruit, best physical recruit, and most improved physical recruit."

Al, Arnold, and Danny came out for a little rah-rah speech from him, and now the audience could get involved and applauded them.

They returned to the squad and Corporal of Horse Tighe said, "Would you like to address the squad, and the guests, sir?"

Captain Forbes-Hart thanked him, probably thinking it's a good job you asked me, or I would have wasted all last night doing my impromptu speech, but he was immediately into his flow as he faced us.

"Today we have seen an excellent display of teamwork that four months ago would have been unthinkable. It is with great pride, that on behalf of Corporal of Horse Tighe and all my training staff here, I can say it has been a great pleasure to watch your daily improvement. From a collection of raw young boys into a mature, smart, efficient and disciplined squad of young men. Speaking for all those involved, we applaud you."

There was a spontaneous applause from the families and guests, and as it subsided Captain Forbes-Hart turned to them. It was at this moment I noticed our three PTIs sat in the back row applauding and smiling, still in PT kit and windjammers, and I felt part of another family. A very different kind of family, but a family none the less, and that at this moment my two families were merging. This was borne out by his next words:

"I am extremely pleased to address all of you here today, to witness a day that I am sure many of you could never have envisaged happening." He paused while everyone laughed.

"The regiment places great store in families, and I want to assure you as much as is possible, that we will look after them. There is no greater investment in life than our children, but today they are young men, and I know how proud you are of each and every one of them, and quite rightly so. I am sure you cannot wait to speak to them, so lastly, thank you all once again. Corporal of Horse Tighe carry on."

Corporal of Horse Tighe shouted, "Squad salute," then faced us with a huge smile on his face that he must have kept in a drawer for the last four months.

"You have earned today, now go and enjoy it, for the last time. SQUAAAD-DISMISS."

There was a moment's silence as we realised it was all over. In front of our families, it had gone better than we could have hoped.

Then chaos as we looked like a poor version of a square-dance team, trying to shake hands, pat each other on the back, and get to our families, all jumping around at the same time as pent-up tension was released.

I finally reached Mum, who had tears running down her face, and a huge smile. I gave her a hug, then a much longer one, until we got our emotions under control.

I stepped back and Aunt Bet said, "Hey I hug too," and I was back in hug mode.

I had my composure back as Uncle Fred shook my hand. "That was quite a display John, I'm so pleased we were able to see it."

"So am I Uncle Fred; it was hard work, but now it's all been worthwhile."

Then I saw Dad, as he handed Helen to Mum, and we looked at each other smiling and before I could hold my hand out, Dad put his hands on my upper arms and said, "I am really proud of you, son.

Almost in shock I blurted out, "I know Dad, I know," and then we shook hands.

It was lunchtime by now. Some decided to walk around the barracks first, and we went to the cookhouse.

I heard Timmy call. He had pulled two tables together, and as only his brother had been able to attend, we joined them round the tables. I introduced him to my family and met his brother Andy. We all settled down to eat and it was a happy, noisy place, with multiple conversations and lots of introductions, and parents finding they had a lot in common.

Captain Forbes-Hart came across and introduced himself to Uncle Fred.

"Lieutenant Commander Swindells, I am pleased to meet you."

Uncle Fred thanked him, and introduced Aunt Betty. "As you can appreciate this is John's special day, and I am enjoying every moment of seeing my sister so happy." Then he introduced him to "Ex-Leading Wren Cath Green, and ex-Petty Officer John Green, Royal Navy.

"This led to a whole group of people beginning to chat about their military service, and for a moment we might as well not have been there, although it was becoming obvious that many of our families had a lot in common.

Everything was very informal by now, and Corporal of Horse Tighe came across for a chat. I introduced him to my family and he said, "You never told me you were from a naval family."

I laughed and said, "You never let us get a word in."

He was then consumed by a large group of people who wanted to speak to him.

As we were on the edge of it again, Timmy, Andy, and I went for some food and saw Omelette standing behind the hot plates.

Timmy shouted, "Hey Omelette, Jimmy's sister is looking forward to meeting you."

"Yes, come on over, I'll introduce you to her."

We all made our way back through the crowd. As we reached the table I said, "Helen, meet Omelette."

He looked as if he wished the floor would open up and swallow him.

Mum saw this and smiling said, "Don't take any notice of John, it's nice to meet you, Omelette." Then she started to laugh saying, "Omelette?"

He told her, "I've not been posted here very long, and every time I cook breakfast, I keep breaking the eggs," which had us all, including Omelette smiling.

He strolled off and Don who was nearby heard Mum and said, "*John*?"

"Yes," I replied.

"I thought it was Jimmy?"

"Only since I joined up."

Don said, "Well I'll be—"

Timmy cut in saying, "Not in here Don," and we were all laughing again.

We said our goodbyes to Don and his family, as he would be in Germany by the time we returned, and we walked to the door.

As we were getting the pushchair set up, the doors opened and a leggy brunette in high heels and a mini-mini skirt, plus a low-cut blouse that left nothing to the imagination, came tripping in. She was followed by Jay, "facking" Pete and two parents and we realised we were in the presence of the "delectable Desiree."

It was a short, wide area by the door and immediately my family were chatting away to Pete's parents, and Jay introduced us to Desiree. Timmy was nearest and as they shook hands, she saw that Timmy's eyes were out of focus and said, "Should I introduce them to you separately," and Andy nearly choked.

"This is Jimmy Green, and we shook hands as she said, "Is this your child?"

"No, my sister," I turned Helen to face her and said, "Helen, meet Maude."

Desiree looked at me quizzically, "Maude?"

"Yes, she can only say little words," and as she leaned over to speak to Helen, I leaned over and whispered in her ear. She began to laugh, then began to say something and started laughing again. As we said our goodbyes, I looked at them walking away and she was talking to Jay, who looked back also laughing.

While we were ready to move on, Ginger came in with his sister and her boyfriend and we had another chat. As they were chatting to my family, Timmy tapped my arm and we saw Desiree stroking Jay's backside as they looked into the dining room.

"Yes," I whispered to him, "She'll be pulling more than a pint for him tonight."

Once outside, we all walked around the barracks showing them the equitation wing, the LAD (Light Aid Detachment) area, plus the Hound of the Baskervilles gate, all with accompanying stories.

The mess had been opened and we strolled through the WOs/NCOs mess where they could see the silverware and hear tales of bygone battle honours. My family thoroughly enjoyed the history of it all. As we got outside the mess, I was pushing Helen and chatting to Mum.

Timmy said, "Before we leave, what did you say to Desiree?"

"I just told her to be careful when she leans over Helen, as she's breast feeding, and she'll think it's her birthday."

Mum slapped my arm saying, "John, you didn't."

"As if, love," I said, as I looked at Timmy nodding yes.

Timmy and Andy left soon after, as they had to travel to Newcastle. We were in no hurry and went down to the NAAFI. This proved to be a really good move, as when we got inside, Alice, Jenny, and a couple of their family members were there and asked us to join them. We spent a very good forty-five minutes reminiscing about the course.

Alice especially enjoyed this as her husband was ex-navy, but had died five years previously, and she enjoyed a great chat with Mum, Dad, Fred, and Betty—so good that Jenny went and brewed up.

Eventually we left and went to the block to collect my civvies. It had been a superb day from start to finish, from the easy-paced start to getting ready, a drill parade without putting a foot wrong, a terrific meal, and a wonderful family day out, with so many people from so many different walks of life.

In retrospect it was not just today, it was the culmination of four months of hard work. A system that I had to adjust to, with a group of people I had never met, way out of my comfort zone, in a place far from home, but I had dealt with it.

My mind was having problems imagining that cocky teenager, who had spent most of Christmas arguing with his parents, and who knew everything, was no longer.

The one thing I absolutely knew for sure was that this was a major turning point. My life would never again be the same, and I was looking forward to it.

On entering the block, we were helped upstairs by Corporal Miles, who walked around and chatted with the family about what we had achieved on the course. I changed my boots, checked money and passes, and showed Mum my photos while she had another happy cry. I locked my locker, ready for my return, and Corporal Miles helped me carry the chair back downstairs and reminded me to book out on leaving.

We walked back to where the car was parked as Mum and Aunt Betty remarked on how nice the instructors were and, "So helpful." I wondered who they were talking about, but why spoil a great day discussing mental health issues?

I put my gear in the boot, and Dad and I walked down to the Guard Room still talking to people on the way. The rest of the family got into the car, and the car arrived at the Guard Room the same time as we did.

I went in to sign out, and Corporal of Horse Tighe was there. He shook hands with Dad while I was signing out in the book, then went and thanked the others for being here.

I walked out with Dad and Corporal of Horse Tighe shook hands with me saying, "Enjoy your leave, I will see you in two weeks."

I was at the back door of the car and looking back up the road at the hustle and bustle that accompanies a busy army barracks, remembering a very nervous youth full of anxiety, trepidation, and no little fear...but that was four months ago.

That was then, that is not today, and suddenly I was aware of a hand on my shoulder and Dad saying:

"Son, the boy has gone."

Printed in Canada